1968

This book may be kept

A Delta Book · 1964

translated by Sylvia Townsend Warner

MARCEL PROUST
on art and
literature
1896-1919

A DELTA BOOK
Published by
Dell Publishing Co., Inc.
750 Third Avenue
New York 17, New York

Copyright © 1958 by Meridian Books, Inc.
Reprinted by arrangement with World Publishing Company, Cleveland and
New York
Library of Congress Catalog Card Number: 57-6687
Delta ® TM 755,118
Translation © Chatto and Windus, Ltd., 1957
Originally published in French by Librairie Gallimard, Paris, 1954,
under the title CONTRE SAINTE-BEUVE
Manufactured in the United States of America
Cover photograph by Atget
First printing—March, 1964

C ontents

Contents

 cknowledgment

I wish to record my especial gratitude to Mrs. Sydney Schiff, for the criticism, advice, and encouragement she gave during the early stages of this translation, and to Mr. George D. Painter, who generously spared time from his own work on Proust to read through the typescript, rescuing me from many blunders and misapprehensions, and supplying much relevant information, which I have gratefully incorporated in the Notes. And I must thank my publishers for their patience.

I also owe it to my publishers to explain that it was at my insistence that quotations from French poetry are translated in the text (the originals will be found among the Notes). As Proust quotes extensively from Les Fleurs du Mal, *this may seem an ostentatious impiety. But it was exactly those quotations that decided me. They occur as part of Proust's chain of thought about Baudelaire; and for some links in a chain of thought to be obscured by a language presumably foreign to the reader would defeat the purpose of translating the rest.*

S.T.W.

Translator's preface

In September 1905, Proust's mother died. He was thirty-four, and an invalid. "She takes my life away with her," he wrote on the day after her death. And in a letter of a few days later he cites with melancholy and yet approving acquiescence the remark of Madame Proust's nurse, that to his mother he was always four years old.

The purpose of such remarks is analgesia, and very likely the nurse remarked to other hearers that the poor lady died worn out by the exigencies of a grown-up son who wouldn't get off his mother's lap. In fact, the life that Madame Proust took away with her and which it became her son's life work to recapture was a prolonged adolescence round which she had extended a sheltering wrap of childhood. This wrap of childhood imparted a brilliant illusion of precocity to that adolescence persisting long after actual dates could justify it, and in *La Recherche* it is exactly this which Proust renders in the Marcel who goes into society, so that as one reads, one is continually exclaiming to oneself, "How could he have got so far, how did he know all this already?" During those years of social success and social exploration, he certainly discarded the wrap when he went out, but it was as certainly waiting to reinfold him when he returned home. After his health broke down in 1902 there are signs that he grew impatient with it—sickness is intolerant of illusions—but by then his mother had made her own shelter in it. Then, with her death, it was torn away from an aging adolescence, in the course of which he had published a book and made a name and fought a duel, and written a novel, and which must often have seemed as long-drawn-out as a wet afternoon seems to a sick child, lying in bed and hearing the noises of other people's living. And he was left to himself.

Three years later he wrote to Georges de Lauris—and, in almost identical terms to Madame de Noailles—that although he was very ill, he wanted to write an essay on Sainte-Beuve, but was uncertain what form to cast it into. It could be an orthodox critical essay, or it could "begin with an account of a morning, Mamma would come to my bedside and I would tell her about the article on Sainte-Beuve I want to write, and enlarge it to her. Which do you think would be best?" In a subsequent letter to Lauris he said: "What is most likely to come out one day is *Sainte-Beuve* [the study] because it irks me to have that packed trunk in the middle of my mind, and I must decide whether to set out or to unpack."

By then, the contents of the trunk had been accumulating for eight years at least, lavendered and mothballed with reasons for dissent. In a letter of the summer of 1905 to Madame Strauss he quotes a smug sentence and exclaims, "Isn't that typical of Sainte-Beuve?" The years after *Jean Santeuil* had been laid aside were barren, or he felt them to be so. He published some articles, he became interested in Ruskin, and translated *The Bible of Amiens*. "Nothing I am doing is real work; just documentation, translations, etc. . . . It is enough to rouse my thirst for accomplishment without of course gratifying it in any way. From the moment I emerged from that long torpor and turned my eyes inwards towards my thoughts, I felt the complete void of my life, while hundreds of characters for a novel, thousands of ideas, beg me to give them a body." Towards the end of this volume there is an obviously autobiographical fragment, *The Wane of Inspiration*, which must relate to this period. Two characters suddenly appear in the last sentence, begging to be given life, and immediately the fragment breaks off. But the packed trunk was in his mind, and though to be a critic is a come-down from being a creative artist, and ranks one among the Sainte-Beuves, he had a great many things to say about and round-about Sainte-Beuve, and things to say against him, against the man as well as against the method. The first part of *Sainte-Beuve and Baudelaire* is written with such sustained fury against the behaviour of the man, and has obviously been meditated at such white heat, that animus may well have been a determining factor in his decision to extend an essay into a series of essays, and eventually, into a book.

Yet it is doubtful how long, and when he was so ill, he would have gone on writing as a critic, if by that time he was not again writing as a novelist. It was as a novelist that he conceived that alternative conversational form the essay might take, and then, while keeping the essay orthodox and intact, approached it by *Talking to Mamma*, and that, by *The Sunbeam on the Balcony*, and that, by *The Article in Le Figaro*. For the essay on *The Method of Sainte-Beuve* comes in a group of manuscripts which shows him at work on material which afterwards made part of *La Recherche*. Combray, which the sunlight falling on a weathercock has associated with Venice, appears in *Talking to Mamma*, Gilberte—unfathered, for in this state of *La Recherche* there is no Swann—in *The Sunbeam on the Balcony*, a nameless Balbec in *The Days*. Backward from *The Days* the direction of mind is towards Combray. Except for the episodic *Countess*, all this wing of what is to be a triptych is supported on the narrative fact, related backwards, that Marcel leaves the bed in which he has spent the night, although by this time he only sleeps by day, and goes to his mother's room.

The centre of the triptych is completed by *Sainte-Beuve and Baudelaire*, in which Mamma is inaudibly present, the unfinished study of Gérard de Nerval, and the long and splendid *Sainte-Beuve and Balzac*, in which Mamma is only vaguely invoked, though her presence has a structural importance, because it occasions the apparent hesitation and formality which orchestrates the introduction of the theme of homosexuality. Then, as though fuelled with Balzac's gusto, Proust charges straight into the Guermantes Way, and proceeds along it with scarcely a turning-aside, rather as though, having laughed at Balzac's prosy divagations, he were temporarily abjuring poetical divagations of his own. By this point he is up and dressed, and no longer an invalid, but reverted to the young man of whom it was said in Paris, "He made up the number at table for Madame Strauss, he was invited for his wit."• Mamma, yielding place to the grandmother who is to be her second embodiment, has loosed her hold, removing the wrap of childhood and the consequent glitter of precocity; the Marcel of *Contre Sainte-Beuve* who goes to the Princesse de Guermantes's reception is both less sophisticated and more mature than the corresponding Marcel of *La Recherche;* and when, under the name of M. de Quercy, the figure of M. de Charlus rears up behind the Guer-

• Marthe Bibesco. *The Veiled Wanderer.*

mantes foothills, he is so compassable, stimulating and congenial a subject that it is obvious that Proust has compassed his own homosexuality. The great oration on homosexuals is to reappear in *La Recherche*, along with much else in these two chapters. But here, in *Contre Sainte-Beuve*—so it seems to me (as Proust says Balzac's mother told him to say)—the writing conveys an effect of force and pace and commandingness which Proust never shows us again; possibly because on later consideration he decided against repeating it, possibly because, passing out of the gravitational field of Balzac, he was never again in a way to repeat it.

The penultimate chapter uses material which Proust had recorded as *Pages Written* in a note for the early version of *La Recherche*: "*Norman hydrangeas; the grand-daughter of Louis Philippe; Fantasie; the mother's face beneath the rake's*"; but its main theme is one which underlay in *The Countess*: "*the disappointment a possession is; kissing the face.*" At the opening of the last chapter the elegiac strain is arrested by a most significant modulation. Marcel visits the castle of Guermantes; it ceases to be a name, yet it does not become a disappointment: it exists, not as a thing but as a thing remembered. It exists in the remembrance of the past. And at the end of this chapter Proust's love for his mother, which till now has been invoked, described, dwelt on, is at last expressed with a tenderness which he, perhaps, released from filiality, dependence, and obligation, was at last able to feel—though it is strikingly typical of the way in which his whole life was suspended in the *pot-au-feu* of his creative mind that he here reverts to something he wrote in a letter to Montesquiou a few days after her death.

In the autumn of 1909 Proust wrote to Lauris: "Vatelle won't take *Sainte-Beuve*, which no doubt will remain unpublished. It is too long, four or five hundred pages." An author who is so amply uncertain how many pages have been written is an author who has written in breakneck pursuit of what he has to say. There is both objective and subjective evidence of this in *Contre Sainte-Beuve*. Gaps are left to be filled up, quotations are unchecked (incidentally, the extent of what Proust quotes by heart is an index of his amazing memory), names are not quite fastened to characters (the two Villeparisis ladies), nor actions to places (the momentary shift to a Combray Saturday in *The Sunbeam*); and, as an artist's drawing will often include a third hand or the outline of an alternative profile at a different tilt, there are seeming repetitions which are really alternative renderings (though the fact that this text has been assembled, and from manuscripts which sometimes offer as many as eight or nine alternative versions, is no doubt an explanation of some of these inconsistencies and repetitions). The subjective evidence is of much deeper interest. At this period Proust, menaced by ill-health, was haunted by a sense of urgency. " 'For the night cometh when no man may work,' " he quotes in a letter to Lauris. "Georges, I am already half-way into that night." An author who can take his time or who takes time to revise, hides his tracks. He re-writes, or cancels, or evades those passages where inspiration failed him, where he was at a loss, where he was struggling to make sure not only how he wanted to say a thing, but exactly what it was he wanted to say. In *Contre Sainte-Beuve* the tracks remain. We can see where the author paused, trudged, tried for another foot-hold; and then, suddenly, there are no tracks at all, he is off, he is airborne. As translators cannot be airborne, I cannot hope to have conveyed the whole range of these vicissitudes, nor the immediacy of the original; but I have made it my main attempt to pre-serve this uneven fluctuating texture, because it is a record of the actual state of Proust's creative mind, just as *Contre Sainte-Beuve* itself records a hitherto unknown stage of his development. M. de Fallois, to whose editing—an editing so onerous and intimate that one almost thinks of it as a form of co-operation —we owe this new aspect of Proust (for as he truly says, there is no such thing as a new book by Proust), comments in his preface on the handwriting of the manuscripts. It has none of the ample, majestic flowing ease of the handwriting of *Jean Santeuil*, he says; it has grown taut and intricate, and festoons itself round the first spurt of the author's intention, and the manuscript is loaded and heavy with corrections which dangle from the lines like clusters from a vine, like a swarm of chrysalises; and one cannot look on it unmoved, for it is the very handwriting of *La Re-cherche*.

CONTRE

Sainte-Beuve

Prologue[1]

Every day I set less store on intellect. Every day I see more clearly that if the writer is to repossess himself of some part of his impressions, get to something personal, that is, and to the only material of art, he must put it aside. What intellect restores to us under the name of the past, is not the past. In reality, as soon as each hour of one's life has died, it embodies itself in some material object, as do the souls of the dead in certain folk-stories, and hides there. There it remains captive, captive for ever, unless we should happen on the object, recognise what lies within, call it by its name, and so set it free. Very likely we may never happen on the object (or the sensation, since we apprehend every object as sensation) that it hides in; and thus there are hours of our life that will never be resuscitated: for this object is so tiny, so lost in the world, and there is so little likelihood that we shall come across it.

Several summers of my life were spent in a house in the country. I thought of those summers from time to time, but they were not themselves. They were dead, and in all probability they would always remain so. Their resurrection, like all these resurrections, hung on a mere chance. One snowy evening, not long ago, I came in half frozen, and had sat down in my room to read by lamplight, and as I could not get warm my old cook offered to make me a cup of tea, a thing I never drink. And as chance would have it, she brought me some slices of dry toast. I dipped the toast in the cup of tea and as soon as I put it in my

mouth, and felt its softened texture, all flavoured
with tea, against my palate, something came over me
—the smell of geraniums and orange-blossoms, a sensation of extraordinary radiance and happiness; I sat
quite still, afraid that the slightest movement might
cut short this incomprehensible process which was taking place in me, and concentrated on the bit of sopped
toast which seemed responsible for all these marvels;
then suddenly the shaken partitions in my memory
gave way, and into my conscious mind there rushed
the summers I had spent in the aforesaid house in the
country, with their early mornings, and the succession, the ceaseless onset, of happy hours in their
train. And then I remembered. Every morning, when
I was dressed, I went down to my grandfather in his
bedroom, where he had just woken up and was drinking his tea. He soaked a rusk in it, and gave me the
rusk to eat. And when those summers were past and
gone, the taste of a rusk soaked in tea was one of the
shelters where the dead hours—dead as far as intellect
knew—hid themselves away, and where I should certainly never have found them again if, on that winter's evening when I came in frozen from the snow,
my cook had not offered me the potion to which, by
virtue of a magic past I knew nothing about, their
resurrection was plighted.

But as soon as I had tasted the rusk, a whole garden,
up till then vague and dim, mirrored itself, with its
forgotten walks and all their urns with all their flowers, in the little cup of tea, like those Japanese flowers which do not re-open as flowers until one drops
them into water. In the same way, many days in
Venice, which intellect had not been able to give back,
were dead for me until last year, when crossing a

courtyard I came to a standstill among the glittering uneven paving-stones. The friends I was with feared I might have wrenched my ankle, but I waved to them to go on, and that I would catch up with them. Something of greater importance engaged me, I still did not know what it was, but in the depth of my being I felt the flutter of a past that I did not recognise; it was just as I set foot on a certain paving-stone that this feeling of perplexity came over me. I felt an invading happiness, I knew that I was going to be enriched by that purely personal thing, a past impression, a fragment of life in unsullied preservation (something we can only know in preservation, for while we live in it, it is not present in the memory, since other sensations accompany and smother it) which asked only that it should be set free, that it should come and augment my wealth of life and poetry. But I did not feel that I had the power to free it. No, intellect could have done nothing for me at such a moment! Trying to put myself back into the same state, I retraced my steps a little so that I might come afresh to those uneven shining paving-stones. It was the same sensation underfoot that I had felt on the smooth, slightly uneven pavement of the baptistry of Saint Mark's. The shadow which had lain that day on the canal where a gondola waited for me, and all the happiness, all the wealth of those hours—this recognised sensation brought them hurrying after it, and that very day came alive for me.

It is not merely that intellect can lend no hand in these resurrections; these past hours will only hide themselves away in objects where intellect has not tried to embody them. The objects which you have consciously tried to connect with certain hours of your life, these they can never take shelter in. What is more, if something else should resuscitate those hours, the objects called back with them will be stripped of their poetry.

I remember how once when I was travelling by train I strove to draw impressions from the passing landscape, I wrote about the little country churchyard while it was still passing before my eyes, I noted down the bright bars of sunlight on the trees, the wayside flowers like those in *Le Lys dans la Vallée*. Since then, calling to mind those trees streaked with light and that little churchyard, I have often tried to conjure up that day, that day *itself*, I mean, not its pallid ghost. I could never manage it, and I had lost all hope of doing so, when at lunch, not long ago, I let my spoon fall on my plate. And then it made the same noise as the hammers of the linesmen did that day, tapping on the wheels when the train halted at stations. The burning blinded hour when that noise rang out instantly came back to me, and all that day in its poetry—except for the country churchyard, the trees streaked with light, and the Balzacian flowers, gained by deliberate observation and lost from the poetic resurrection.

Now and again, alas, we happen on the object, and the lost sensation thrills in us, but the time is too remote, we cannot give a name to the sensation, or call on it, and it does not come alive. As I was walking through a pantry the other day, a piece of green canvas plugging a broken window-pane made me stop dead and listen inwardly. A gleam of summer crossed my mind. Why? I tried to remember. I saw wasps in a shaft of sunlight, a smell of cherries came from the table—I could not remember. For a moment I was like those sleepers who wake up in the dark and do not know where they are, who ask their bodies to give them a bearing as to their whereabouts, not knowing what bed, what house, what part of the world, which year of their life they are in. For a moment I hesitated like this, groping round the square of green canvas to discover the time and the place where my scarcely awakened memory would find itself at home. All the sensations of my life, confused, or known, or forgotten, I was hesitating among all of them at once; this only lasted a minute. Soon I saw nothing more; my memory had fallen asleep again for ever.

How often during our walks have not my friends known me to halt like this at the turning-off of an avenue, or beside a clump of trees, and ask them to leave me alone for a minute. Nothing came of it. I shut my eyes and made my mind a blank to recruit fresh energies for my pursuit of the past, then suddenly reopened them, all in an attempt to see those same trees as if for the first time, I could not tell where I had seen them. I could recognise their shapes and their grouping, their outline seemed to have been traced from some beloved drawing that trembled in my heart. But I could tell no more of them, and they themselves seemed by their artless passionate attitude to say how sorry they felt not to be able to make themselves clear, not to be able to tell me the secret that they well knew I could not unriddle. Ghosts of a dear past, so dear that my heart beat to bursting, they held out powerless arms to me, like the ghosts that Aeneas met in the underworld. Was it in the walks near the town of my happy childhood, was it only in that imagined country where, later on, I dreamed that Mamma was so ill, close to a lake and in a forest where it was light all night long, a dream country only but almost as real as the country of my childhood which was already no more than a dream? I should never know more of it. And I had to rejoin my friends who were waiting for me at the turn of the road, with the anguish of turning my back for ever on a past I might see no more, of disowning the dead who held out their powerless fond arms to me, and seemed to say, Recall us to life. And before I fell into step and into conversation with my friends, I again turned round for a moment to cast a less and less discerning glance towards the receding crooked line of mutely expressive trees still undulating before my eyes.

Compared with this past, this private essence of ourselves, the truths of intellect seem scarcely real at all. So, and above all from the time when our vitality begins to dwindle, it is to whatever may help us to recover this past that we resort, even though this should entail being very ill-understood by intellectual people who do not know that the artist lives to himself, that the absolute value of what he sees means nothing to him and that his scale of values is wholly subjective. A nauseating musical show put on by a provincial company, or a ball that people of taste would laugh at, may be far more quickening to his memories, far more relevant to the nature of what he dreams of and dwells on, than a brilliant performance at the Opera House or an ultra-elegant evening party in the Faubourg Saint-Germain. A railway time-table with its names of stations where he loves to fancy himself getting out of the train on an autumn evening when the trees are already stripped of their leaves and the bracing air is full of their rough scent, or a book that means nothing to people of discrimination but is full of names he has not heard since he was a child, can be worth incommensurably more to him than admirable philosophical treatises, so that people of discrimination will remark that for a man of talent he has very stupid likings.

Perhaps it will cause surprise that I, who make light of the intellect, should have devoted the following few pages precisely to some of those considerations that intellect, in contradiction to the platitudes that we hear said or read in books, suggests to us. At a time when my days may be numbered (and besides, are we not all in the same case?) it is perhaps very frivolous of me to undertake an intellectual exercise. But if the truths of intellect are less precious than those secrets of feeling that I was talking about just now, yet in one way they too have their interest. A writer is not only a poet; in our imperfect world where masterpieces are no more than the ship-wrecked flotsam of great minds, even the greatest writers of our century have cast a net of intellect round jewels of feeling which only here or there show through it. And if one believes that on this important point one hears the best among one's contemporaries making mistakes, there comes a time when one shakes off one's indolence and feels the need to speak out. Sainte-Beuve's method is not, at first sight, such an important affair. But perhaps in the course of these pages we may be led to realise that it touches on very important intellectual problems, and on what is perhaps for an artist the greatest of all; this relative inferiority of the intellect which I spoke of at the beginning. Yet all the same, it is intellect we must call on to establish this inferiority. Because if intellect does not deserve the crown of crowns, only intellect is able to award it. And if intellect only ranks second in the hierarchy of virtues, intellect alone is able to proclaim that the first place must be given to instinct.

1

I *n slumbers*

At the time of that morning which I want—why, I do not know—to fix in my memory, I was already ill, staying up all night, going to bed at sunrise, and sleeping during the day. But then I was still very close to a time, which I hoped to see return and now think of as having made part of another man's life, when I got into bed at ten p.m. and slept on, except for a few brief wakings, till morning. Often I fell asleep almost as soon as I had put out the light, so quickly that I had no time to tell myself that I was growing drowsy; so that half an hour later, awakened by the thought that it was time to go to sleep, I would try to throw away the newspaper which I supposed I was still holding, saying to myself, "It's time to put out the lamp and settle down for the night," and be much surprised to see only a darkness there, soothing to my eyes and even more soothing to my mind, which received it as something causeless and incomprehensible, something truly obscure.

I lit the candle and looked at my watch. It was not midnight yet. I heard the distant or less distant whistling of trains that plotted the extent of the lonely countryside where on some fine moonlit night the traveller hurries along the road to the nearest railway station, dwelling on the pleasure enjoyed with the friends he has just left, the pleasures of arriving home. I laid my cheek against the pillow's blooming cheeks, which, forever plump and cool, are like the cheeks of our childhood against which we press our own. Once again I struck a light, and looked at my watch. It was not midnight yet. This is the hour when some sick man, lodged for the night in a strange hotel and roused by a savage assault of pain, sees with rejoicing a streak of daylight under his door. Heaven be praised, it is already morning!—in a minute or two the hotel will be astir, he will be able to ring his bell, some one will come and look after him. He bears with his sufferings. There, surely that was a footstep. . . . At that moment, the streak of light under his door goes out. It is midnight, they have turned off the gas whose light he mistook for the light of morning, and all the long night through he will have to lie anguishing and unaided.

I put out the light, I fell asleep again. Sometimes out of a constrained position of my thigh a woman would be born, as Eve was born from Adam's side; created by the pleasure I was on the point of enjoying, I fancied it was she who offered it to me. My body, feeling its own warmth as hers, tried to recapture her, and I awoke. All humankind seemed remote from me in comparison with this woman whom I had just parted from; my cheek was still hot with her kisses, my body cramped by the weight of hers. Little by little, she faded out of my mind, and the girl of my dream was forgotten as speedily as though she were a flesh and blood mistress. At other times I went sleep-walking into the days of my childhood, resuming, easy as a glove, those sensations which by one's tenth year are irreparably mislaid—insignificant sensations that we would be so happy to feel again, as the man who knows he will not live to see another summer will yearn even for the indoor buzz of flies that tells of the hot sun without, or for the whine of mosquitoes that tells of the scented night. I would dream that our old priest was pulling my curls, a thing which had been the terror and tyranny of my childhood. The fall of Chronos, Prometheus's discovery of fire, the birth of Christ, could not have more enlarged the heavens above man's heretofore bowed shoulders than did the shearing of my curls, severing me for ever from that frightful dread. I must admit that other pains and other fears replaced it; but the world's axis had been shifted. In sleep, I painlessly re-entered this world of the Old Dispensation, only waking from it when, having tried in vain to elude the poor priest, dead for so many years, I felt my locks sharply tweaked from behind. And before falling asleep again, and remembering perfectly well that the priest was dead and my hair short, all the same I was careful to consolidate my sheltering nest of pillow, blanket, handkerchief and wall, before returning to that queer world where the priest was alive and I had curls.

And there are other sensations, belonging to the years gone by, that also come back only in dreams and, unpoetical though they may be, bring with them all the poetry of youth—just as there is nothing so full of the sound of Easter churchbells and the first violets as those last cold days of winter which spoil our holidays and compel us to light the fire before midday. I would not venture to speak of these sensations which from time to time revisited me in sleep if they had not then seemed almost poetic, totally irrelevant to my present self, and colourless as those aquatic flowers whose roots are not attached to earth. La Rochefoucauld said that only our first loves are involuntary. So is it, too, with those pleasures taken in solitude, which later on we only make use of to pass off the absence of a woman, imagining to ourselves that She is with us. But when I was twelve years old, and for the first time, going upstairs to the top floor of our house at Combray, locked myself into the water-closet with its dangling garlands of orris root, it was an unknown pleasure that I went in search of, sufficient in itself and not a substitute for anything else.

It was an unusually spacious room for a water-closet. The door locked securely, but the window always stood open to accommodate a young lilac which having taken root in the outside wall had pushed its scented head through the aperture. So far aloft, in the attics of the house, I was completely alone, but this element of being out of doors added a delicious uneasiness to the sense of security which those sturdy bolts assured to my solitude. Then, in search of a pleasure that I did not know, I began to explore myself, and if I had been engaged in performing a surgical operation on my brain and marrow I could not have been more agitated, more terrified. I believed at every moment that I should die. But what of that?— my consciousness, exalted by pleasure, knew itself to be wider and more powerful than the universe which I saw remotely through the window, a universe in whose immensity and duration my everyday thoughts were resigned to claiming no more than a gnat's share. Far as the forest might stretch and the clouds round themselves above it, I felt that my spirit extended a little further, was not quite filled by it, had still a little margin to spare. I felt the lovely swelling hill-sides that rose like breasts on either side of the river supported, like mere insubstantial reflections, on the dominating stare of my pupils. All this world reposed on me, and I was more than it, and could not die.

I paused to draw breath. Wishing to sit down without being incommoded by the sun which was shining full on the seat I quoted to it: " 'Take yourself off, my boy, to make room for me;' "[1] and I drew the curtains, though the lilac bough prevented me from shutting the window. At last a shimmering jet arched forth, spurt after spurt, as when the fountain at Saint-Cloud begins to play—which we can recognise (since there is a personality in the untiring flow of its waters that their unyielding curve gracefully, incessantly, portrays) in the portrait Hubert Robert made of it, only there the admiring crowd had [   ][2] which speckle the old master's picture with little seed-pods, pink, reddened, or black.

In that moment I felt a sort of caress surrounding me. It was the scent of lilac-blossom, which in my excitement I had grown unaware of. But a bitter smell, like the smell of sap, was mixed with it, as though I had snapped the branch. I had left a trail on the leaf, silvery and natural as a thread of gossamer or a snail-track, that was all. But on that bough, it seemed to me like the forbidden fruit on the Tree of Knowledge; and like the races that give non-human forms to their deities, for some time afterward it was in the guise of this almost interminably extensible silvery thread which I had to spin out of myself by going widdershins to the normal course of my life that I pictured the devil.

Despite that smell of a broken branch and that smell of wetted linen, it was the gentle lilac-scent that prevailed. It came to me as familiarly as when I went to play in the park on the outskirts of the town, where, even before one caught sight of the white gate with its lilac trees nearby, swaying their plumed heads and

supple frames like elderly ladies who still preserve
the mannered graces of their youth, the lilac-scent
came to meet us, welcoming us to the path that led
upstream beside the river—there, where the bottles
that boys laid in the current to catch minnows gave a
double impression of coolness, because not only do they
contain water, and make it seem like glass, as table
carafes do, but are contained in water, which makes
them seem almost liquid; there, where the tadpoles,
annulled and invisible in the water a moment before, clotted in a seething nebula round the bread
pellets we threw in, and a few paces before we crossed
the little wooden bridge where, at the corner, in
high summer, a fisherman in a straw hat sprouted
among the sloe-bushes. He would nod respectfully to
my uncle, who doubtless knew him, and signal to us to
make no noise. But for all that, I have never known
who he was, I have never met him in the town; and
while even the precentor, the beadle, and the choir-
boys had, like Olympian Gods, a humbler existence
where I had dealings with them as the farrier, the
dairyman, and the grocer's sons, so, a Roland for an
Oliver, just as I never saw the small stucco gardener
in the soliciter's garden engaged in anything but gar-
dening, I never saw the fisherman doing anything but
fish, in those summer months when the pathway was
tufted with leafy sloe-bushes, with his straw hat and
his alpaca coat, at the time of day when even the
clouds and the chimes idled in the empty sky, when
carp, revolting against the monotony of the hour,
leaped vehemently, hysterically, into the alien element of air, when governesses consulted their watches
and said that it was not tea-time yet.

edrooms

Though from time to time sleep conveyed me painlessly back into those years when I knew terrors and
pleasures that now exist no more, for the most part
the bed, the armchairs, the whole room could scarcely
have been more obscured in slumber than I. A particle
in that sleeping whole, I only woke up for long enough
to be momentarily and appreciatively conscious that
everything was asleep, to listen to the creaking of
wainscot that one only hears in a sleeping room, to
stare at the kaleidoscopic darkness, and to hasten back
to partake in the insensibility of my bed, where I lay
with outstretched limbs like a trellised vine. In those
brief wakings I played no more part than an apple or
a pot of jam on the shelf might play, which on being
summoned to a moment's dim awareness, and having
ascertained that the cupboard was dark and that the
wainscot creaked, would find nothing more urgent to
do than to sink back into the voluptuous insensibility
of the other apples and the other pots of jam.

Sometimes my slumber was so deep or took possession of me so abruptly that even the sense of my
whereabouts was mislaid in it. I sometimes wonder if
the immovableness of things around us is not wished
on them by our conviction that they are what they are
and no other. The fact remains that whenever I woke
up without knowing where I was, all—things and
years and places—swirled round me in the darkness.

My body, still too torpid to move hand or foot, lay
guessing at its surroundings. All those which it had
known from childhood onward offered themselves in

turn to its groping memory, reassembling round it every place I had ever slept in, even those which for years I had not called to mind and might never have called to mind till my dying day, although they were places I ought not to have forgotten. It remembered the room, the doorway, the passage, the last waking thought which reappears as the first thought on waking. From the lie of the bed it recalled where the crucifix hung, and the smell of the alcove in that bedroom at my grandparents' house, in those days when there were still bedrooms and parents and a proper time for everything, when one loved one's parents not because they were intellectually congenial but because they were one's parents, when one went to bed not because one felt inclined to but because it was bedtime, and signified one's willing acceptance of the complete rites of slumber by climbing up two steps into the great bed and drawing together the blue rep curtains with blue stamped velvet borders, and when, if one fell ill, the old regimen, ignoring those immoral remedies which enable you to get up and go about your business in a false belief that you are no longer unwell, kept one abed, with a night light on the Sienna marble mantlepiece, for three and four days together, lying under blankets in a sweat fostered by harmless herb-teas, distillations of flowers and of the field-lore of sixty generations of old women. It was in this bed that my body supposed itself to be lying, and in a flash it had recovered what in those days was my first thought when it woke and stretched itself: it was time to get up, light my lamp and prepare my lesson before starting for school, if I did not want a bad mark.

But my body's memory recalled another posture; I

turned over to assume it, the bed had changed its position, the room its shape. It was that room, so lofty and
so narrow, that pyramid of a room, where I slept
when I went to Dieppe for change of air after an illness, and whose shape my soul had found it so difficult,
for the first two nights, to settle down in. For one's
soul is under a compulsion to fill and refurbish every
new receptacle it may be called on to inhabit, to
breathe its scents into it and to attune to its pitch; and
till then I know how one can suffer during those first
evenings, while one's soul is still a stranger, and has
to fall in with the colour of the upholstery, the tick
of the clock, the smell of the counterpane, and strive
and strive again, expanding, lengthening, contracting
itself, to take on the shape of a pyramidal bedroom.
But if I am in that room and getting over an illness,
then Mamma is lying near me! I cannot hear the
sound of her breathing, nor yet the sound of the
waves. . . . But already my body has conjured up
another attitude; now it is seated, not lying down.
Where, then?—in a wicker chair in the garden at Au-
teuil? No, it is too hot for that. In the cardroom of
the club at Évian, where they must have put out the
lights without noticing me where I had fallen asleep.
. . . But the walls close in, my armchair makes an
about-turn and has its back to the window. I am in my
room at Réveillon. I have gone up as usual for a rest
before dinner; I must have fallen asleep in my chair;
perhaps they have finished dinner.

It would not have been held against me. Many
years had gone by since the days when I lived with my
grandparents. At Réveillon we did not have dinner till
nine o'clock, after coming back from the walk for

which we set out at almost the hour when formerly I would have been returning from my longest excursions. The pleasure of coming back to the great house when it stood out against a sunset sky that reddened in the fishponds, and then reading for an hour by lamplight before seven o'clock dinner, was replaced by another, more hermetical pleasure. We would set out at nightfall, down the village street. Here and there a shop, lit from within like an aquarium and filled with rich glinting lamplight, displayed behind its glass front people extended by long shadows who, moving slowly through their element of golden light and unaware that we were watching them, single-mindedly performed for our benefit the dazzling private theatricals of their improbable everyday lives.

Then I came to the fields; on the one side, sunset had died away, over the other, the moon was already shining. Presently, they were entirely flooded with moonlight. An undulating blue-grey irregular triangle of sheep flocking homeward was all we encountered. I walked on like a ship bound on its solitary course. With my shadow following me like a wake, I had already traversed a stretch of enchanted ground and left it behind me. Sometimes the lady of the castle walked beside me. We were soon beyond those fields whose furthest boundaries I had never reached in the longest of my former walks, my afternoon walks, and beyond that church, and that manor house, which I had known only as names, and I thought could have no place except on a map of dreamland. The landscape altered, it was full of ascents and descents, and from time to time, when we had scaled a hillside and looked down on the mystery of a deep valley carpeted with moonlight, we would pause for a moment, that lady and I, before going down into that opalescent cup. At some remark made by the impassive lady, I realized in a flash that I had unwittingly become part of her intimate life, a life in which I could not have conceived myself installed and whence she would already have dismissed me by the morrow of the day I left her castle.

Thus my body builds around it room after room: wintry rooms where one loves to hold the outer world at bay, where one keeps the fire going all night and wraps about one's shoulders a cloak of warm air, smoke-coloured, smoke-scented, and shot with ruddy gleams; summer rooms where one loves to be gathered to the breast of nature, rooms where one sleeps, a bedroom I had in Brussels whose proportions were so pleasing, so spacious and yet so cosy, that it seemed a nest to hide in and a world to explore.

All this had been conjured up in no more than a few seconds. Then for a moment I feel myself lying in a narrow bed with other beds on either side. Reveille has not sounded yet, and I must get up at once if I am to have time to drink a glass of coffee and milk in the canteen before going out on a route march through the countryside with the band playing ahead.

The night had drawn to an end while these various rooms filed slowly through my recollection, and my body faltered among them, still uncertain where it had woken up, until my memory gave it the word that it was in my bedroom of time present. Once there, it reconstructed it from floor to ceiling, but having started from its own, none too certain, position, it had miscalculated the position of everything. I had settled that round me was, here, the chest of drawers, there, the fireplace, yonder, the window. Then, just above the place I had allotted to the chest of drawers, I saw a streak of daybreak.

3

The days

That slender streak above the window-curtains tells
me by its degree of brightness what sort of day it is,
and tells me the mood of the morning even before re-
porting on its sky; yet I could do without it. Still
lying with my face to the wall, and even before the
streak of light has shown itself, I can tell, by the
sound of the first approaching tram, and the ring of
its bell, whether it comes drudging through the rain
or has set out for a blue horizon. For not only the
time of year but every kind of weather provides
it with a different atmospheric density, like a particular musical instrument on which it will play its per-
sistent tune of rumble and ring, and this same tune
will not only sound different to us, but will take on a
colour and a purport, and express quite a different
feeling if it is muffled like a drum by fog, if it melts
and sings like a fiddle—and it is quite ready to assume
that light, glinting tone-colour—in an air that rip-
ples with breezes, or if it pierces the blue ice of a
sunny day in winter with the gimlet-note of a fife.
The first street noises bring me the tedious rain
that benumbs them, the frosty sunlight in which
they ring out, the despondency of the fog that
quenches them, the gusty sweetness of a mild blowing
day, where they are scarcely moistened by a passing
shower before a puff of wind wipes them over and a
sunbeam dries them.
It is on days like this, above all if the wind in the
chimney is sounding an irresistible bugle-call which
makes my heart beat quicker than any young girl's

through whose opened windows come strains of dance-music and the rumble of carriages conveying others to the ball she has not been invited to, that I would like to have spent the night in a train and to be arriving in the first light at some town in Normandy, Caudebec, or Bayeux, whose old steeple and ancient name would deck it for me as if with its traditional Caux coif, or Queen Matilda lace cap; whereupon I would set out to walk along the coast beside a stormy sea until I came to the fishermen's church, round which the waves that seem to billow on in the transparence of the painted windows where they buoy up the blue and purple warships of William the Conqueror and his host, have drawn piously, protectingly, aside to leave untouched between their encircling green surges that crypt of submarine smothered silence and damp where a little water still stagnates here and there in the rock-pools of the holy-water stoups.

And the morning's weather does not even need the tint of its daylight and the sound of the street noises to disclose itself and summon me towards the season and the climate whose ambassador it seems to be. Feeling a calm and slowed-down conduct of affairs in that little city of nerves and blood-vessels which I carry within me, I know that it is raining, and I wish myself at Bruges where, as if in a picture by Breughel, a couple of pullets, some moorhens, and a porker would be roasting for my luncheon before a furnace as red as a winter sun. If through my slumber I have already felt all those little citizens, my nerves, brisk and wideawake before I am, I rub my eyes and look at my watch to find out if I can get to Amiens in time to see the cathedral beside the frozen Somme, with its statues sheltered from the wind under their canopies, basking in the midday sun against its golden wall and patterning it with a whole vine of shadow. But on misty mornings I would like to awaken as a newcomer in some castle where I had not arrived until after nightfall; and getting up late, shivering in my nightshirt, blithely returning to scorch myself at the fire blazing on the hearth, while the frozen winter sunlight comes in to warm itself on the near-by carpet, I would see from the window a stretch of unknown country and between the wings of the house, which make a splendid appearance, a huge forecourt where stablemen bring up the horses which will presently take us into the forest to look at fishponds and a monastery, my early-arisen hostess meanwhile giving orders to her household that they are not to disturb me by making a noise.

There are times, when a morning of spring has strayed into winter and the clapper of the man who sells goat's-milk sends a purer note than a Sicilian shepherd's flute into the blue sky, when I would like to cross the snows of the Saint Gothard and come down into a flowering Italy. And already, touched by this morning sunbeam, I have jumped out of bed, I perform a thousand frisks and capers that I see corroborated in the looking-glass, I delightedly utter quite uninspired remarks, and I sing—for the poet is like the statue of Memnon; one ray from the rising sun is enough to make him sing.

When all the other men who, one above another, inhabit me have in succession been reduced to silence, when, one after another, they have been felled by intense bodily pain or by sleep, the one who finally remains, who still keeps his feet, is I vow! someone ex-

actly like that mannikin whom I used to see displayed
in opticians' shop-windows when I was a child, who
opened his umbrella in wet weather and on fine days
lifted his hat. If it is a fine day, in vain do my shutters
keep out every breath of air; my eyes may be closed
and a frightful attack of asthma, brought on by just
this same fine weather, by a lovely golden haze I
stifle in, may by dint of suffering almost deprive me
of consciousness, may deprive me of all possibility of
speech; I can no longer utter a word, nor frame a
thought, I am too exhausted even to summon up a
wish for rain that would put an end to my attack; then,
in this vast silence broken only by the sound of my
gaspings for breath, I hear from far down in the
depth of myself, a small voice saying merrily: "It's a
fine day . . . it's a fine day." Tears of pain run down
my cheeks, I cannot speak, but if I could snatch a moment's breath, I would sing; and the optician's mannikin, who is all that is left of me, takes off his hat
and proclaims the sun.

So when later on I took to staying up all night and
spending all day in bed, though I did not see the light
of day I felt its proximity with an appetite for light
and living all the sharper because it could not be
gratified. With the first pallid, scarcely emerging,
chimes of the angelus that pass overhead, faint and
swift as the dawn-wind, scattered like the raindrops
of a morning shower, I began to hanker after the
pleasure felt by those who start before sunrise for a
day's outing, who arrive punctually at the meeting-
place in the yard of a little hotel in the country and
walk up and down waiting for the horses to be
harnessed to the carriage, rather proud to be showing

those who had doubted their promises of overnight that they have not overslept. It's going to be fine. On fine summer days an afternoon nap is as romantic as a siesta.

What did it matter to me that I was in bed and my curtains drawn? The hour of day had only to declare itself by a ray of light or a whiff of scent, and I knew it for the hour it was, not just in my imagination but in the authenticity of time present, with all the possibilities of living that it offered to mankind, not a fancied but a real hour that I would partake in, like a warrant the more added to the truth of pleasure.

I didn't go out, I didn't have lunch, I didn't leave Paris. But when the rich air of a summer forenoon had finally polished and isolated the artless smells of my wash-stand and my wardrobe, and these reposed, quiescent and distinct, in a pearly chiaroscuro which the light sifting through my large blue silk curtains had finished "glazing over," I knew this was the time when school boys, such as I had been a few years earlier, and professional men, such as I might have become, were getting out of the train or the river-steamer on their way to have lunch at home in the outer suburbs, and that consulting their watches under the limetrees of the mall or in front of the sweltering butcher's shop to make sure they were "on time" they tasted in advance the pleasure of walking through a whole rainbow of scents in a dark, flower-filled little drawing room where a motionless shaft of light seemed to have anaesthetised the air; and that when they had made their way into the shadowy back-kitchen where as in a damp cave sudden iridescences catch the eye and cider is chilling in stone water-troughs—chilling to such purpose that when they drink it, as they soon will, out of those charming, slightly discoloured, rather clumsy glasses that tempt one, as some female flesh does, to press on from the half-measure of kissing to biting, it will go down cleaving to mouth and throat like an icy aromatic jelly —they tasted in advance the cool freshness of the dining room where the air—a block of frozen light, streaked like an agate with the various odours of the tablecloth, the sideboard, the cider, and that of the gruyère cheese too, which seemed mystically abetted by the prismatic reflections of the glass knife-rests beside it—would be lightly veined with the smell of cherries and apricots when the fruit dishes were brought in. Bubbles would rise through the cider, in such multitudes that others were left hanging on the side of the glass, whence one could have scooped them up with a spoon, as a net lowered into the swarming vitality of tropical seas brings up thousands of ova; and seen from the outside, they would freckle the glass like a Venetian glass, and give it a look of extreme fragility by embroidering its cider-flushed surface with a thousand tiny dots.

If I got up for a moment and drew back my curtains to put myself in tune with the light, it was as a composer, who hearing in his head the symphony he is writing on paper scarcely needs to strike a note in order to make sure he is in tune with the real pitch of instruments. At the same time I put myself in tune with those other realities for which solitude whets the appetite, and whose possibility, whose reality, gives a value to life: the women one does not know. Now one of them is going by, glancing from right to left, unhurried, changing her course like a fish in clear water. Beauty is not like a *ne plus ultra* of what we suppose beautiful, an abstract type of the beauty before our eyes; on the contrary, it is something novel and, until life puts it before our eyes, unimaginable. That tall girl, for instance, in her later teens, with a pert expression, and pale cheeks, and crisply curling hair. Oh, if I were up! . . . But at least, I know that the days abound in such chances, and my appetite for life grows thereby. For because every beauty is a separate type, because there is no one Beauty but many beautiful women, a beautiful woman is an invitation to a happiness which she alone can fulfill.

How delightful they are, and how painful, those balls where not only pretty girls with fragrant cheeks throng past us, but the fugitive, invisible ranks of all those unknown lives which we long to explore. Sometimes, in the silence of an eager regretful glance, a girl will unlatch her life to us, but only our desire can enter. And by itself, desire is blind, and to desire a girl whose very name is unknown to us is no better than to wander blindfolded in a place of which one knows that it would be paradise to be able to revisit it, and that nothing will enable us to recognise it again. . . .

But she, how little we know of her! We would like to know her name, which would at least allow us to trace her, and perhaps is such that she would despise ours, the parents, whose rules and customs she obeys and follows, the house she lives in, the streets she walks in, the friends she meets and those other, happier, friends who visit her at home, the place in the country where she goes in summer and which sets her at even greater remove from us, her tastes, her thoughts, all the things that denote her identity, make up her life, catch her eye, contain her presence, fill her mind, take the weight of her body.

Now and then I went to the window and lifted a corner of the curtain. I saw, going by in a spatter of gold, on their way to a catechising or a lecture, with their governesses following them, with every careless movement expurgated from their supple gait, some of those young girls who seem to belong to a small enclosed order of society, and to be blind to the common herd they walk among, except to laugh at it unrestrainedly, and with an insolence which they look on as the hallmark of their superiority; young girls who with a glance seem to establish a distance between you and themselves which their beauty makes a matter for regret; not young girls of the aristocracy; for the harsh distinctions of riches, of splendour, of elegance, are nowhere so completely cancelled as among the aristocracy: aristocracy may pursue wealth for amusement's sake, but attaches no value to it, and without fuss or favour genuinely puts it on the same level as our ungraceful poverty; not young girls of the world of intellectuals, for some of those going by might be very hail-fellow goddesses; not even young girls of the purely moneyed world, for money venerates what it hopes to purchase, and is still not so far distant from hard work and respectfulness. No, but young girls brought up in that world which can keep you at the furthest and most merciless remove, a clan of the moneyed world which, thanks to the pretty figure of a wife or the idleness of a husband, has begun to rub shoulders with the aristocracy in the hunting-field and will try to marry into it tomorrow, today still keeps up the middle-class grudge against it but already suffers agonies lest a plebeian surname should obscure the fact that its wives are on the same visiting-list as a duchess, lest a father's profession, solicitor or stock-jobber, should be taken to mean that he lives like other solicitors or stock-jobbers, people whose daughters one doesn't want to meet. It is difficult to get into this set because the father's associates are already banned from it, and the duchess would have to stoop too low to open a way for you. How often at the very moment when their beauty enchanted me, have not these young girls, fined down by several generations of living in luxury and playing games, made me feel with a single look the whole extent of the really impassible territory between them and me—and for me all the more impassible as the grandees I knew did not know them and could not give me an introduction.

I catch sight of one of those beings whose particular face tells me that a new happiness is possible. Beauty multiplies the possibilities of happiness by its particularity. Each being is like an unsurmised ideal that opens before us, and to see a delightful face going by that we do not know opens up a prospect of new lives we long to be living. They disappear at the turn of the street but we hope to see them again, we are left with the thought that there are a great many more lives to be lived than we supposed, and this enhances our self-esteem. A new face that has gone by is like the charm of an unvisited country which a book has disclosed. We can read its name and a train goes there. It doesn't matter if we don't set off. We know the country is there, we have a further reason for living. So I looked out of the window to make sure that the real, the potential life, whose proximity I never ceased to

feel, held countless possibilities of different ways of
being happy. A pretty girl the more vouched for the
reality and multiformity of happiness. Alas, we shall
never know all the happinesses—the happiness of being led on by the gaiety of that fair-haired chit, of being known by the solemn eyes in that stern sombre
face, of holding that slender frame on one's knee, of
knowing the laws and ordinance of that aquiline nose
and those steely eyes and that high white forehead.
But at least they give us new reasons for living.

At times the rank smell of petrol came in—that
smell which spoils the country, according to modern
thinkers who believe that the human soul can exercise
free will as to what brings joy to it, etc., who believe
that truth is objective, not subjective. But the perceived is so instantly transformed by the perceiver
that the smell of petrol came into my room quite simply as the most intoxicating of all the summer smells
of the country, the smell that summed up both its
beauty and the joy of speeding over it, of being on
one's way to a longed-for destination. Even the smell
of hawthorn would but have called up in my mind a
sort of motionless, circumscribed happiness, a happiness tethered to a hedge. That delicious smell of
petrol, sky-coloured, sun-coloured petrol, was the
whole vast stretch of the countryside, and the joy of
setting out, of travelling on and on among cornflowers and poppies and crimson clover, of knowing that
I would arrive at the wished-for place where the
woman I loved awaited me. All that morning, I remember, a drive through those fields of La Beauce had
kept me away from her. She had stayed behind,
thirty miles off. From time to time there came a great
puff of wind that flattened the sunlit corn and sent

a shiver through the trees. And in that vast flat countryside where the furthest horizons seem to perpetuate the same landscape beyond the reach of sight, I
felt that this puff of wind had come directly from
where she awaited me, that brushing her face before
it brushed mine it had met with nothing on its way
from her to me except those limitless fields of corn
and cornflowers and poppies, which were like a single
field at whose two extremities we might have sta-
tioned ourselves in fond expectation, at a distance too
wide for sight to travel but which a puff of wind had
covered, sweet as if it were a kiss she had sent me, as
if her breath had travelled to my cheek—and which
I would cover so quickly in the car when the time
came to go back. I have loved other women, I have
loved other landscapes. The charm of drives in the
country has never lain so much in the presence of the
woman I was in love with, which from my fear of boring or displeasing her soon became so painful to me that
I did not try to prolong it, as in the hopefulness of
going towards her, where I would remain on some
pretext of necessity, and in the hope of being invited
to return with her. Thus a landscape depended on a
face. Perhaps, too, that face depended on a landscape.
In my conception of its charm, the place where I
would see it, that it would endear to me, where it
would succour my life, that it would share with me,
where it would bring me joy, was an integral part of
the charm itself, and of my hopes of life, and underlay my wish to love. Thus the charm of a human being vibrated in the depth of a landscape; thus a landscape committed all its poetry to a human being; thus
each of my summers took the face and form of a
human being and the form of a landscape—or, rather,

the form of one selfsame dream in which my desire for a human being, my desire for a landscape, quickly coalesced. One year, spindle-shaped clusters of red or blue flowers showing above a sunny wall, and leaves glistening with moisture had been the leit-motif that expressed all I asked of nature; the following year, it was a melancholy lake under the morning haze. One after another, the pleasures that I had tried to carry into such landscapes, or renounced the landscapes to remain with, or grew enamoured of because I believed (often erroneously, but even when I knew I had been mistaken, the illusion remained) that they were native there, all these the smell of the passing automobile had restored to me, whilst inviting me towards pleasures to come—for it is a smell of summer, of power, of freedom, and nature, and love.

4

The Countess

Our flat on the second-floor was in the side block of one of those old town-houses, the like of which is now scarcely to be found in Paris, where the forecourt was encumbered with as many little lean-to workshops (perhaps the swelling tide of democracy had brought them in, perhaps they were survivals from the time when a nobleman extended his patronage over a retinue of small craftsmen) as the approaches to cathedrals which have not been "cleaned up" by reformers and restorers, beginning at the lodge gates with a cobbler's shop hedged round by lilacs, where the concierge mended shoes and reared poultry and rabbits, while at the further end of the courtyard there dwelt, as one would expect and, as I supposed, by right of immemorial freehold though in fact on a recent lease, the "titled lady" who at that date was always established in a little "house in a quiet corner," and who, driving out in her great barouche and pair, distributed smiles from under the brim of a hat that was trimmed with irises like those in the cobbler-tailor-concierge's window-box, and waved a vaguely acknowledging hand to the water-carrier, to my parents, to the concierge's children, to show that though she did not stop she was not proud.

Then the rumble of her carriage wheels died away and the courtyard gates were closed again, and while the barouche went from house to house at the leisurely pace of her immense horses, its length extending over the width of a housefront, the footman's hat level with the first-floor windows, she hallowed the insensitive streets with an odour of aristocracy, pausing for visiting-cards to be dropped, summoning shopkeepers to her carriage door for orders, passing friends who were bound for an At Home she was going to, or were even on their way back from it. But the barouche turned down a side street, for the Countess wished to take a turn in the Bois first and do the At Home on her way back, when there would be no one left, and the last carriages would be leaving the door. Taking, elbows well in, her hostess's hands into a clasp of suede gloves, demonstrating admiration for her clothes by a light pat here or there, like a sculptor displaying a statue or a dressmaker trying-on a bodice, no one knew better than she how to say, with that grave candour that went so well with her gentle eyes and her low-pitched voice: "Really, it wasn't *possible* to get here sooner, with the best will in the world" —meanwhile casting a lovely blue backward glance over the whole concatenation of obstacles which had impeded her but which she would not go into, being too well-brought-up to talk about herself.

As our flat was in the inner courtyard it overlooked her dwelling. When I think about her today, I realise that she held a certain particular charm—though one had only to talk to her for it to evaporate—and that she was totally unaware of it. She was one of those people who have a little magical lamp, but who will never know about its light. And when one gets to know them and talks to them, one follows suit, one no longer sees the mysterious light, the little charm, the faint colour; and all their poetry is lost. One must leave off meeting them and suddenly see them again as they were in the past, in the days when one did not know them, for the little light to shine again and the quality of poetry to be restored. So it has to be, apparently, in the case of things, and places, and griefs, and loves; those in possession of them do not see the poetry; it only shines at a distance. This is what makes life so disappointing for those who have the gift of seeing the little poetic light. If we think about the people we have felt a wish to know, we are compelled to admit that once there was a Fair Unknown whose acquaintance we sought, and who vanished as soon as we met him. He recurs to the mind's eye like a portrait of someone we have never met again, and with whom our friend X . . . has certainly nothing in common. Familiar faces, you have eclipsed your looks of aforetime. Our whole life is passed in allowing the force of habit to obliterate those splendid canvases on which a first impression portrayed persons unknown; and when for a moment we have enough energy to scrape off all the clumsy repainting that covers the original physiognomy, we see emerging the faces of those whom at that time we still did not know, as the first impression engraved them; and we feel they are the faces of strangers. . . . You, my intelligent friend —intelligent, that is, as the rest—whom I daily talk to, what have you kept of the impetuous young man with hallucinated eyes bolting from their sockets whom I saw hurrying down a theatre gangway, like a knight by Burne-Jones or an angel by Mantegna?

Besides, even when we love, a woman's face changes so quickly. The face we love is a face that we have made up for ourselves out of a certain way of glancing, a certain detail of a cheek, a certain something about a nose; she is one of the thousand women who might spring at our bidding out of one woman; and in the twinkling of an eye, she will be loved under some other face. Just now, it was her dusky pallor and the way her shoulders implied a disdainful shrug. Today it is a mild, almost shy, full-face, where the contrast between pale cheeks and black hair no longer plays any part. How many women in turn represent one woman for us, and how far away is she we saw when we first set eyes on her. The other night, when I was taking the Countess back from an evening party to where she lives still and where I have not lived for so many years, in the midst of an embrace, I held her face away from mine, in an attempt to see her as something at a distance from me, a portrait of a lady, and as I saw her long ago when she stopped in the street to say something to the dairywoman. The violet eyes, the classic nose, the disdainful mouth, the tall figure, the air of melancholy—I wanted to see them combined in their former harmony, and then while my eyes still held the retrieved image of the past, to fasten my lips on hers and kiss the woman whom then I would have kissed. But alas, the faces we kiss, the places we live in, even the dead for whom we put on mourning, retain nothing of what made us hope to love them, hope to live with them, dread losing them. When the art that claims to be realistic suppresses that inestimable truth, the witness of the imagination, it suppresses the only thing of value; and on the other hand, if it records it, it enriches the meanest material; it could give a value to snobbery if instead of describing it in its relation to fashionable life—where, like real love, real travel, real sorrow, it counts for nothing—it tried to recover it in the light that never was—the only true one—that plays from the longing eyes of a young snob on the violet-eyed Countess as she sets out in her carriage on a summer Sunday.

Naturally, when I first saw the Countess, and fell in love with her, all I saw of her face was something as fleeting and evasive as what an artist pleases to pick out when he paints a *profil perdu*. But for me it was that—the kind of serpentining curve that comprised the briefest of glances, the arch of a nose, and a little pout at a corner of the mouth, and left out everything else; and when I met her in the courtyard or in the street, wearing different clothes and with a face which in the main was still unknown to me, I seemed to be meeting someone I did not know, while at the same moment my heart stopped because beneath the disguises of a hat trimmed with cornflowers and the face of a stranger I had glimpsed the possibility of the serpentine curve and the corner of a mouth that the other day had been puckered in a pout. Sometimes I spent hours vainly lying in wait for her, and suddenly there she was, I had seen the little wavy line that ended its course in the violet eyes. But soon this first arbitrary face which to us is a person, always turning the same profile where there is always the same slight lift of an eyebrow, the same dawning smile in the eye, the same preliminary pout always at the one corner of the mouth—and all this scissored out of the face and its repertory of possible expressions as arbitrarily, as instantaneously, as capriciously, and as unalterably as if it were a sketch that catches an impression and cannot vary—this is the person we see in the beginning; and then, a few days later, we see another expression and another face. The antithesis of hair so black and cheeks so pale, which was at first the dominant thing about it, we pay no further heed to; it is no longer the sparkle of a mocking eye, but the sweetness of a shy glance.

As the love she inspired in me enhanced the idea of what was wonderful in her titled rank, I saw her little house at the bottom of our courtyard as something inaccessible, and had I been told that by a law of nature commoners like me could no more set foot in it than take wing into the clouds I should not have been unduly surprised. I was at that blissful age when one knows nothing of real life, when things and people still wander at large and uncategoried through one's mind, but are differentiated and have some part of their character in some way imposed on them by the names they bear. I was rather like Françoise, our old servant, who believed that between the title of Marquise, borne by the Countess's mother-in-law, and the kind of awning called a marquise that shaded this lady's windows, there was a mystical affinity, and that no other kind of person but a Marquise could have such an awning.

Sometimes I was walking quietly down the street, thinking about her and telling myself that today there was no chance of meeting her, when all of a sudden, just as I was passing the dairy-shop, I felt transfixed, as a small bird might do on catching sight of a snake. Beside the counter, on the face of someone who was talking to the dairywoman while choosing a cream cheese, I had seen the quiver and ripple of a little curve that serpentined beneath a pair of bewitching violet eyes. On the morrow, thinking that she might go to the dairy again, I stood for hours at the street-corner, but I did not see her and was going heartbroken home when in crossing the road I had to save myself from a carriage which almost ran over me. And under a hat I did not know and in another face I saw the little serpent asleep, and the eyes, which then scarcely seemed violet at all, but which I was quite sure of; and my heart had stopped even before I was sure. Every time I saw her, I reeled, and turned pale; I would have bowed to the ground before her if I could, and she thought I was "well brought up." In *Salammbô*, there is a snake who embodies the tutelary Genius of a family; in the same way, it seemed to me that the little serpentine curve reappeared in her sister and her nephews. It seemed to me that if I could get to know them I should find them tinctured with her essence. One and all, they seemed different sketches of the same hereditary face. When I recognised her butler's blond side-whiskers nearing me round the bend of the street—her butler, who talked to her, who saw her lunching, as might one of her friends—my heart stopped yet again, as if I had been in love with him too.

Those forenoons, those daytime hours, were only of the nature of strings of pearls attaching her to the most brilliant pleasures of that date; wearing that blue dress, after that drive she went out again to lunch at the Duchesse de Mortagne's; in the evening, when houses are lit up for formal entertainments, she visited the Princesse d'Aleriouvres or Madame de Bruyvres, and after dinner, stepping into her waiting carriage and filling it with a shimmer of rustling silk and pearls and glances, she went to the Duchesse de Rouen's or the Comtesse de Dreux's. Later on, when I had come to regard these same ladies as bores whose houses I no longer wanted to go to and saw that she felt about them as I did, her life lost its glamour for me, and she often preferred to sit and talk with me rather than that we should go out to those festivities where alone, as I had once imagined, she must be completely herself, the residue that I saw keeping me merely as it were in the wings of a theatre, where one can gather no idea of the beauty of the play and the talent of the leading lady. Later on, the process of reason sometimes drew conclusions from her and from her life which, put into words, appear to mean the same thing as my day-dreams: she is exclusive, she only meets people of blue blood. Words, by then, and no more.

5

The article in Le Figaro[1]

I shut my eyes and waited for daylight. I thought about that article I had sent to *Le Figaro*, which they had now kept for a long time. I had even corrected the proofs. Every morning when I opened the paper I had hoped to see it. For the last few days I had given up hope, and I wondered if everything I sent them would be discarded like this. Presently I heard all the household getting up. Mamma would soon come in to see me—for already I only slept by day, and had good-night said to me as soon as I had read my letters. I reopened my eyes. Day had come. A servant entered. Soon Mamma came in too.

There was no need to guess twice if one wanted to know what she was about. As during her whole life she had never once given a thought to herself, and as the sole end of all her actions from the greatest to the least was our welfare—and, from the time when I had become sickly and my welfare had to go by the board, my solace and pleasure—it was easy enough, in the light of this interpretation which I had known from my infancy, to read her intentions in her doings, and to discover myself at the root of her intentions. So when, after she had said good-morning to me, I saw her face take on a look of airy unconcern while she casually put down the copy of *Le Figaro* beside me—but so close that I could not have stirred without seeing it—and when, as soon as this was done, I saw her hurry out of the room like an anarchist who had put down a bomb and, with a violence quite unlike herself, thrust back my old servant, who at that same mo-

ment was coming in, and who did not understand
what this extraordinary event was that was taking
place in my room, nor why she should not be present
at it, I understood at once what Mamma had wished
to conceal from me and knew that my article had appeared, that she had said nothing about it because she
did not want to take the bloom off my surprise, and
that she intended to keep out anyone whose presence
might cloud my joy, or even compel me for reasons of
decorum to veil it. Mamma had never put down my
letters with that free and easy demeanour unless there
had been among them either an article by me, or
about me or about someone I love, or something by
Jammes or Boylesve that would spell enchantment for
me, or an envelope addressed in some welcome handwriting.

I unfolded the copy of *Le Figaro*. Why, here is an
article on my subject! No! This is too bad, my very
words. . . . I shall write to the editor. . . . But I
said this too, and here is my name at the bottom. . . .
It is my article! But for a moment, my thoughts, swept
on by the impetus of this reaction, and perhaps already at this date grown rather the worse for wear,
continue to believe it isn't, just as elderly people cannot arrest a movement once they have begun it. But
quickly I return to the thought: it is my article.

Then I pick up that sheet of paper which by a mysterious process of multiplication, preserving its sin-
gleness while withholding it from nobody, is both one
and ten thousand, which is given to as many newsboys
who ask for it, and carried damp with morning fog
and printer's ink, under the red span of sky over Paris
to all those people who have just woken up and are

about to drink their morning coffee. What I am holding in my hand is not only my own thought, it is thousands of wakened attentions taking it in. And if I am
to realise what is happening, I must abandon myself,
I must be for a moment some one of the ten thousand
readers whose curtains have just been drawn and on
whose freshly awakened mind my thought is about to
dawn in a manifold sunrise which fills me with more
hope and faith than the sunrise overhead. So I pick up
Le Figaro as if I did not know there was an article by
me in it; I purposely avert my glance from the place
where my words appear, trying to discover experimentally where it would be likeliest to fall, and load-
ing the dice by folding the page with that part hinder-
most, as someone who is waiting spaces out the minutes so that he may not be led away into counting them
too fast. I feel my lips purse up in the grimace of my
reader who expects to find nothing in particular, then
my glance falls on my article, in the centre of the page,
and I begin to read. Every phrase conveys the image I
meant to call up. In every sentence the thought I
wanted to express is made clear from the first words;
but as it reaches me in the sentence it is more abun-
dant, more detailed, enriched—since I, the author, am
for the time being the reader, and at the receiving end
merely, and when I wrote I was at the producing end,
and to the same thought which is now re-shaping itself
in my mind I then added harmonious amplifications
which at the sentence's beginning had not entered my
head, and whose ingenuity now amazes me. I feel it is
really impossible that the ten thousand who at this
moment are engaged in reading my article should not
be feeling as much admiration for me as I feel myself.
And the thought of their admiration plugs the little

gaps in my own. If I compared my article with the article I meant to write—as later on, alas! I shall do—instead of delightfully coherent passages I should probably find palsied stammerings which even to the most well-wishing reader could barely hint at what, before I took pen in hand, I supposed myself able to express. That was how I felt when I wrote it, when I revised it; in an hour's time I shall feel so again; but at this moment each sentence that I extorted from myself flows, not into my own mind, but into the minds of thousands on thousands of readers who have just woken up and opened *Le Figaro*.

In my attempt to become one of them, I put my previous intentions behind me, I give myself a blank mind which was ready to read something, no matter what, and which this delightful description, this unusual idea, this stroke of wit, this deep insight, this eloquent passage, coming one on the heels of another, have just assailed, beguiled, filled with the notion of my talent, convinced that I am to be preferred to all other writers. Above this vista of awakening intellects, the thought of my fame dawning on each mind shines on me with a rosier hue than the manifold sunrise flushing each window. If there is a word or two wrong—well, they will not notice it; and in any case, it is not too bad, and better than what they are used to. Now that this substance of ten thousand imagined approvals upholds me, the sense of my impotence, which is the sorrow of my life, changes to a sense of rejoicing in my strength. I escape from my poor opinion of myself, I draw life from words of praise, my mind matches itself by turns to the particular degrees of admiration I attribute to every bosom, and to the eulogies, soon to be paid me, which will discharge me from the painful duty of pronouncing on myself.

But alas, at the very moment when I profit by this discharge, my own work pronounces sentence on me. If I see a picture in my words, it is because I meant to paint it; but it is not there. And if in some places I have indeed managed to bring a description to life, even so, unless the description calls up something the reader already knows and loves, he will find nothing there to recognise and welcome. Re-reading one or two good passages I say to myself, Yes, these words convey what I thought, what I saw; I can rest easy, I have done my part, anyone coming on this will see what I meant, he has but to open *Le Figaro* to find this wealth of thought and imagery. As if thoughts lay on the printed page, as if they had but to meet the eye of a reader in order to be received into a mind where they were not already native. All mine can do is to awaken kindred thoughts in kindred spirits. In others, where my words find nothing to awaken, what an absurd notion of me will be called up! What will they make of it, these statements that mean things which not only will they never be able to understand, but which could not enter their heads? So when they read them, they see— what? And that is why all those readers of mine who know me will say: "It doesn't amount to much, that article of yours." "Very poor stuff." "A pity you wrote it," while I, telling myself they know best, wanting to fall in with their opinion, shall try to read my article with their eyes. But I can no more borrow their eyes than they could have seen with mine. As soon as I begin to read, the entrancing pictures come to life; I marvel at them impartially, one after another, I feel that all is said, that it is there, on the page, that people cannot fail to take it in, that if they gave their minds to it, if I told them to, they would feel as I do.

I would like to think that my marvellous ideas are even now running in every head, but in the same breath I think of all those people who don't read *Le Figaro*, or who will not happen to read it today, who have gone away for a day's shooting, or have not looked through it. Besides, will those who read it, read my article? If my acquaintances notice my name, they will read on, alas! But will they notice it? I congratulated myself on being on the front page but I have a lurking suspicion that there are people who turn at once to page two. True, one has to straighten out the paper to get to the second page, and my name is right in the middle of the front page. All the same, it seems to me that if one is turning over to read page two one notices nothing on the front page except the right-hand column. I put it to the test: I am the gentleman who is in a hurry to see who went to Mme. de Fitz-James's party, I take up *Le Figaro*, meaning to look at nothing on the front page. Exactly! The two right-hand columns catch my eye all right, but as for Marcel Proust, he might as well not be there. But surely, even if one only starts reading on page two, one always looks to see who wrote the main article. Then I ask myself who it was by yesterday, the day before yesterday, and I realise that very often I myself don't read the contributor's name. I vow that henceforward I will always look for it—as a jealous lover, to persuade himself of his mistress's fidelity, leaves off being unfaithful to her. But alas, I know that my attention will not bring about a general attentiveness, and that though in the future I shall always look at the front page this is no reason to assume others will do so too. On the contrary, I do not suppose that real life could be so much in accord with my wishes—as I did formerly, when hoping for a letter from my mistress I wrote it in my mind just as I would have liked it to be. Then, knowing that this could never happen, that not by any chance could she write the very letter I had imagined, in order that what I had imagined might remain within the bounds of possibility, and that she might write me that letter, I gave up imagining. Even if by some chance she had written it, it would not have pleased me, I should have believed I was reading a letter I had written myself. Alas, first love once over, we are so familiar with every phrase that can delight a lover's ear that not one of them, not the most longed-for, can bring us anything from outside ourselves. As soon as they are written in a language that is as much ours as our mistress's, and express thoughts we can hit on as naturally as she, it is inevitable that in reading them we should remain ourselves and, since the fulfilment chimes with the desire, feel little difference between having wished for them and getting them.

I send out the man-servant to buy me some more copies of Le Figaro, telling him that I want to give them away to friends—which is the case; but above all I want to handle the embodiment of my thought in these thousands of damp pages, to have another Le Figaro that a new purchaser would have had if my man-servant had not reached the newspaper kiosk just before him, and to imagine with another copy before me that I am a new reader. Thus, a new reader, I come on my article as if I had not read it, and with a virgin good-will; but in fact the new reader's impressions are not so very different from those of the first, and are

quite as much my own. At heart, I know quite well
that a number of people, some of them my intimate
friends, will make nothing of my article; but even
from these I get the agreeable feeling that today I
shall occupy their minds, if not with my thoughts,
which will be totally inapparent to them, at least with
my name, my personality, and the merit they impute
to some one able to write so many things they do not
understand at all. There is a person to whom this will
give the idea of me that I so much desire she should
have. Just by fact of existing, this article that she will
not understand is a declaration of my merit which will
reach her ears. Alas, a declaration of the merit of
someone she does not love will no more charm her
heart than a page filled with ideas she does not possess
will detain her mind.

Well then, before I settled down for my day's sleep
I would go and kiss Mamma and ask her what she
thought of the article; as I could not experimentally
ascertain if the ten thousand readers of *Le Figaro* had
read it and liked it, I was now impatient to cast some
soundings among people I knew. This was Mamma's
At Home day, and perhaps her visitors would talk to
her about it.

Before going to say goodnight to her, I drew back
my curtains. Now the pink sky overhead gave one the
feeling that the sun had rounded itself and was about
to bounce up by its own elasticity. This pink sky made
me long to travel, for I had often seen it from train
windows, after a night in which I had slept, not as I
do here in the stifling hush of things fast-closed and
brought to a standstill about me, but amid movement,
and borne on myself, like fish that swim as they sleep

and still keep on their course with the rattle of the brook all round them. So, waking or sleeping, I have been lulled by that noise of the wheels, which the ear couples as whim dictates, two and two, four and four, like a chime of bells, following an imaginarily-heard rhythm that seems to hurl one bell on the heels of another, on and on, until another rhythm takes over, which the bells or the noises of the train comply with as obediently. It was after such a night and while the train was carrying me at full speed towards places I longed for, that I saw in the square of the window a pink sky above some woods. Then the track took a turn, and there, instead, was a starry night-sky above a village whose streets were still full of a blue-grey nocturnal dusk. Then I hurried to the opposite window where I saw the lovely pink sky growing brighter and brighter above the woods, and thus I went from side to side to keep it in view, catching it again from the right-hand window when by a change in the train's direction I had lost it from the window on my left. It was one of those moments when one vows to spend one's life travelling. And now this wish came back to me: I would have liked to see once more, under this very sky, that wild ravine in the Jura and the watchman's hut, standing all alone beside the curve of the railway track.

But this was not all that I would have liked to see again. The train halted there, and as I stood at the window where a smell of coal-smoke came in, a girl of sixteen, tall and rosy-cheeked, walked by with steaming cups of *café au lait*. There is no spice in the abstract love of beauty, for it imagines beauty in terms of the already known, and confronts us with a made and concluded universe. But what a pretty girl the more has

to offer is precisely something we had not imagined—
not beauty, something in common with others, but a
person, something particular, a thing by itself, and
also something individual, which exists and in which
we would like to mingle our life. I called out "Coffee,
please!" She did not hear me. I saw this life in which
I counted for nothing, her eyes that had never known
me, her thoughts in which I played no part, going
away from me; I called her, she heard me, she turned
round, smiled and came back, and while I was drinking my coffee and the train was about to start, I stared
her full in the eyes; hers did not flinch, staring back
into mine with a look of astonishment, where, though,
my desire believed it saw fellow feeling. How I would
have liked to purloin her existence, to take her with
me on my journey, call my own, if not her body, at
least her attention, her time, her friendship, her ways.
There was no time to spare, for the train was starting.
I said to myself, I shall come back tomorrow. And
now, two years after, I feel that I will go back there,
that I will try to live in the neighbourhood, and early
one morning, under a pink sky and looking down on
that wild ravine, kiss the apple-cheeked girl who offers
me *café au lait.*

Another man carries his mistress with him, and
when the train goes on and the country girls are left
behind, she serves to smother the desire which they
have aroused; but it is an abdication, a surrender of
one's right to know what the country has to give, a re-
fusal to plumb reality. Those who look to reality for
one pleasure or another, can forget in the arms of a
mistress the girl who smiled as she brought the *café
au lait;* they can satisfy their wish to see the towers of
Amiens by visiting some other cathedral. My realities

are specific; I want to enjoy, not a woman, but such or such a woman, not a Gothic cathedral, but the cathedral of Amiens, in the domain where it is bound to the soil—not its equivalent, not its counterpart, but itself; and with the fatigue of getting there, and in the weather of today, and touched, it and I, by the same burst of sunshine. And often two desires coalesce, as for two years past I have wanted to revisit Chartres, where after I had looked at the porch I would go up the tower with the sexton's daughter.

Now it was broad daylight, and I thought of that countryside wearing the chimerical golden light which tells people who open their shutters that the sun is but newly up, and gauzes the tall sunflowers in the garden, the sloping park, and the motionless Loire in the distance, with that tremor of golden dust they will not see again till the evening; but then no longer possessing this grace of promise which makes them hurry down to the still-silent roadway.

6

The sunbeam on the balcony[1]

I wanted to know, before I went back to bed, what Mamma thought of my article.

"Félicie,[2] where is Madame?"

"Madame is in her dressing-room, I was just brushing her hair. Madame thought that Monsieur was asleep."

As I am still up, I take advantage of it to go into Mamma's room, where my appearance at this time of day, a time of day when by custom I should have been in bed and going to sleep again, is something out of the ordinary. Mamma in a flowing white dressing gown is sitting at her dressing-table, her beautiful black hair spread over her shoulders.

"What's this?—my lamb out of his bed at this hour?"

" 'My master must have thought the sunset was sunrise.' "[3]

"Or perhaps the lamb did not want to go to bed before talking to Mamma about his article."

"What do you think of it?"

"Your Mamma, who does not read great books and make extracts, thinks it is excellent."

"That bit about the telephone—that's not too bad, is it?"

"Excellent. As your old Louise would have said, I don't know where that child can have picked it all up, things that I've never heard of even at my age."

"No, but seriously, if you'd read it without knowing I'd written it, would you have thought it was good?"

"I should have thought it very good indeed, and believed it was by some one much cleverer than my little goose, who doesn't know how to sleep as the rest of the world does, and walks into my room in a nightshirt at this hour of day. Take care, Félicie, you're pulling my hair. Dress quickly, my darling, or go back to bed, because it's Saturday and I haven't too much time. If your gentle readers could see you as you are now, do you suppose they would feel a shred of respect for you?"

For on Saturdays, as it was the day when my father lectured, we had lunch an hour earlier. Because of this small break of routine, we all felt that Saturdays had a peculiar and rather congenial quality. We knew that lunch would be upon us at almost any moment, and that we should be blamelessly enjoying omelet and steak and chips at a time when normally we should not have deserved them till an hour later. And, more than that, this recurrent Saturday was one of these little events which in humdrum lives are focussing points for all the interest, all the merriment, and if need be, all the wit and creative instinct that run to waste in those small provincial communities where nothing ever happens to call them out. Saturday was the established, inexhaustible, darling theme for conversation, and if one of us had happened to be epically-minded no doubt Saturday would have become the subject of a trilogy. Just as the people of Brittany never enjoy a ballad so much as when it is about the feats of King Arthur, the only jokes we found really amusing were jokes about Saturday; for these had something tribal about them and helped us to feel ourselves notably different from strangers and barbarians, all those, that is to say, who lunched on Saturday at the usual hour. The consternation of a neighbour who, not knowing that we lunched earlier on Saturday, came in during the morning for a talk and found us at table was one of our stock jokes. Françoise chuckled over it by herself for several days after. And we were so sure of raising a laugh with it, and a laugh of that congenial type where all can share in an almost sectarian sense of piety about a local custom, that we went out of our way to refer to it, we embellished the neighbour's consternation, we dramatized it and invented dialogue. To a "What? Only two in the afternoon? I should have thought it was much later," we would reply: "Of course. But it's a Saturday. That's what threw you out."

"Just a minute," I said. "There's one other thing. Supposing that you did not know me, that you did not know that an article of mine was in the offing—do you think you would have noticed it? It seems to me that one never reads that bit of the paper."

"Little goose, how do you think one could miss seeing it? It is the first thing one's eye falls on. And a five column article, too!"

"Yes, that won't please M. Calmette. He thinks it doesn't do in a daily paper, that readers don't like it."

At this, Mamma's expression became seriously vexed.

"Then why did you do it? Really, it's not very kind, since he is so friendly to you, besides, you know, if people don't like it, if there are complaints about it, he won't ask you for another. Perhaps there's something you could have left out." And she took up the paper, a copy she had got for herself so that she would not have to ask for mine back.

The sky had clouded over, I heard those gusts of wind in the chimney that bear my heart away seawards and make me want to start off for the coast, when, glancing back at the copy of *Le Figaro* that Mamma was reading to see if there was anything I could have left out, my eye fell on a paragraph I had not noticed. *The Storm: Brest. A gale has raged since yesterday evening, ships in harbour have broken from their moorings*, etc. No young girl waiting to be asked to her first ball could feel more wildly excited at seeing her card of invitation than I, when I see those words: *The Storm.* They give shape and substance to what I dream of. And the shock of emotion they bring me is painful, since with my longing to depart comes that uneasy dread of travelling which for years past has, at the last moment, impeded every departure.

"Mamma, there is a storm. And since I am up, I really think I must take advantage of it, and go to Brest."

Mamma looks over her shoulder at Félicie, who laughs.

"Félicie, what did I tell you? If Monsieur Marcel sees there is a storm, he'll want to be off."

Félicie looks with awe at Mamma, who always knows everything beforehand. Besides, the family scene of Mamma and me together with me kissing Mamma from time to time has worked on her feelings, and Mamma, as I realise, is slightly irritated by this, so that she ends by saying that her hair will do now and she will finish putting it up by herself. I am still restless, torn between two imagined pictures, one of which draws me towards Brest while the other leads me back to bed; in the first I am drinking a cup of boiling hot coffee after lunch while a sailor waits to take me to see the breakers dashing on the rocks and the sun is just coming out, in the other it is the time when everyone is going to bed and I must needs go up to a strange room, lie down between damp sheets and know that I shall not see Mamma in the morning.

And just then I saw, quivering on the sill of the
French window, a pulse like a heartbeat, dim and
colourless, but continually dilating and enlarging, and
which one felt was going to become a sunbeam. And
indeed a moment later it half invaded the sill, and
then, after a brief hesitation, a shy drawing-back,
flooded it all over with a pale light in which swam the
rather indistinct shadows of the iron-work balcony
railings. A breath of wind scattered them, but they
had already gained confidence, and came back; and as
I watched I saw this light on the window-sill grow
brighter, rapidly yet glidingly and steadily asserting
itself, like that musical effect which often comes at the
close of an overture; a note that has entered so softly
that one felt it as a crescendo before one heard it as a
note, and then it grows and grows, and reaches its final
fortissimo with such unfaltering speed that a moment
later the overture has ended on its deafening and triumphant cry. In the same way, a moment later the
sill of the balcony was painted all over, and as if for
ever, with that steadfast gold which a summer day
compounds from its long splendours, and the shadows
of the balcony iron-work whose tracery had always
seemed to me uniquely hideous, were almost beautiful
against it. Their one-dimensional exposition of the
curves and coils which in the iron-work itself one
scarcely noticed, had such delicacy, and there was such
precision in the maintenance, even into the finest little tendrils, of their intricate convolutions, that they
seemed to reveal the pleasure felt by a perfecting
craftsman, one of those artists who delight in a meticulous finish and can endow an exact rendering of an
object with a beauty independent of the object itself.
And the shadows lay on that shining ground with such

sharpness of form, such tactile value and palpability, that they seemed to have stretched themselves out on it in a sort of happy unanimity and silent repose.

Whatever pains we may take to talk like ourselves, when we write we fall in with certain old-established usages, and perhaps the thought of describing the look of something that has made an impression on us is one of those things, like cooking meat or wearing clothes, which would not have occurred to anyone if civilisation had taken a different course. In any case, it seems unlikely that the closest description of the shadows cast by the balcony railings on the sunlit stone could give much idea of the pleasure they had given me. For if of all the common-or-garden forms of vegetation which clamber up to windows, cling to porches, twine round casements, these are the most insubstantial and fleeting, none is more vital and significant, and nothing acquaints us more intimately with the actual moods of nature and the changing climate of a day than this golden caress from the sun, these delicate fronds of shadow on our windowpanes, a vegetation that flashes into bloom at all times of year, and which in the gloomiest winter days of one's childhood, when it had been snowing all the morning, suddenly told us that after all we should be able to go for a walk in the Champs-Élysées and that very likely we should see, turning out of the Avenue Marigny, a little girl whose face sparkled with health and merriment under her tam-o'-shanter, and who in spite of her governess's threats was already taking slides along the icy pavement, the little girl whom we had cried about all the morning, thinking that the weather would prevent us

seeing her. The years when one is allowed out even in
bad weather, when either one is not still in love, or it
is not always at Prisoner's Base in the Champs Élysées,
or else it is not there alone, that one can meet the
young lady one is in love with, come later on.

But even when one is no more than a little boy,
one sometimes happens to attain the unhoped-for, apparently inaccessible goal of one's life, and on the wet
day is asked to tea at that house which one would never
have believed one could enter, and which spreads its
charmed circle so widely around it that a mere mention
of the street where it stands, or of streets nearby, or its
postal district number, re-echoes through one with a
painful sickly charm. Love was enough to make it
marvellous in our eyes; but when through a majestic
semi-darkness—for I speak of the days before it was
fashionable to have floods of light and a blue drawing-
room—even at midday we groped our way up the stair
with the awe of a neophyte, the solemn shades of the
anteroom where it was impossible to make out whether
the person standing in front of the Gothic mystery of
an old oak chest was a footman waiting for his mistress
who was paying a call, or the master of the house who
had come to meet us, deepened awe to emotion, while
in the drawing-room, which one could not enter without negotiating several door-hangings, the ermined
canopies of the aforesaid tapestry hangings, the stained
glass in the windows, the lapdog, the tea-table, and the
painted ceiling seemed like so many vassals and pre-
rogatives of its feudal Dame, as if this dwelling had
been the only one of its kind and derived its nature
from the character, the rank, the identity of the lady of
the house, by what algebra might call a simple and
determinate progression. Besides, love is enough to

make us see the smallest peculiarities as enviable supe-
riorities. The fact that we had nothing like this at
home seemed to me the admission of a social inequality
which if known to the little girl I admired would irrevocably cut her off from me as from a lower type of
animal, and as I could not persuade my barbarous parents to give up the mortifying discrepancies of our flat
and of our way of life, I chose the liar's part, and being
sure that she would never discover the shameful truth
by coming to visit us, I brazenly left her to suppose
that in my home, as in hers, the drawing-room chairs
were always in loose-covers, and that we never drank
chocolate at tea-time.

But even when an unhoped-for gleam of sunlight
round about two o'clock no longer lightened on me
like a reprieve coming to a man in the condemned cell
because on wet afternoons there was this possibility of
going to tea with my little friend, how often in the
course of my life have not projects that one thought
must be abandoned, been recoined, delightful excursions that had seemed past praying for been made possible, orders been given for the horses to be put to the
carriage, all because of a sunbeam falling on the window? Days without sun, which are like days without
clothing, have a crudity that provokes one's desire to
enjoy them, to sink one's teeth into them—days we call
dull days, grey days when, without the sun appearing,
people walking in the streets look like a catch of her-
ring in a silver net whose glitter is painful to the eyes;
but for all that, how glad one has been to feel the
tremor of sunlight, still not yet sunshine, on the window, as though one were listening to the afternoon's
uncertain heartbeat while studying its vague smile in
the sky.

Across the road from the window the avenue has nothing beautiful about it; the wall that shows between the tattered autumn trees has been newly-painted in far too bright a pink and is plastered with blue and yellow posters. But the sunbeam has shone out, firing and fusing all the colours together; out of the red trees, the pink wall, the yellow and blue of the posters and the patch of blue sky that shows between the clouds, it has built up a fairy palace, with all the rainbow loveliness and glowing colour of Venice itself.

Thus, it was only by describing how the shadows patterned the balcony that I could express how I felt when the sun came out while Félicie was brushing Mamma's hair. A pattern, a one-dimensional thing, could easily be the medium for that impression, since it was not with my eyes of the moment that I saw it. Just as in those Celebrity Concerts where the famous singer, whose voice is not as strong as it was, is supported in her rendering of a special item by the voices of a choir off-stage, countless faint memories reaching back one behind another to my earliest childhood received the impression of that sunbeam at the moment when I saw it with my actual eyes, and imparted to it a sort of volume, to me a sort of depth and plentitude, and reality, made up of all the reality of those days that were loved and mused over and felt in their authenticity, their promise of pleasure, their intimate, uncertain heartbeat. No doubt, my sensibility of to-day, like the singer's voice, is elderly and the worse for wear; but all these impressions reinforce it and impart something lovely to it. Perhaps, too, they may grant me that ravishing thing: a pleasure of the imagination, a pleasure of no reality, the only true pleasure of the poets; in a minute of real life they may grant me one of the rare moments that bring no disillusionment in their train. And from this impression and others like it something common to them all is liberated, something whose superiority to our everyday realities, even the realities of thought, and passion, and sentiment, we shall never be able to account for. Yet this superiority is so positive that it is almost the only thing we can never doubt. And when we recognise this thing, this common essence of our impressions, we feel a pleasure like no other pleasure, and while it stays with us we know that death is negligible. And after we have read pages containing the loftiest thoughts and the noblest sentiments and have remarked, "That's really quite good," if, suddenly and without our knowing why or wherefore, from some seemingly casual word a breath of that essence is wafted to us, we know that this is Beauty.

It is profoundly pleasant on the day when that Fair Unknown who surpassed us in every respect becomes known and mastered, so that it is we who surpass him. All those ways of life, and that house we dreamed of making our way into, lie under our hand and are yielded up to us; we walk into the forbidden temple as if it were a tavern. The young lady's parents, who seemed implacable deities to us, barring our way more constantly than the Furies, are changed to kindly Eumenides who ask us to call on her, to come to dinner, to talk to her about books—as in Huxley's example of delusive mania where the madman saw the prison wall change into a kindly old lady who begged him to be seated. Those dinners, those afternoon teas, that were high mysteries because she took part in

them, and which set us at such a far remove from her
that we speculated about them as if they were some
hidden aspect of her life, turn into dinners and afternoon teas to which we are invited, at which we are the
guest of importance, consulted about fellow-guests,
dates, and dishes. Her friends, those girl friends for
whom she appeared to feel a special affection that we
could never hope to arouse and with whom we felt
sure she laughed at us, play second fiddle, they are
asked to meet us, and we take part in the private walks
and hostile gatherings. We are one of the friends, the
dearest, the most admired. The awe-inspiring concierge touches his cap to us, we are made at home in
the room we have glanced into from outside. That
love we felt is inspired by us, that jealousy her friends
aroused in us we implant in them, that parental influence—it is we, her parents say, who can influence her,
the holidays, those appalling absences, will be spent
where we are going ourselves. And a day will come
when that unhoped-for right of entry into a girl's life,
be she the postman's daughter or the peer's, the girl at
Rochemur or the girl at Cabourg, will mean no more
to us than a pass we never make use of; who knows, we
may even choose to forfeit that right of entry for ever
by a quarrel.

    We penetrate into the whole of that impenetrable
life and make ourselves master of it. It is no more than
meals and strolls and conversations and pleasures and
a friendly relationship that is more gratifying than
other such relationships because the desire we had for
it gives it a special flavour; but the anguish has vanished and with it the dream. It is ours—we lived for it,
we tried not to come a cropper, not to fall ill, not to be
tired, not to look ugly. God has given us grace to get

there, safe and sound, at our ease and blooming with
health, in the stage box; everything has combined to
make us look elegant and talk wittily. We said to ourselves: "Afterwards, let come what may—death, sickness, ugliness, contumely." And behold, the prize does
not seem worth the purchase, and we wish we had kept
what is spent. We sigh for the bloom of health, the elegance, the smooth cheeks, the flourish of youth, saying
to ourselves, If only we could have kept them, since the
rest is gone. And to console ourselves we say, At any
rate, it was what I longed for. So that the state of being unsatisfied is essentially part of the desire, why, indeed, it is the completest typification, the most perfect
rationalization of a desire; accordingly, we have attained to what we wanted, we are satisfied, we shall
not spend our lives in going one step forward and two
steps back, in stooping from the quarry to the carrion
which cheats our hunger. That is why one must live
among desirable desires, attend balls at the best
houses, walk about the streets, observe passing loveliness and lay stratagems to see it again, in order to afford one's soul the sense of having accomplished—
though to be disillusioned—the most perfect thing
this world can offer and the best matched to the claims
of desire; that is why one must watch flower-like beings moving through a garden and gather them, look
out of windows, go to dances, say to oneself, "There
go the loveliest possibilities," and enjoy them. Sometimes by force of cunning one can bring down in a
single evening its three most inaccessible fruits. Besides,
one only desires occasional conquests, to prove to oneself that one can implement desire. To human beings,
fulfilment of desire comes as a day's outing does to a
maid-servant. One gazes and meditates, since to the

human being it is a matter of individuals, and one must use one's eyes; and one settles upon a being, and a date, and renounces greater pleasures to have enjoyed this. A particular caress from a particular person—less than that, a particular movement, a particular lowering of her voice, this is what we want for the morrow, a sample of the fulfilment we ask of life; to be introduced to a certain young girl and to transform her from unknown to known, or rather, to be ourselves transformed from unknown to known, from slighted to well-thought-of, from beggar to chooser; this is the little hand's grasp by which we are seized and possessed of an intangible future; and the only levy we shall lay on it, just as going to Brittany means that hour of five o'clock in the afternoon when we shall see the shaft of sunlight levelled midway on the oak trees of the shady avenue. And as the one makes us set out on a journey (or makes us, if we know the woman, go with her to that place where she will see us at our best and where we shall give each other one of the pleasures of life, fulfilled with her because we have chosen her among all others), the other, this little thing, will make us give up things of importance rather than miss a fulfilment, rather than give up, in short, the one little being on whom our arbitrary desire has settled, and in whom we sum up love and the loveliness of women, as the whole world is summed up in that sunlight on a palace in Venice which makes us determine on our journey.

7

Talking to Mamma

Félicie took a step or two back, for the sun prevented her from "seeing what she was at." Mamma broke into a laugh.

"Exactly! Here's my lamb working himself up, and why? The storm has blown itself out, there's not a leaf on the tree stirring. Aha! When I heard the wind last night, I foresaw it all, I said to myself, There'll be a scribble from Marcel, for he'll never let a chance of upsetting himself or falling ill slip through his fingers: 'Telegraph at once to Brest to find out if there is a rough sea.' But your Mamma can tell you that there isn't the least trace of a storm. Look at that sun!"

And while she was speaking, I saw the sun—not face to face, but where it enamelled the iron weathercock on the house opposite with tawny gold. And as the world is only a sundial of innumerable aspects, to see this was enough to know that in the square at Combray, the draper's shop, its awning let down because of the heat, was even then about to close for the interval of high mass, that the draper who had just changed into his Sunday coat was showing customers, amid a smell of brown holland, the latest thing in handkerchiefs, keeping his eye on the clock meanwhile, and that the sellers in the market were busy laying out their eggs and poultry while there was still no one about in front of the church except for that lady in black who in a country town may be seen slipping out of church at any time of day. But now it was not this that the enamel of brilliant sunlight on the weathercock of the opposite house made me want to see again.

For since those days I have often seen that brilliant
ten o'clock sunlight enamelling, not the church slates
but the golden angel on the campanile of Saint Mark's,
when my window-shutters above the alley alongside
the Palazzo X . . . in Venice were opened. And from
my bed I could see one thing only, the sun—not face
to face but in an enamel of flame on the golden angel
of the campanile of Saint Mark's, who in an instant
exactly informed me of the hour and permeating light
of that Venetian day, bringing me on his dazzling
wings a promise of beauty and of greater joy than
ever he brought to Christian hearts when he came
heralding: "Glory to God in the highest and on earth
peace, goodwill toward men."

For the first few mornings this glitter of gold on the
angel recalled the glitter, less vivid, but marking the
same hour of day, on the slates of the parish church,
and all the time I was dressing, the angel's golden
beckonings, so dazzling that I could not focus my sight
on them, seemed to promise that I should hurry downstairs and out into a fine morning, go as far as the mar-
ket-place, full of shouts and sunlight, see the shadow
cast by the shop buildings, some closed, some still
open, and the draper's awning, and then go back to
the coolness of my uncle's house. And no doubt, in a
sort of way, it was this that Venice had given me as
soon as I had thrown on my clothes and gone down to
the marble steps that the water now laps over, now
leaves bare; but it was from things of beauty and
works of art that I received these same impressions of
a fine morning. For the street in full sun was this
stretch of sapphire, whose colour was so soft, yet so
positive, that I could lave my eyesight in it and at the
same time impose the whole weight of my stare on it,

like a tired body on a bedstead, without the blue weakening or giving way; and even feel it restored to my eyes, supported, like a body that abandons to the supporting bed the whole weight of even its slightest, innermost muscles, by that unsurrendering blue. And the shadow cast by the draper's awning or the barber's pole was a mere darkening of the sapphire where the head of a bearded god is thrust from a palace doorway, or the little blue flower that the shadow of a delicate piece of carving prints on the sunny surface of a pavement: and for the welcoming coolness of my uncle's house there were wafts of sea-air, and shafts of sunlight streaking long shadowy expanses of marble, and expounding, as in a picture by Veronese, the counter-doctrine to Chardin's doctrine that even the most commonplace things can be beautiful. And even those humble details by which we identify the familiar window in the little house in a country town—its haphazard spacing between the windows that flank it, its clumsy wooden window-rail or, what's worse, an iron one, lavishly and meanly ornate, the latch that was missing from the shutters, the colour of the curtain that was looped up by a central rosette and fell in two wings—all these things by which on every return we know our windows from all the other windows and which, when later on it is our window no longer, we cannot see or even remember without being touched by their witness to a time that was and now is not—this simple yet most eloquent role which as a rule is entrusted to the plainest objects, in Venice it was assigned to the Pointed Gothic arch of a window that appears in every museum as one of the masterpieces of medieval architecture.

After the train had left [   ] and before we

reached Venice, Mamma read me that dazzling passage
in which Ruskin successively compares it to a coral
reef in the Indian seas and to an opal. When our gondola halted us beneath it, naturally it could not retain
the beauty it had worn a moment before in my imagination, since we cannot see a thing with the eyes of the
body and at the same time with the eyes of the spirit.
But at noonday, when my gondola brought me back
in time for lunch, from far away I often caught sight
of Mamma's shawl, with a book weighting it down
against the wind, lying on the alabaster balustrade, and
above it the window's rounded cusps expanded in a
smile—like a friendly countenance, full of trust and
goodwill.

From far away and as soon as I had passed Salento, I
saw it awaiting me and watching my coming, and to
the smiling window the jet of its ogival curve added
the distinction of a slightly veiled glance. And because
Mamma sat behind its balustrade of various-coloured
marbles, waiting for me and reading the while, wearing the pretty straw hat that netted her face in a white
veil and was intended to make her look "dressed"
enough for meeting people in the restaurant or out
walking—because, after a moment's uncertainty about
the voice that was hailing her, as soon as she knew it
was mine she wafted me a tenderness that rose from
the depth of her heart and which, though it was
brought to a halt on the frontiers of her physical domain, on her face, at her fingertips, she tried to bring
as close to me as possible in a smile that stirred her lips
towards me and in a look that sought to lean out to me
through her binoculars—because of all this, the marvellous arched window, unique conflict of Gothic and

Moorish, and the splendid lattice-work of porphyry trefoils above it, that window has taken on in my memory the sweetness taken on by those things whose hour chimed with ours, a single hour in whose bosom we and the window were gathered together, that sunned, before-luncheon hour in Venice, that hour which somehow put us on friendly terms with it. For all its wealth of lovely design, for all its architectural renown, I remember that window as I might remember a man of genius whom we had met at a watering-place and lived with on terms of familiarity for a month, during which time he had come to feel some degree of friendship towards us. And if when later on I saw it again, I wept, it was simply because the window said to me, "I remember your mother so well."

Those palaces along the Grand Canal whose part it was to give me the light and sense of morning have become so much a part of it that now it is no longer the sunlit church slates flashing like black diamonds, and the market square, that, seeing the glitter of the weathercock across the street, I want to see again, but only Venice, the promise that the golden angel fulfilled.

But as soon as I saw Venice again, I remembered an evening when, after a quarrel with Mamma, I said to her, out of spite, that I was going away. I had gone downstairs, I had changed my mind about going, but I wanted to prolong Mamma's distress at my supposed departure so I remained below, on the landing-stage where she could not see me, while a tenor in a gondola sang a serenade that the sun, on the brink of disappearing behind the church of the *Salute*, had paused to listen to. I felt Mamma's distress dragging on, wait-

ing became unbearable, and I could not bring myself
to get up and go to her and say, "I am not leaving." It
seemed as if the serenade could not come to an end
nor the sun go down, as if my agony of mind and the
hues of twilight and the singer's notes had been fused
for ever in a searing, ambiguous and unalterable alloy.
To escape from the memory of that brazen minute I
should not always, as now, have Mamma at hand to
turn to.

The unbearable recollection of the distress I had
caused her brought back an agony that only her presence and her kiss could heal. . . . I felt how impossible it would be to set out for Venice, for any place
on earth, where I should be without her. . . . I am no
longer a happy creature, dallying with a wish; I am
only a vulnerable creature in torments of mind. I look
at Mamma. I clasp her in my arms.

"What is my silly-billy thinking of, what nonsense
is this?"

"I should be so happy if I never saw anyone again."

"Don't say that, my lamb. I am very fond of these
people who are nice to you, in fact, I would like to see
you with more friends who would come in and talk,
without being too much for you."

"All I want is my Mamma."

"But your Mamma would rather think of you seeing
other people, who could tell you things she doesn't
know, things you could explain to her about after they
had gone. And if I had to go away on a journey, I
would like to think that my lamb wasn't feeling bored
without me, and know before I went how he would
spend his days and who would come and talk with

him as we are talking now. It's a bad plan to live quite alone, and you of all people need a little amusement because your life is sadder and more solitary, even as it is."

My mother was sometimes very unhappy, but we never knew of it for in conversation she was all wit and kindness. On her deathbed she quoted Molière to me, and Labiche. " *'He chose the very nick of time to go away in.'* " [1] "My little lad mustn't be afraid, his Mamma won't leave him. 'It would be a fine set-out if I were at Étampes and my spelling at Arpajon!' " [2] Later on she became unable to talk. Once only when she saw that I was constraining myself to keep back my tears she made a face at me, half frowning, half smiling; and though by then she could not speak plainly, I caught the words:

" *'Though not a Roman, act the Roman's part.'* " [3]

"Mamma, do you remember how you read *La Petite Fadette* and *François le Champi* to me when I was ill? You had sent for the doctor. He prescribed medicines to bring down my temperature, and a light diet. You said nothing. But I knew very well from your silence that you were only listening for politeness' sake, and that you had already made up your mind that I should not take any medicine, and that as long as I was feverish I should not eat. And all you gave me was milk, till one morning when you decided in your wisdom that I had a cool skin and a steady pulse. And then you allowed me a small sole. But you put no trust whatsoever in the doctor, and your listening was a pious fraud. It was the same story when Robert was ill, you allowed him to lay down the law, and as soon as he had gone away—'My dears, he may be a great deal more learned than I am, but your Mamma is in the right.' Now, don't deny it! When Robert comes in, we'll ask him if it wasn't so."

Mamma could not help laughing at the picture of her hypocritical behaviour towards the doctor.

"Of course your brother will hear you out, because the pair of you always band together against your Mamma. You may laugh at my doctoring, but ask M. Bouchard for his opinion of your Mamma, and if he doesn't think she knows how to look after children. All very fine for you to tease me, but those were happy days when you were well, when you were under my management and had to do as your Mamma told you to. Were you any the worse for that, eh?"

And as she has finished putting up her hair, Mamma conveys me back to my bedroom.

"Mamma, my pet, you know it's late. I don't need to remind you about noises."

"No, goose! While you're about it, why not ask me not to show anyone in, not to play the piano? Do I make a habit of letting you be disturbed?"

"But those workmen who were coming in over-head?"

"They have been put off. Orders for the day have gone out, everything seems to be under control. '*A point of order, no disorder in the town.*' [4] And try to sleep on as long as you can, you won't hear a mouse stirring till five o'clock, six, if you like. We will make your night last for as long as you please.

'*Madam night, a word in your ear,*
Prythee, rein your coursers in,
Till their sober trot stretch out
This honeyed night that's now beginning
Into the longest night of the year.' [5]

"And then my lamb will end by thinking it's too long and asking for a little noise. I can hear you saying,

'Surely this night is most unduly long.' " [6]

"Will you be going out?"

"Yes."

"But you won't forget to say that no one is to come into my room?"

"No, I've got Félicie on guard outside already."

"Perhaps it might be as well if you would leave a little note for Robert, to make sure he knows, and doesn't walk straight into my room."

"Walk straight into your room?

'Can he be unaware how strict a law
Fences our Monarch here from men in awe,
And that for mortal rash enough to come
Unbidden to his sight, death is the doom?' " [7]

Of all Racine's plays, it is *Esther* that Mamma loves best, and after these quotations from it, she begins to hum—diffidently and as though she were afraid that too loud and bold a voice would scare away the tune that is in her mind like a heavenly presence—*"He is appeased, he pardons,"* from the ravishing choral settings that Reynaldo Hahn composed for it. It was when I was ill in bed that he sang them for the first time, sitting at the little piano near the fireplace, while Papa having come in on tiptoe sat in that armchair and Mamma stood listening to the enchanting voice. She tried over a solo part, diffidently, as though she were one of the young girls at Saint-Cyr rehearsing before Racine; and her beautiful Jewish features stamped with Christian sweetness and Jansenist fortitude made her a very Esther in this domestic, almost clois-

ter-like little performance, that she had devised to entertain the sickly tyrant who lay there abed. My father
did not dare to applaud. Mamma stole a furtive glance
at him to gather his happiness to her heart. And taking up the refrain whose text applied so truly to my
life at home, Reynaldo sang,

> *"O lovely peace,*
> *Beauty for ever bright,*
> *Happy are they who guess thy joys in store!*
> *O lovely peace,*
> *Pure ray of endless light,*
> *Happy are they who keep thee evermore!"* [8]

"Darling Mamma, I must have one more kiss."

"Now, really, my lamb, this is silly, you mustn't
overtire yourself. When I come back I shall want to
hear that you are in blooming health and feeling as
strong as a horse."

She leaves me; but my thoughts return to my article, and suddenly I have an idea for another one. *Contre Sainte-Beuve.* I re-read him not long ago, I made,
contrary to my usual habit, a great many rough notes
and put them away in a drawer, and I have some interesting things to say about him. I begin to think
out the article. More and more ideas occur to me. Before half an hour has gone by the whole article has
taken shape in my head. I want to ask Mamma what
she thinks of it. I call, there is no sound, no answer. I
call again, I hear stealthy footsteps, they pause outside my door, and the door creaks.

"Mamma."

"Did I hear you calling me, my darling?"

"Yes."

"You know, I was afraid I might be fancying it, and
that my lamb would say:

93

'Whose footsteps trespass here?
What impious mortal bent on death draws near?
You, Esther? And unlooked for?' "[9]

"Not at all, darling Mamma.

'What fear you? Were these laws for you designed?
Do I not love you with a brother's mind?' "[10]

"For all that, if I had waked you, I doubt if my lamb would have held out his golden sceptre so sanctimoniously."

"Listen! I want to ask your advice. Sit down."

"Wait till I've found the armchair. It's not very easy to see in here, I may say. Should I tell Félicie to bring the electric lamp?"

"No, don't. I might not be able to go to sleep again."

"Still Molière," she said laughing. " *'Forbid the torches to approach, sweet lady.'* "[11]

"You're settled? Good! Now this is what I want to tell you about. I've had an idea for an article, and I want your opinion on it."

"But you know that I can't give you advice about such things. I'm not like you, I don't read great books."

"Now listen! The subject is to be: Objections to the method of Sainte-Beuve."

"Goodness! I thought it was everything it should be. In that article by Bourget you made me read, he said that it is such a marvellous method that there has been no one in the nineteenth century who could make use of it."

"Oh yes, that's what he said, but it was stupid. You know the principles of that method?"

"Go on as if I didn't."

8

The method of Sainte-Beuve

I have reached the moment, or if you prefer it, I find myself in circumstances where one may fear that the things one most wanted to say—or at least if not they themselves, should a flagging sensibility, which bankrupts talent, no longer allow it, then in their stead those that stood next, which by comparison with this higher and holier ideal one had come to think little of but which after all one has not read anywhere, which one may suppose will never be said unless one says them oneself, and which obviously stem just as much as from one's mind, though from an even shallower region of it—one may suddenly be prevented from saying. One regards oneself as no more than the trustee, who from one moment to the next may disappear, of an intellectual hoard which will disappear with him; and one would like to say check to one's previous idleness's force of inertia by obeying that noble commandment of Christ's in the Gospel of Saint John: "*Work while ye have the light.*" Thus it seems to me that about Sainte-Beuve, and presently much more in respect of Sainte-Beuve than about him, I might have things to say which perhaps are not without their importance; whilst in pointing out where, in my opinion, he sinned as a writer and as a critic, I might perhaps manage to say some things, things I have long had in mind about what criticism should do and what art is. In respect of Sainte-Beuve, and as he so often did, I would in passing make use of him as a reason for discussing certain aspects of life, and I might be able to say a few words about some of his contemporaries, on whom I too have some opinions; and then, after having dealt critically with the others, and this time leaving Sainte-Beuve quite out of it, I would try to say what art might have been to me, if [   ] [1]

"Sainte-Beuve abounds in discriminations, of a deliberate nicety, the better to mark even the most delicate shades of thought. He multiplies anecdotes in order to multiply points of view. He devotes his attention to what is individual and particular, and these minute investigations he subjects to a certain Ideal of aesthetic law, by means of which he forms his conclusions and compels us to subscribe to them."

I have availed myself of this definition and this eulogy of Sainte-Beuve's method in M. Paul Bourget's article because the definition is short and the eulogy official. But I could have cited dozens of other critics. To have devised the Natural History of Intellectuals, to have elicited from the biography of the man, from his family history, and from all his peculiarities, the sense of his work and the nature of his genius—this is what we all recognise as Sainte-Beuve's special achievement, he recognised it as such himself, and was right about it, besides. Even Taine, who meditated a more systematic and better classified natural history of intellectuals, and whose racial theories, moreover, Sainte-Beuve disagreed with, can but say the same thing when he comes to praise him. "M. Saint-Beuve's method is no less valuable than his writings. In that respect, he was an innovator. He carried the methods of natural history into the history of moral philosophy.

"He has shown us how to set about knowing the man; he has indicated the series of circumstances which shape the individual and must be successively examined if that individual is to be understood: first, his race, and his inherited traditions, which can often be made out by studying his father, his mother, his brothers and sisters; then his early upbringing, his home surroundings, the influence of family life and of all that shapes childhood and youth; later, the earliest group of notable men among whom his gifts unfolded, the literary flock to which he belonged. Then comes the study of the man thus formed, the search for clues which lay bare his innermost being, the revulsions and attractions which reveal his dominant passion and his particular turn of mind; in short, an analysis of the man himself, pursued into all its consequences, through and despite those false appearances which literary bent or public prejudice never fail to interpose between our vision and the actual countenance."

But he added: "The practice of this sort of botanical analysis on the human individual is the sole means of reconciling the moral and the positive sciences, and it has only to be applied to peoples, races, and epochs, for its virtues to be made manifest."

Taine said this because his theoretician's conception of reality admitted no truth that was not a scientific truth. However, as he was at the same time a man of taste, and admired various manifestations of the spirit, in order to account for their value, he thought of them as the auxiliaries of science (see the Preface to *L'Intelligence*). He thought of Sainte-Beuve as an inaugurator, as a remarkable man "for his date" —one who had almost hit on his, Taine's, own system.

But the philosophers who have failed to discover what there is in art that is authentic and independent of anything scientific, have to tell themselves that literature, criticism, etc., are like the sciences, where the man before is inevitably less advanced than the man who succeeds him. But in art there is no such thing as an originator, a precursor (at any rate in the scientific sense of the words): everything being comprised in the individual, every man takes up the continuous attempt of art or of literature on his own account, and for him the works of his predecessors are not, as they are for the scientists, a fund of truth which those who come after may profit by. A present-day writer of genius has it all on his hands. He is not much further forward than Homer.

And besides, what is the use of calling up all those who see in this the originality and the superlative merit of Sainte-Beuve's method? We have only to let him speak for himself.

"In regard to the classical authors, we lack adequate means for such a study. With the truly ancient Masters, those of whom only a mutilated statue remains to us, to go, book in hand, in search of the man is in most cases an impossibility. So we are reduced to commenting on the works, admiring them, and picturing the author and the poet behind them. We can thus reconstruct figures of poets and philosophers, busts of Plato, Sophocles or Virgil, in keeping with our lofty ideal; the imperfect state of our knowledge, the scantiness of sources, the lack of the means of information or reconstruction, allows of no more. A wide river, which in most instances is unfordable, separates us from the great men of Antiquity. Let us salute them from one bank to the other.

"With the Moderns, it is quite different. Here, a critical system based on material sources has other duties. To know a man the more, and to know him thoroughly, above all if he be a notable and celebrated person, is an important matter and one not to be lightly dismissed.

"So far, the moral study of character is a piecemeal affair, confined to the description of individuals, or at most, a few types: Theophrastus and La Bruyère go no further. A day is coming, which I believe I have caught glimpses of during the course of my researches, when scientific knowledge will be established, when the major family systems of the intellect and their chief sub-divisions will be determined and known. Then, being given the leading characteristics of an intellect, we shall be able to deduce several others from it. With man, of course, we shall never be able to proceed exactly as with animals or with plants: a moral being is more complex; he is what is called a free agent, which in any case presupposes a great versatility of possible combinations. Be this as it may, we shall come in time, I fancy, to constitute ethical science on a more ample scale: today it is where botany was before Jussieu, or comparative anatomy before Cuvier— at the anecdotic stage, so to speak. For our own part, we compose simple monographs, but I catch glimpses of links and of affinities, and an intellect more far-reaching, more enlightened, but retaining its grasp of detail, may one day discover the great biological divisions that correspond with the family systems of the intellect."

"I do not look on literature," said Sainte-Beuve, "as a thing apart, or, at least, detachable, from the rest of the man and his nature. . . . One cannot provide oneself with too many means or too many objectives if one is to know a man—by which I mean something other than a pure intelligence. So long as one has not asked an author a certain number of questions and received answers to them, though these were only whispered in confidence, one cannot be certain of having a complete grasp of him, even though these questions might seem at the furthest remove from the nature of his writings. What were his religious views? How did he react to the sight of nature? How did he conduct himself in regard to women, in regard to money? Was he rich, was he poor? What governed his actions, what was his daily way of life? What was his vice, or his weakness? No answer to these questions is irrelevant in judging the author of a book, nor the book itself, short of a treatise on pure geometry, above all, if it be a literary work, that is, one into which everything enters."

Sainte-Beuve's great work does not go very deep. The celebrated method which, according to Paul Bourget and so many others, made him the peerless master of nineteenth-century criticism, this system which consists of not separating the man and his work, of holding the opinion that in forming a judgment of an author—short of his book being "a treatise on pure geometry"—it is not immaterial to begin by knowing the answers to questions which seem at the furthest remove from his work (How did he conduct himself, etc.), nor to surround oneself with every possible piece of information about a writer, to collate his letters, to pick the brains of those who knew him, talking to them if they are alive, reading whatever they may have written about him if they are dead, this method ignores what a very slight degree of self-acquaintance teaches us: that a book is the product of a different *self* from the self we manifest in our habits, in our social life, in our vices. If we would try to understand that particular self, it is by searching our own bosoms, and trying to reconstruct it there, that we may arrive at it. Nothing can exempt us from this pilgrimage of the heart. There must be no scamping in the pursuit of this truth, and it is taking things too easily to suppose that one fine morning the truth will arrive by post in the form of an unpublished letter submitted to us by a friend's librarian, or that we shall gather it from the lips of someone who saw a great deal of the author. Speaking of the great admiration that the work of Stendhal aroused in several writers of the younger generation, Saint-Beuve said: "If I may be allowed to say so, in framing a clear estimate of this somewhat complex mind and without going to extremes in any direction, I would still prefer to rely, apart from my own impressions and recollections, on what I was told by M. Mérimée and M. Ampère, on what I should have been told, had he lived, by Jacquemont—by those, in short who saw much of him and appreciated him as he really was."

Why so? In what way does the fact of having been a friend of Stendhal's make one better fitted to judge him? For those friends, the *self* which produced the novels was eclipsed by the other, which may have been very inferior to the outer selves of many other people. Besides, the best proof of this is that Sainte-Beuve, having known Stendhal, having collected all the information he could from M. Mérimée and M. Ampère, having furnished himself, in short, with everything that according to him would enable a critic to judge a book to a nicety, pronounced judgment on Stendhal as follows: "I have been re-reading, or trying to re-read, Stendhal's novels; frankly, they are detestable." He returns to it elsewhere, and there admits that *Le Rouge et le Noir*, "so entitled for no very apparent reason and with a latent symbolism, *has at least some go in it*.[2] The first volume is interesting, in spite of its affectation and improbabilities. *It contains an idea*. For this opening of his novel, Beyle, *so I have been assured*, had exactly the model he wanted in some person he knew, and *while he stuck to his model he managed to appear convincing*. The speedy introduction of this shy youth into a world he had not been brought up for, etc., *all this is well conveyed, or would be, at least, if the author*, etc. . . . These are not living beings, but cleverly-made automatons. . . . In the shorter novels, which have Italian themes, *he succeeded better*. . . . Of all Beyle's novels, it is *La Chartreuse de Parme* from which *some people have drawn* the greatest idea of his talent as a novelist. It is obvious how far I am from sharing M. de Balzac's enthusiasm about Beyle's *La Chartreuse*. When one has finished reading it, one turns again—in my opinion, most naturally—to the French style, etc. . . . One requires some degree of rationality, etc. such as is to be found in Manzoni's story, *I Promessi Sposi*, all Walter Scott's best novels, or in some delightful and perfectly simple story of Xavier de Maistre's; the remainder is merely the work of a clever man."

And this concludes with these two utterances. "While thus criticising, with some freedom, Beyle's novels, I am far from censuring him for having written them. His novels are makeshifts, but they are not vulgar. Like his critical writings, they are eminently fitted for those who find in them. . . ." And, the closing words of this essay: "Beyle had a fundamental rightness and sure-handedness in his treatment of intimate relationships which one must never fail to acknowledge, the more so when one has spoken out one's mind about him." All things considered, a good fellow, that Beyle! Perhaps it was not worth the trouble of meeting M. Mérimée so often at dinner parties and at the Académie Française, of so often "getting M. Ampère to talk," to reach this conclusion; and when one has read it one is less perturbed than was Sainte-Beuve at the prospect of a coming generation. Barrès, with an hour's reading and no "information," would have made a better fist at it than you, M. Sainte-Beuve! I don't mean that Sainte-Beuve was wrong in everything he said about Stendhal. But when one recalls with what enthusiasm he spoke of Mme. Gasparin's stories, or Toepffer's, it is clear enough that if all nineteenth century literature bar *Les Lundis* had been destroyed by fire, so that it was from the *Lundis* that we had to assess the relative importance of nineteenth century writers, we should see Stendhal ranked below Charles de Bernard, below Vinet, below Molé, below Mme. de Verdelin, below Ramond, Sénac de Meilhan, Vicq d'Azyr, below how many more, and, to tell the truth, none too distinguishable between d'Alton Shée and Jacquemont.

I shall show besides that he took the same line towards almost all his contemporaries who were genuinely original—a fine record for a man who laid down that the critic's whole function is to point out the great men of his own time, and in these cases the grudges he cherished against some other writers were not present to lead him astray.

"An artist," said Carlyle, ["is sent hither specially that he may discern for himself, and make manifest to us, this same Divine Idea which lies at the bottom of all Appearance,"][3] till in the end he only looks on the world as "affording an illusion to describe." [4]

At no time does Sainte-Beuve seem to have understood that there is something special about creative writing and that this makes it different in kind from what busies other men and, at other times, busies writers. He drew no dividing line between the state of being engaged in a piece of writing and the state when in solitude,[5] stopping our ears against those phrases which belong to others as much as to us, and which whenever we are not truly ourselves, even though we may be alone, we make use of in our consideration of things, we confront ourselves and try to catch the true voice of the heart, and to write down that, and not small-talk. "As for myself, during those years which I can count happy (before 1848) I endeavoured, and, as I believed, successfully, to shape my existence serenely and worthily. From time to time to write something congenial, to read what was congenial and solid, above all, not to write too much, to cultivate friendships, to reserve some of one's intellect for day-to-day contacts and know how to expend it ungrudgingly, to bestow more on private than on public relations, to keep one's finest, most sensitive part, the cream of oneself, for private life, to employ, discreetly, what remained of one's youth in happy interchanges of intellect and feeling, so did my fancy paint its dream of a gentleman of letters, who possesses a true sense of values and does not allow profession or work in hand to encroach too far on his mental or spiritual development. Since those days, necessity has become my master, and compelled me to renounce what I regarded as the sole felicity or the exquisite consolation of the melancholy man and the man of wisdom."

This implication that there is something more superficial and empty in a writer's authorship, something deeper and more contemplative in his private life[6] is due to nothing else than the special-pleading metaphor of Necessity. In fact, it is the secretion of one's innermost life, written in solitude and for oneself alone, that one gives to the public. What one bestows on private life—in conversation, that is, however refined it may be (and the most refined is the worst, since it falsifies the life of the mind by getting mixed up in it: Flaubert's conversations with his niece and the clockmaker had no harm in them) or in those drawing-room essays, whittled down to suit a particular circle and scarcely more than conversation in print—is the product of a quite superficial self, not of the innermost self which one can only recover by putting aside the world and the self that frequents the world; that innermost self which has waited while one was in company, which one feels certain is the only real self, and which artists—and they only—end by living for, like a god whom they less and less often depart from, and to whom they have sacrificed a life that has no purpose except to do him honour. Admittedly, from the time Sainte-Beuve began writing the *Lundis*, he did not only change his way of life; he attained to the idea—not a very elevated one—that a life of forced labour, such as he was leading, is inherently more fertile, and, for such characters as are indolent by choice, necessary, since without it they

would not yield their fruit. "What happens to him,"
he was to say, writing about Fabre, "was rather like
what happens to some young women when they marry
old men; in a very short time they lose their bloom,
no one can say why, and the cooling breezes that play
on them do more harm than the untempered blasts of
a life of passion could do.

> *'I fancy that old age invades us through the eyes,*
> *And that they age too soon who dwell among grey*
> *heads'*

said Victor Hugo. So it was with the youthful talent of
Victorien Fabre; he pledged himself irrevocably to an
ageing type of literature, and his very fidelity was his
ruin."

In spite of the incredible outcry he raised against
what Balzac wrote in *La Cousine Bette*, Sainte-Beuve
is much given to saying that the life of a man of letters is lived at his desk. "We have recently seen, we
have intercepted, André Chénier's methods of work
and study; we have looked on at the accumulated
and painstaking preliminary attempts in the workshops of his muse. How different is the study whose
doors M. de Lamartine throws wide open to us, and
into which, so to speak, he almost forces us to enter.
'For a few days,' he writes, 'I am resuming my poetical life. You know better than any one that it has
never been more, at the most, than a tithe of my real
life. The worthy public, which instead of creating man
in its own image, as Jehovah did, distorts him to suit
its fancy, believes that I have spent thirty years in
matching rhymes and contemplating the heavens. I
have not given as many months to it, and I have

felt about poetry as I have felt about prayer, neither more nor less.' " But Sainte-Beuve remained unable to understand that world apart, shuttered and sealed against all traffic with the outer world, the poet's soul. He believed that it could be counselled, stimulated, repressed, by other people. "If it had not been for Boileau and for Louis XIV, who considered Boileau to be his Superintendent of Parnassus, what might not have happened? Would even the most richly-talented have yielded in equal measure all that has since constituted their most durable title to fame? Racine, I fear, would have written further *Bérénices*, La Fontaine fewer Fables and more Tales, Molière, even, would have indulged in more *Scapins* and perhaps might never have scaled to the austere heights of *Le Misanthrope*. In short, each of these splendid geniuses would have been most prolific where he was most defective. Boileau, the common-sense, that is, of a poet-critic authorised and reinforced by that of a great monarch, controlled them all, and constrained them to their best and weightiest productions by his respected ubiquity." And so, by failing to see the gulf that separates the writer from the man of the world, by failing to understand that the writer's true self is manifested in his books alone, and that what he shows to men of the world (or even to those of them whom the world knows as writers but who can only resume that character when they put the world behind them) is merely a man of the world like themselves, Sainte-Beuve came to set up that celebrated Method which, according to Taine, Bourget, and the rest of them, is his title to fame, and which consists, if you would understand a poet or a writer, in greedily catechising those who knew him, who saw quite a lot of him, who can tell us how he conducted himself in regard to women, etc.—precisely, that is, at every point where the poet's true self is not involved.

His books, especially *Chateaubriand et son groupe littéraire*, seem like drawing-rooms opening out of each other, whither the author has invited various conversationalists, who are questioned about the distinguished persons they have known and whose evidence is foredoomed to clash with evidence given by others, and thus to show that in the case of men whom we are wont to praise there is much to be said on both sides, or that those who don't agree must represent a different type of mind.

And there are discrepancies, not betwixt the two sources, but coexisting in the bosom of one visitor. Leaving no stone unturned, Sainte-Beuve remembers an anecdote, goes to find a letter, invokes the witness of some grave eminent person who was philosophically warming his toes, but is more than ready to put in his word or two to prove that a person who has just said one thing meant quite another. M. Molé, top-hat in hand, recollects that Lamartine, hearing that Royer-Collard was standing for election to the Académie, wrote off at once to ask him to vote for Royer-Collard, but when the day of election came, voted against him; and on another such occasion, having voted against Ampère's admission, sent Mme. de Lamartine to Mme. de Récamier's to congratulate him.

It will be seen that Sainte-Beuve never altered his shallow conception of the creative mind; but his pinchbeck ideal was irrevocably forfeited. Necessity compelled him to renounce his way of life. Obliged to give in his resignation of the directorship of the Mazarin Library, in order to earn his bread he first accepted an invitation to lecture at the University of Liège; then he began to write the *Lundis* for the *Constitutionnel*. From that day forward the leisure that he had aspired to was replaced by implacable toil. One of his secretaries wrote: "I cannot help remembering this illustrious writer dressing in the morning, scribbling on some newspaper margin a pencilled note of a fact, an idea, a sentence which had come to him ready made, and whose due place in the article in hand he had decided on in his mind. I would arrive. That scrap of newspaper, so easy to mislay, would have to be kept. M. Sainte-Beuve would say to me: 'This is what I shall put in just here.' It was part of my job as secretary to recollect at once, as soon as I got there, on the hop, even before *we* had set to work, the article that had been in hand for the last two days. But the great man soon put me in the way of it, and before long I was accustomed to these mental bursts of speed."

No doubt, this industry compelled him to put forth a throng of ideas which, had he persevered in the idle life that was his first choice, might never perhaps have seen the light of day. He seems to have been impressed by the way some minds had profited by such forced productivity (Fabre, Fauriel, Fontanes). During ten years' time, everything that he would have husbanded for his friends, for himself, for a long-projected book that doubtless he would never have written, had, week after week, to be licked into shape and sent out into the world. Those stores where we keep precious thoughts, the thought round which a novel should have crystallised, the thought he would have unfolded in a poem, another whose beauty had suffused a day for him, welled up from the depth of his mind while he read the book he was to write about; and heroically, to embellish the offering, he sacrificed his dearest Isaac, his last Iphigenia. "I shape my arrows out of any stick," he said. "I am down to my last cartridges." One could say that into the making of these rockets which during the course of ten years went off with such matchless brilliance every Monday he put—and from that moment, lost—the material of books that would have been more permanent. But he knew quite well that not all of it was lost, and that since some particle if not of immortal diamond at least of very good paste had gone to the making of these things of a day, these things of a day would be gathered up into a volume and readers would find the very good paste as bright as ever. And, in fact, they have become these books, which are at times such good reading, at times really delightful even and afford moments of such genuine entertainment that I am sure some people would say, in all good faith, of Sainte-Beuve, what Sainte-Beuve said of Horace: "Among modern nations, and particularly in France, Horace has become a breviary of good taste, poetry, and practical worldly wisdom."

Their title, *Les Lundis*, reminds us what they were for Sainte-Beuve: the feverish enchanting work of a week, and the triumphant Monday morning's awakening in that small house in the Rue de Montparnasse. On a Monday morning, at that hour when in winter only a wan daylight shows above the drawn window-curtains, he opened his *Constitutionnel*, and felt that at that same moment, in rooms all over Paris, the words he had enlisted were proclaiming the brilliant ideas he had hit on, and exciting in many breasts that admiration which he, who has hatched a better idea than he has ever seen hatched by anyone else, and has expounded it in all its force, with all those details which even he had not at first perceived, all in the most advantageous light, and with a chiaroscuro which he has lovingly stroked in, feels for it himself. He did not, of course, know the thrill of the beginner, whose article has been in the editor's hands for so long that, expecting every day to open on it and never doing so, in the end he despairs of its appearance. But one morning his mother coming into his room, had put down the paper beside him with an unwontedly casual air, as if there were nothing worth reading in it; but for all that, she placed it so much in his eye that he would be bound to read it, and then hurried out of the room, vehemently pushing away the old servant who was just about to come in. And he had smiled—for he realised that his darling mother was determined that he should suspect nothing, that he should have all the surprise of his joy, that he should be left alone to savour it and not be teased by other people's remarks while he read nor compelled out of pride to conceal it from those who might tactlessly have wished to share it with him. Meanwhile above the grey daylight, the sky is glowing like redhot coals, and through the foggy streets copies of the newspaper, still damp with printers' ink and the early morning drizzle, are speeding in their thousands—more nourishing and more appetising than the hot rolls, that while the lamp still lights the table, one breaks into one's morning coffee—to carry his thoughts into every dwelling. In haste he sends out to buy more copies, so that he can plant his finger on this astonishing miracle of multiplication, equip himself with the

spirit of a new reader, cast an unprepared eye on this
other copy and find the same thoughts in it. And as
the swelling, filling, brightening sun has leaped by the
little impetus of its enlargement above the purpled
horizon, he sees his brain-child at the same moment
triumphing in every mind, rising like a sun and completely steeping it in its colours.

Sainte-Beuve was no longer a beginner, and no
longer felt these joys. But still, in the first wintry
dawning he pictured Mme. de Boigne in her tall four-
poster opening *Le Constitutionnel;* he told himself
how at two o'clock that afternoon the Chancellor
would pay his call and discuss it with her, how during
the evening he would have a note from Mme. Allart
or Mme. d'Arbouville telling him what people had
thought of it. And so his articles appeared to him as
a sort of arc, springing indeed from his thinking and
his writing, but plunging its further end into the
minds and admiration of his readers, where it completed its curve and took on its final colouring. It is
the same with articles as it is with those sentences that
thrill us when we read them in newspaper reports of
debates in the Chamber: "*M. le Président du Conseil,*
Minister of Home Affairs and Religious Cults. You
will see. . . . (*loud cries of: 'No, no!' from the Right,
loud applause from the Left, prolonged uproar.*)"
Here the preceding attributes of the speaker and the
subsequent record of strong feelings are as much part
of the whole effect as the spoken words themselves.
The sentence is in no way concluded by "You will
see," it is barely at its beginning, and the "loud cries
of: 'No, no!', etc.," is its culmination—finer than its
middle section, and worthy of its opening. In the
same way, the beauty of a piece of journalistic writing

does not lie wholly in the article; cut off from the minds where it finishes its course, the article is but an armless Venus. And as it is to the mob (even though it may be a highly select mob) that it owes its completed effect, that effect is always slightly vulgar. It is the imagined approving silences of this or the other reader that the journalist has in mind when he weighs his words and tries out their equivalence to his thoughts; and thus his work, composed with the unwitting collaboration of other people, is less personal.

As just now we saw Sainte-Beuve believing that cultured society, which he enjoyed, was indispensable to literature and had, throughout the centuries, now as the Court of Louis XIV, now as the intellectual circle of the Directory, continually kept it on the right track, in the same way this seventh-day creator who often did not even rest on the Sabbath day and on Monday received his meed of glory in the satisfaction he gave to the right-thinking and the stripes he laid on the froward—looked on all literature as though it came out in a weekly, something that might be reread but must have been written for a present day, with due regard for the best class of reader, and to please, and without staking too much on the future. He put literature into the category of the temporal. "Be prepared for an interesting poetical season," he writes to Béranger. "Arrayed in the lists are . . ." and being at heart a sound Classic, he says: "After that, there is but little of that poetry which, for my part, I practice; it is not your kind, either, it is the poetry of a rowdy reeling generation without much critical faculty." We are told that when he lay dying he wondered if literature would be loved in times to come, and to the Goncourts he said, about *Madame Ger-*

vaisais: "Come back thoroughly refreshed and in good fettle. This Roman novel will come in the nick of time, and it seems to me that the literary world is in such a lively state of intelligent curiosity about you that it only needs one clever hit to ensure a magnificent success." Literature for him was a contemporary affair, and assessable by the standing of the author; there was, in short, more to be said for being a great political figure and writing nothing than for being a political malcontent and writing a book on ethics . . . , etc. So he differs from Emerson, who said one must hitch one's waggon to a star. He tried to hitch his waggon to what is nearest at hand, to politics: and said, "I thought it interesting to collaborate in a great social movement." He harped on what a pity it was that Chateaubriand, Lamartine, Hugo, should have taken up with politics, but in reality politics play less part in their writings than in his criticism. Why did he say of Lamartine: "The talent is left out"? [7] Of Chateaubriand: "These *Mémoires* in fact, are not very kind and that is their main defect. For *as far as talent goes,* mingled with a vein of bad taste, and with verbal abuses of all kinds—which for that matter are to be found in almost all M. de Chateaubriand's writings—there are many pages bearing the stamp of the master, the claw-mark of the old lion; sudden flights side by side with childish whimsies, and passages of such grace, such magical suavity, that one owns the enchanter's voice and wand." "I really should not be able to discuss Hugo."

[In the literary drawing-rooms] he was popular, but he was respected, too. "I must tell that if you value the opinion of others, we value yours," so wrote

Mme. d'Arbouville to him, and he tells us that she
gave him as a motto: *Wish to please, and remain free.*
In actual fact he was so seldom free; that for instance,
a couple of pages further on he, who during Mme.
Récamier's lifetime trembled to say a harsh word
about Chateaubriand, once they were both dead,
changed his tune. Whether it is this he referred to in
his *Notes and Thoughts*—"After having been an advocate I have a great wish to become a judge," I don't
know. The fact remains that he unsaid, word for
word, what he had earlier maintained. Having had to
write an account of Chateaubriand's *Mémoires d'Outre-Tombe*, which had been read aloud at Mme. Récamier's, on reaching Chateaubriand's words: "But
surely these are quaint minutiae, vaunts that ring hollow in an age when no one is allowed to be the son of
his father? What vanities in a progressive, revolution-
ary age," he protested, thought these scruples exhib-
ited too much delicacy: "Not so! In M. de Chateaubriand the quality of chivalry is inalienable; his good
breeding has always been evident but has never hin-
dered him from better things." Reviewing the *Mémoires d'Outre-Tombe* after the deaths of Chateaubriand and Mme. Récamier, on coming to the passage
in question—"Had I, like my brother, inherited my father's infatuation, my family muniment chest would
leave me no choice but to believe myself a descend-
ant of the ducal house of Brittany," he interrupts the
august narrator—but this time, not to exclaim: "What
could be more natural?" "How's this?" he says to him.
"Then what are you doing now, if not swelling out a
remnant of that infatuation, as you call it, by boasting
that you are cured of it? That is boasting twice over,
and the infatuation you upbraid your father and

brother with was at least more straightforward." And
if he did not revoke his eulogies of Pasquier, the Chancellor, one of those whom he most signally, discrimi-
nately, continuously, praised to the uttermost, I
think myself it was because Mme. de Boigne's interminable longevity prevented him. "Mme. de Boigne
complains that she never sees you now," the Chancellor wrote to him (as George Sand wrote: "Musset
often wants to call on you and pester you into coming
to us, but I don't let him, though I would be ready
enough to abet him if I weren't afraid it would be to
no purpose"): "Will you come and pick me up at the
Luxembourg? We could have a chat, etc." The Chancellor died, Mme. de Boigne lived on. Three articles
about the Chancellor, laudatory enough to gratify the
disconsolate lady; but after Pasquier's death we read
in the Portraits: "Cousin said . . ." and at a Magny
Dinner he said to Goncourt: "You know, I would not
exactly class him among men of letters. In Chateaubriand's circle they could barely put up with him," at
which Goncourt cannot withhold the comment: "How
ghastly to be survived by Sainte-Beuve."

But as a rule his thin-skinnedness, his natural incon-
stancy, his rapid intolerance of what at first he could
not have enough of, meant that he "regained freedom" during people's life-times. One didn't need to
die, it was enough to have fallen out with him, and
that is how we get the conflicting articles on Hugo,
Lamartine, Lamennais, etc., and on Béranger, of
whom he wrote in a *Lundi:* "To turn the fire of those
who may recall that at one time, over fifteen years ago,
I painted Béranger in rosy hues and without a shadow
in the picture, I would point out that it is for this precise reason that I propose to paint him again. Fifteen

years is quite long enough to change a sitter's appearance, or at any rate to bring out his features; above all, it is long enough for an artist who claims to catch likenesses to revise himself, develop himself, in short, to put himself through a profound modification. When I was a young man, I mingled great warmth of feeling and great enthusiasm in my paintings of poets, nor do I repent of it; I even put in a dash of connivance. Today, I admit, I put in nothing, except a sincere intention to see and paint things and persons as they are, as, at any rate, they now appear to me to be." Without this "freedom regained" as a counterbalance to "wishing to please" he could not have commanded so much respect. One must add that together with a certain tendency to bow to powers that be he had a certain tendency to make light of them, and combined worldly and Tory leanings with liberal and freethinking leanings. To the former, we can attribute the vast acreage that the political eminences of the July Monarchy occupy in his works, where one cannot take a step through the drawing rooms into which, with his belief that enlightenment springs from discussion, he has gathered together the illustrious conversationalists, without meeting M. Molé, and every conceivable Noailles—whom he reveres to the point of thinking he would be in fault to quote the whole of Saint-Simon's portrait of Mme. de Noailles in one of his articles; while alongside of this, in compensation for this, he inveighs against aristocratic candidates for the Académie (though on the occasion of the very proper election of the Duc de Broglie), saying: "These people will end by getting themselves nominated by their doorkeepers."

Even in regard to the Académie, his position is am-

biguous: now as a friend of M. Molé's who thinks it a
joke that Baudelaire should stand for election (though
Baudelaire was a great friend of his) and tells him
that he has already good cause for pride since the
members of the Académie were pleased with him—
"You have made a good impression, is that nothing?";
then as a friend of Renan's who thinks that Taine
lowered himself by submitting his *Essais* to be pronounced on by Academicians who are incapable of
understanding them, who inveighs against Monsei-
gneur Dupanloup for keeping Littré out, and says to his
secretary as soon as he engages him: "On Thursdays,
I go to the Académie. My fellow-members are a poor
lot." He writes puffing articles for this and that person,
and has himself admitted it, but refuses with fury to
put in a good word for M. Pongerville, remarking:
"He shall not be admitted today." He has what he
calls his sense of dignity, and manifests it with a sol-
emnity which is sometimes ludicrous. When he relates
that after a stupid accusation of having accepted a
bribe of a hundred francs, he sent a letter to the *Journal des Débats:* "with an unmistakable ring in it,
such as only an honest man can write," well and good.
Well and good, that when accused by M. de Pontmartin[8] [   ] or that when believing himself in-
directly attacked in a speech by M. de Villemain, he
exclaimed: [   ]. But he is ludicrous when
having warned the Goncourts that he would write un-
favourably of *Madame Gervaisais,* and having learned
through a third party that they had said to the Princesse Mathilde: "Sainte-Beuve knows quite well . . . ",
he flies into a white-hot fury over the phrase, "a slating," bursts out, "I do not go in for slating." It is one
of these Sainte-Beuves who replied to the [   ].[9]

At times I wonder if after all Sainte-Beuve's best work is not his poetry. All play of wit is at an end. Things are no longer approached obliquely with a hundred ingenuities and conjuring-tricks. The sorcerer's magic circle is broken. As though the persevering falsehood of his thought had derived from the artificial dexterity of his style, when he leaves off writing prose, he leaves off telling lies. As a student obliged to put his thoughts into Latin is obliged to lay them bare, Sainte-Beuve for the first time comes face to face with reality, and feels straightforwardly about it. There is more honest feeling in the *Rayons Jaunes*, in the *Larmes de Racine*, in any of his poems, than in his prose works. Yet if falsehood forsakes him, all his advantages fly from him too; like some habitual drinker put on a milk diet, along with his artificial vigour, he loses all his strength. *"How clumsy is the creature, and how ugly."* [10] Nothing could be more touching than this technical destitution in the great spell-binding critic, practised in all the elegancies, fine shadings, drolleries, all the emotional effects, all the paces and graces of style. All are gone. Out of his vast store of culture, his technical accomplishment, nothing is left to him except the ability to reject anything pompous, stale, or extravagant, and there is an austere refinement in the choice of imagery that in a way recalls the studied perfection of André Chénier's poetry, or that of Anatole France. But all that is an Act of Taste, and not his own. He tries to do what he admires in Theocritus, or Cowper, or Racine. Of his own, of what was involuntarily and profoundly his own, almost the only thing is clumsiness. It comes back and back, as if it were a natural tone of voice. But this handful, this charming handful of his poems

—charming, and also sincere—this skilful and sometimes successful attempt to express the purity of love, the sadness of dusk in a great city, the spell of memory, the thrill of reading, the woe of unbelieving old age, shows, because one feels it is the only genuine thing about him, the emptiness of the whole of his marvellous, enormous, ebullient work as a critic; since all these marvels come back to this: *Les Lundis*, the outward show; a little poetry, the reality. In the scales of eternity, a critic's verses outweigh all the rest of his works.

9

Sainte-Beuve and Baudelaire[1]

A poet you only half love, and in regard to whom it is a matter of common consent that Sainte-Beuve, who was very intimate with him, gave proof of a most enlightened, most discerning admiration, is Baudelaire. Well—if Sainte-Beuve, touched by Baudelaire's admiration, his deference, his graceful attentions, his tributes, now of poems, now of gingerbread, and by the ecstatic way he wrote about *Joseph Delorme* and *Les Consolations* and the *Lundis*, replied with affectionate letters, he never responded to Baudelaire's reiterated entreaties that he should devote even one article to him. Baudelaire, the greatest poet of the nineteenth century, and his friend to boot, has no place among the *Lundis*, where so many Comte Darus, d'Alton Shées, and the like, have theirs; no place, at least, except as an accessory figure. Once, at the time of the Baudelaire trial, Baudelaire begged Sainte-Beuve to write a letter in his defence. Sainte-Beuve felt his connection with the court of Napoleon III forbade it, and contented himself with drafting in anonymity· a plan for the defence,[2] authorising Baudelaire's lawyer to make use of it, provided his name was kept dark, in which he said that Béranger had been quite as daring as Baudelaire, adding: "Far be it from me to detract from the renown of a great poet"—no, he meant Béranger, not Baudelaire—"a national poet,

· "Sainte-Beuve, glad to be able to come to his friend's aid without compromising himself," as M. Crépet artlessly says, under the impression that he is saying something in praise of Sainte-Beuve's behaviour.

endeared to all hearts, whom the Emperor had deemed worthy of a public funeral, etc." But he wrote a letter to Baudelaire about *Les Fleurs du Mal*, which was later included in the *Causeries du Lundi*, with emphasis on the fact that it had been written with the idea of reinforcing the defence (to qualify the strain of praise, no doubt). He begins this letter by thanking Baudelaire for his inscribed copy, cannot bring himself to utter a word of praise, says that these poems, which he had read before produce when put together "a quite different impression," says this is obviously sad and distressing, but that Baudelaire knows that already, and keeps this up for a page without a single adjective to justify a supposition that he thought it a good book. All we learn is that Baudelaire was very fond of Sainte-Beuve and that Sainte-Beuve knows that Baudelaire had a great deal of good in him. At last, about halfway down the second page, he lets himself go, at last says a word of appreciation (and this is a letter of thanks, and addressed to someone who has shown him so much affection, so much deference): "By doing this with subtlety"—appreciation number one, but it could be read ambiguously—"with refinement, with a fastidious talent,"—the first word of praise, if praise it be, but it won't do to cavil, for it's almost the only one—"and with an almost *chiselled* freedom of expression, in *conversing*"—the italics are Sainte-Beuve's—"or sonneteering about horrors . . . ," then, paternally: "You must have suffered much, my dear lad." Then come a few criticisms, then great compliments on just two poems: the sonnet, *Tristesse de la Lune*, "which might have been written by an English contemporary of the young Shakespeare," and *A celle qui est trop gaie*,[3] of which he says: "Why is not this poem in Latin, or rather, in Greek?" I forgot to say that a few lines earlier he remarked on Baudelaire's "polished craftsmanship." And as he is fond of conceits, he ends with: "But I repeat, there is no call to pay compliments to someone one loves"—and who has just sent you *Les Fleurs du Mal*, and when paying compliments to mediocrities by the dozen is how you have spent your life.

But that is not the end of it; for no sooner did Sainte-Beuve learn that there was an intention of publishing his letter, than he asked to have it back again, probably to see whether he had not been carried away into praising overmuch (this, though, is merely my private guess). Be that as it may, when he included it in the *Causeries du Lundi*, he thought he ought to introduce it—I would say plainly, water it down yet further—by a little preamble in which he says that this letter had been written "with the idea of reinforcing the defence." And though in this preamble he is no longer addressing *his friend* the poet, so there is no longer any need to scold him and a compliment or two might not come amiss, this is how he writes about the *Fleurs du Mal*. "The poet Baudelaire . . . spent years in distilling from every subject and every flower"—that means, in writing *Les Fleurs du Mal*—"a poisonous essence and even, it must be said, a quite *agreeable* poisonous essence. He was, moreover"—(still at it!)—"a man of parts,"(!) "and with a great capacity for affection"—(and really this is all that need be said about the author of *Les Fleurs du Mal*: Sainte-Beuve has already told us to the same tune that Stendhal was unassuming and Flaubert a good fellow). "After he had published the collection called *Fleurs du Mal*"—("I know you write poems," a man of fashion said to Mme. de Noailles: "Have you ever felt tempted to bring out a little collection of them?")—"he had to reckon with more than critical opinion, for the law intervened as if *these spiteful innuendos, wrapped up in elegant verse, constituted a real menace.*" Then comes the passage apparently explaining away the praises (so at least I read it) on the grounds that they were intended to be of service to the accused. Observe, by the way, that "spiteful innuendos" doesn't go too well with: "You must have suffered much, my dear lad." How often Sainte-Beuve tempts one to cry out, What an old ass! or, What an old blackguard!

Another time (and very likely because he had been publicly censured by Baudelaire's friends for having lacked the courage to stand up for him in court, as Barbey d'Aurevilly and others did) Sainte-Beuve wrote an article about the various candidates who were standing for election to the Académie Française. One of these was Baudelaire. Sainte-Beuve, who in any case liked giving lessons in literature to his fellow-Academicians, just as he liked giving lessons in liberalism to his colleagues in the Senate—because though he was imbedded in his world, he was greatly superior to it, and had whims, attacks, itching-fits of modern art, anti-clericalism, and revolutionism—Sainte-Beuve referred briefly and charmingly to the *Fleurs du Mal:* "this little lodge, which the poet has built himself on the tip of the Kamtschatka of literature, I call it 'the Baudelaire Folly'" (always these "sayings," sayings that clever people can quote with a chuckle—*He calls it the Baudelaire Folly*—except that though the type of conversationalists who dine out on such sayings could have used one about

Chateaubriand or Royer-Collard, they did not know who Baudelaire was). And he wound up with these extraordinary words: M. Baudelaire, so much is certain, "improves on acquaintance, so that those who were expecting some strange eccentric to come in, found themselves meeting an exemplary candidate, polite, deferential, a nice fellow, refined of speech and with perfectly correct manners." I cannot believe that in writing those words, *nice fellow, improves on acquaintance, perfectly correct manners*, Sainte-Beuve was not giving way to the sort of verbal hysteria which from time to time made him find an irresistible pleasure in talking like an illiterate grocer, and saying of *Madame Bovary*: "the opening has some delicate touches."

But the process is always the same: utter some words of praise, "as from a friend," about Flaubert, or the Goncourts, or Baudelaire, then say that in private life besides, they are the nicest of men, the firmest of friends. In the retrospective article on Stendhal, it's still the same thing: "more reliable in his proceedings." And having advised Baudelaire to withdraw his candidature, as Baudelaire followed his advice and wrote to withdraw it, Sainte-Beuve mingled congratulation and consolation as follows: "When your final expression of thanks, couched in such modest and courteous terms, was read out, they"—the Academicians in session—"said out loud, Excellent! *So you have left a good impression behind you. Isn't that something?*" Wasn't it something to have left an impression of modesty, of being "a nice fellow," on M. de Sacy and on Viennet? And for Sainte-Beuve's part, wasn't it something for Baudelaire's great friend to have given advice, always, of course, in anonymity,

to his lawyer, to have jibbed at any article on the
Fleurs du Mal, or even the Poe translations, but to
have said at last that the Baudelaire Folly was a
charming little lodge, etc.?

Sainte-Beuve thought something was a great deal.
And what is more disconcerting—and it bears out
what I have been saying—Baudelaire, fantastic as it
may seem, agreed with him. When Baudelaire's
friends resent Sainte-Beuve's cowardice at the time of
the trial, and let loose their resentment in print, Baudelaire is frantic, writes again and again to Sainte-
Beuve with assurances that he had no hand in these
attacks, writes to Malassis, writes to Asselineau:
"Just think how disagreeable this business could be
for me. . . . Babou knows quite well how much attached I am to Uncle Beuve, what store I set on his
friendship, what pains I am at to hide my own views
when they are at variance with his, etc. It seems as
though Babou were bent on protecting me from
someone who has done me innumerable kindnesses."
He writes to Sainte-Beuve that far from having sug-
gested Babou's article, he had convinced the author
"that you have always done everything that you
should and could do. Only a short time ago I was
telling Malassis of that great friendship you honour
me with, etc."

To assume that Baudelaire was not sincere just
then, and that it was with an eye to the main chance
that he was anxious to humour Sainte-Beuve and let
him believe he thought he had acted rightly, only
brings us back to the same thing; it shows how much
store Baudelaire set on an article by Sainte-Beuve
(which he could not get, either), or, failing an article, on the few sentences of praise that eventually were

granted him. And you know what they amounted
to. Yet shabby as they seem to us, they enraptured
Baudelaire. After the "improves on acquaintance, nice
fellow, Baudelaire Folly, etc.," article, he wrote to
Sainte-Beuve: "I am indebted to you for yet another
kind office. When will there be an end to this? And
how can I thank you? A brief note, dear friend, to tell
you what an especial kind of pleasure you have
brought me. . . . As for what you call my Kamtschatka, if such rousing encouragements often come
my way, I believe I shall feel equal to enlarging it into
a whole Siberia, etc. When I see how energetic you
are, how fertile, I am thoroughly ashamed"—(of his
literary unproductiveness!)—"And I, irreclaimably
enamoured of *Rayons Jaunes* and *Volupté*, of the poet
and novelist Sainte-Beuve, must I now compliment
the journalist? How have you managed to reach that
pitch of style, etc.? I thought it had all the eloquence
of your conversation, etc.," and he ends with: "Poulet-
Malassis is burning to publish your wonderful article
as a pamphlet." His gratitude does not stop at a letter,
he sends an unsigned article on Sainte-Beuve's article
to the *Revue Anecdotique:* "The whole article is a
masterpiece of good humour, liveliness, sagacity, good
sense and irony. All those who have the honour to be
intimately acquainted with the author of *Joseph Delorme*, etc." Sainte-Beuve makes a grateful acknowl-
edgement to the editor, and winds up, still true to
form in his fondness for straining the sense of a
word: "I greet and respect the kindly Anon." But Baudelaire, not sure whether Sainte-Beuve had detected
him, writes to say the article was his.

All this bears out what I have told you, that any man
who shares his skin with a man of genius has very lit-

tle in common with the other inmate, yet it is he who is known by the genius's friends, so it is absurd to judge the poet by the man, or by the report of his friends, as Sainte-Beuve did. As for the man himself, he is just a man and may perfectly well be unaware of the intentions of the poet who lives in him. And perhaps it is best so. Deducing the poet's greatness from the greatness of his work, we argue that he is king among men, we look on him as a king and expect him to behave with majesty; but if the poet is to keep an objective vision of the reality he depicts, and remain unselfconscious, he ought on no account to see himself in this light. So he sees himself as a poor man who would be highly gratified if a duke asked him to dinner or the Académie gave him an award. And if this humility is a condition to his sincerity, and to the sincerity of his work, let it be called blessed.

Did Baudelaire misconceive himself to this extent? In theory, probably not. But if his modesty and deference were strategic, in practice his misconception went quite as far, since he, who had written *Le Balcon*, *Le Voyage*, *Les Sept Vieillards*, saw himself on a footing where a place in the Académie or an article by Sainte-Beuve would mean a good deal to him. And I would say that it is the best and the most intelligent who are like this, quick to come down again from the sphere in which they write *Les Fleurs du Mal*, *Le Rouge et le Noir*, *L'Éducation sentimentale*—and we, knowing only the books, the man of genius, that is, and not misled by the disguise of the man he lodges in, can assess how high that is above the world where *Lundis* and *Carmens* and *Indianas* are written—in order to accept, out of deference, out of strategy, out of natural courtesy, or out of friendship, the spuri-

ous superiority of a Sainte-Beuve, or a Mérimée, or a
George Sand. This very natural duality has something
very disconcerting about it. Look at the un-Baude-
laired Baudelaire being respectful to Sainte-Beuve,
and at so many others intriguing for a decoration,
Vigny begging for a puff in a daily paper when he had
just written *Les Destinées*. (I don't remember exactly,
but I think I'm right.)

Like the heaven of Catholic theology, which is made
up of several heavens one above another, our spiritual
man, in the outward man imposed on it by our body,[4]
with its head penning up our thinking within a little
ball, our spiritual man is made up of several people
one above another. Perhaps this is even more obvious
in the case of those poets who have an extra heaven,
a mezzanine heaven between the heaven of their genius and that of their intellect, their virtues, their
everyday shrewdness—the heaven of their prose.
When we read Musset's *Contes*, we still, from time to
time, because of that indescribable something, become aware of the flutter, the silkiness, the readiness
for flight in wings that remain furled. Anyhow, this
has already been said, and much better:

*And even when the bird walks one still knows him
winged.*[5]

A poet writing prose (naturally, I don't mean when
he is making it into a form of poetry, like Baudelaire in his *Petits Poèmes*, Musset in his plays, but
Musset writing his stories, his critical essays, his addresses to the Académie) is someone who has put by
his genius, who no longer requires of it the things
it invents in the privacy of its own magic world, but
who still bears it in mind and puts us in mind of it
too. Some turn of phrase will suddenly remind us

of a famous line of poetry, not perceptible, not there, but whose unspecified indeterminate shape seems to extend like an atmosphere behind a statement that could quite well have been made by anybody, giving it a kind of grace and stateliness and emotional evocativeness. The poet has flown away, but one can catch sight of his lustre behind the clouds. Nothing of it remains in the man, the everyday man who goes out to dinner and has his ambitions; and it is from this one, who has kept none of it, that Sainte-Beuve claims to extract the essence of the other.

I know why you only half love Baudelaire. In his letters, as in Stendhal's, you have come on merciless passages about his relations. And he is merciless in his poetry, merciless with the utmost sensibility, his ruthlessness the more startling since one feels that he had felt to his nerves' ends the sufferings he makes a mock of and describes with such composure. To be sure, in such a poem as the magnificent *Les Petites Vieilles* no item of the old women's sufferings escapes him. It is not only their vast unhappiness:

> *Those eyes are well-heads which thousands of tears have brimmed. . . .*
> *Each of them could have made a river with her tears;*[6]

he lives in their bodies, winces with their nerves, quakes with their trembling limbs:

> *scourged by the villainous winds,*
> *Trembling at the rolling din of omnibuses,*
> *Like wounded animals, they drag themselves along.*[7]

Yet for all the beauty of statement and characterisation in this picture, he does not recoil before any cruel detail:[8]

Or they dance with no will to dance, poor jingle-
bells . . .
And she there, still straight-backed, proud, knowing right
from wrong . . .

And have you not remarked many a crone's coffin
Almost as small as those in which we lay a child?
A parity of biers employed by learned Death
To adumbrate an odd beguiling bent of mind . . .

Unless with thoughts engaged upon geometry
I wonder, at the sight of these erratic limbs,
How many times and how diversely the workman
Must needs adjust the box to all we put in it;[9]

But above all:

But I who from afar survey you tenderly,
Keeping an anxious watch on your uncertain steps,
And just as if I were your father—strange, O strange!—
Taste all unknown to you a surreptitious joy.[10]

And it is because of this that to love Baudelaire—
as Sainte-Beuve would say, from whom I forbid myself
to take over this formula for my own purposes, as I
have often been tempted to do, because I mean to
keep any sort of witticisms out of this article I'm planning, but here I am not guying Sainte-Beuve, it is a
thing I have noticed, I remember and could tell you
instances of it, and now it has darted into my mind—to
love Baudelaire, to love him, I mean, to the point
of infatuation, in these most piteous and human
poems, is not necessarily a token of great sensibility. The picture he draws of those sights which I am
convinced really pained him is so powerful, and yet
so divorced from any expression of feeling, that
purely ironic and sensation-hunting minds, truly hard
hearts, can take pleasure in it. The line about the old
women:

Rubble of humankind, ripe for eternity,[11]

is a noble line, and dear to the high-minded and the generous-hearted. But how often have I not heard it quoted, and with full appreciation, by a woman who was extremely intelligent, but of all the women I've met the stoniest-hearted, the most devoid of kindness or conscience, and who, adding it to her repertory of jests and gibes, amused herself by letting fly with it, after the exit of this or that old woman whom she loathed, as a prophecy of impending death. To feel every variety of pain, but to have such mastery over oneself that one can watch it undistressed, to be able to bear the pain that an impulse of malice has artificially provoked (when one quotes it, one overlooks the cruelty of that lovely line:

The fiddle trembling, like a heart that one gives pain to. . . .[12]

Oh, that quivering of a heart one has given pain to! —a minute ago, it was only the nerves of old women, quivering at the rolling din of omnibuses); perhaps this subordination of sensibility[13] to truth and statement is ultimately a sign of genius, of the force of art overcoming a personal compassion. But there are stranger things than this in Baudelaire. When he is giving the noblest possible expression to certain feelings, he seems to be describing them from outside and without being involved in them. One of the finest lines on charity, one of Baudelaire's vast unrolling lines, is this:

So that when Jesu comes thou mayest at his feet
Outspread a cloth of state wrought by thy love for man.[14]

But could anything be less charitable (intentionally so, but that doesn't matter) than the frame of mind in which this was written?

> *Eagle-like from on high an angry angel swoops*
> *Down on the wrong-doer, plucking him by the hair,*
> *Shaking him and saying: "Thou shalt learn right from*
> *   wrong!*
> *(Am I not thy guardian angel?) Do as I say!*
> *Know this, that thou must love, swallowing thy disgust,*
> *The poor, the wicked, the misshapen, the dullard,*
> *So that when Jesu comes thou mayest at his feet*
> *Outspread a cloth of state wrought by thy love for*
> *   man."* [15]

He understands the nature of all these virtues, yes, indeed, but he seems to banish their spirit from his poetry. There is the whole fervour of piety in these lines from the *Petites Vieilles:*

> *All these thrill me. But yet among these heirs of dust*
> *Some there are who, sucking a nectar out of woe,*
> *Have said to Piety, laying hold on her wings:*
> *"O soaring Griffin, bear my soul up to the skies!"* [16]

It is as though he were employing this extraordinary and unprecedented power of language (a hundred times more powerful than Hugo's, for all that people may say), in order to state for all time a feeling that he tries not to feel at the time he speaks of it, and which he paints rather than expresses. He finds these unmatched phrases for all the pains, for all the balms—phrases torn up by the roots from his own heaven and hell and unfindable in any other man's, phrases from a planet which he alone has lived in and which is like nothing we know of. Over every type of humankind he puts one of these great phrases, all warm and supple, full of scent and sap, one of these bags that could hold a bottle of wine, or a ham; but though he says it with lips that can speak like thunder, one would say he is trying to speak from the lips outward, though at the same time one feels he has experienced it all, understood it all, and has the most quivering sensibility and the profoundest comprehension.

One by her country long-schooled in adversity,
One whom a husband had overburdened with woes,
Another by her child pierced through Madonna-wise,
Each of them could have made a river with her tears![17]

Long-schooled is exquisite, so is *overburdened*, so is *pierced through;* each envelops the idea in one of his dark, glittering, nourishing great phrases.

Among these splendid poetic idioms I have been talking about, invented by him and enveloping the bare facts he catalogues with their warm, multicoloured great phrases, a certain number are really idioms bearing on the classic idea of *patria:*[18]

One by her country long-schooled in adversity. . . .

Some glad of heart to flee an infamous country. . . .

The poor man's purse, and the dear land of his
fathers. . . .[19]

like the splendid idioms[20] on the idea of the Family: *Others, the horror of their childhood*—which quickly take their place in the category of biblical idiom, and all those figures of speech which make up the force and vehemence of a poem like *Bénédiction,* where everything is on a larger scale because of that solemn diction:

In the meat and in the drink they set before him
They have intermingled ashes and gobs of spit;

With sanctified airs they cast away what he touches,
They reproach themselves when they set foot in his
steps.

His wife lifts up her voice in places of resort:
"I will make my market as idols did of old. . . .

Why in my travail did I not bring forth a whole
Clutch of vipers rather than have nourished this
MOCK!"* [21]

side by side with the Racinean lines, so often to be
found in Baudelaire:

All those whom he would love set eyes on him with
dread.[22]

the great flamboyant lines, *"like monstrances,"* which
are the glory of his poetry:

And in the pit of hell heaps up by her own deeds
The pyre reserved to those mothers who wrong their
child.[23]

and all the other elements of Baudelaire's genius that
I would so much like to tell over to you, one by one,
if time allowed. As it is, this poem contains some of
those beautiful images from the Catholic liturgy
which are wings to him:

Of Thrones and Virtues and of Principalities. . . .[24]

I know that sorrow is the classic dignity
Of man which neither earth nor Hades can corrode,
And that if I would wear the crown laid up for me
I must weave in all time and every universe.[25]

(Not an ironical image of suffering, this, like those I
quoted about charity, and Christian piety, but still
very impassive, and owing its beauty mainly to idiom
and allusions to mediaeval religious art, more pictorial than emotional.) I am not going into the poem

on the Madonna, as this is a specific instance of the deliberate use of all these Catholic idioms.

But soon,[26] those marvellous images!

Serpents I drag after me, which bite my sandals,[27]

(that word, *sandal*, he was so fond of: *How beautiful are thy feet without sandals, O King's daughter!* [28] The infidel leaves his slippers outside the church door, *and these serpents under thy feet as under the feet of Jesus*,[29] *incalcabis aspidem*, "*thou shalt bruise the head of the serpent*")—but little by little, leaving out those that are too familiar (and perhaps the most essential), I think I could begin to conjure up for you, phrase by phrase, this world of Baudelaire's mind, this country of his genius, of which each poem is only a part and which as soon as we read it rejoins other parts we know already; just as when we see in an unfamiliar canvas hanging on the wall of some drawing-room a particular classical mountain reddened by sunset and a poet with a womanish face followed by two or three muses—a picture, that is, where antiquity is taken naturally, these muses being people who really lived, and strolled out in the evening by twos or threes with a poet, etc., and all this at a moment of time, at a given hour, in the fleetingness that gives a kind of reality to timeless myth, we feel this is a fragment of Gustave Moreau's country. But for this, I would have to give you all the harbours, not only *a harbour thronged with sails and masts*, and those

> *Where ships swimming in gold and watered silk, hold out*
> *Their vast arms to embrace the splendour of a clear*
> *Sky and the quiver of interminable heat*,[30]

but those which are only doorways

That the sea-faring suns have fired with countless hues,[31]

and *the doorway opening upon unknown skies,* and the African palm-trees, pale as ghosts:

> *The absent coco-palms of stately Africa*
> *Behind the obscuring towering wall of fog.*[32]

> *The scattered phantom-shapes of absent coco-*
> *   palms. . . .*[33]

and evening, from its first kindling light, when the sun casts

> *Its soft church-candle shine*
> *Over the frugal board, and the old serge curtains.*[34]

till the moment when it is made *of pink, and mystical blue,* with those snatches of music which are always lingering in Baudelaire's evenings, and which inspired him to what is perhaps the most ravishing flight since Beethoven's *Eroica* Symphony:

> *the rich metallic strains*
> *Of regimental bands which sometimes flood our parks*
> *And, in the golden dusks when one draws breath again,*
> *Shed a brief heroism into the town-bred heart.*[35]

> *The trumpet calling through the solemn evenings*
> *Of holy harvest-tides such thrilling sweetness has:*[36]

and wine, not only in all those admirable poems that praise the grape from the moment when it ripens *on the flaming hillside* till the moment when the *labourer's warm breast* becomes its *sweet tomb,* but wherever it, and every elixir, every *vegetable ambrosia* (another charming typical phrase of his) steal into the making of a metaphor, as when he says that the thought of death

> *exalts us, fires our brains,*
> *Puts heart in us to keep walking till fall of night,*[37]

and the blue horizons plastered with white sails,

> Frigate or brig whose distant shape
> Quivers against the blue,[38]

and the negress; and the cat, like a Manet canvas. . . . Besides, what didn't he paint? I have skipped the tropics, as being a too-familiar aspect of his genius, too familiar to you and me, at any rate, since I had such difficulty in breaking you in to La Chevelure; but didn't he describe the sun in its hell of the far north as *a red and frozen lump?* If on moonlight he has written lines which are like that precious stone that holds in a flinty sheath, as under glass, the opal-matrix which is like moonlight on the sea, and through whose centre, like a thread of a different existence, there filters a rainbowed light which is like a ray of Baudelaire, he has painted a quite different moon, *like a new minted medal;* and if I have left out L'Automne, which you, like me, know by heart, there are his lines about spring, lovely, and in quite another manner:

> Springtime will fleet into the distance like a
> wraith. . . .[39]
> Spring, spring the adored, no longer has her
> fragrance. . . .[40]

And besides, how can one count up all these phrases, when there is nothing he spoke of (and he spoke with the whole span of the soul) that he did not present by a symbol, and that symbol always so concrete, so striking, so living, and in the strongest, most usual, most dignified language?

> Staff in the exile's hand, lamp to the inventors, . . .
> Thou of whom outlaws learn that lofty tranquil glance
> Which damns a race entire around a scaffold-foot,[41]

and of death:

> *It is that famous inn writ in the register*
> *Where we at length shall eat and sleep and sit us down;*
>
> *And which trims up the bed for poor and naked folk;*
> *The glory of the gods, the granary of souls,*
> *The doorway from which men look out on unknown*
> *skies!* . . .[42]

and of his pipe:

> *I smoke as cottage chimneys do.* . . .[43]

And all his women, and his springtimes with their scents, and his mornings with the dust blown from the garbage-tins, and his towns tunnelled like ant-hills, and his "voices" that promise worlds, those that speak out of book-shelves, those that call the ships after them, those that say the earth is a sweet-flavoured cake, those that say:

> *here are for the plucking*
> *Hesperidean fruits that your heart hungers for.*[44]

And all the true, modern, poetic colours, it was he, remember, who discovered them—unobtrusive, delicious, his pinks above all, with blue, or gold, or green:

> *You are an autumn sky, clear and pink and lovely.* . . .[45]

> *And balconied twilights, with the pink mists rising,*[46]

and all the evenings that have a rosy sky.

And within this world there is another, even more secluded, the world of scents; but that, we should never come to the end of; and if we should take no matter which poem of his (I don't mean his great major poems that you love as much as I do, *Le Balcon, Le Voyage,* but the lesser ones), you would be astounded to see at every third or fourth line a famous line, not wholly Baudelairean, so that (compared with lines that are perhaps more typically and supremely his) you would not know where it came from:

Rich caskets without gems, lockets that hold no tress,[47]

a parent line, it would seem, being so universal and so new, of thousands of other kindred lines, though no one else has done them so well; and lines in every manner, lines like:

And the wide skies that bring eternity to mind,[48]

which you might think was Hugo's, like:

And your compelling eyes, such as a portrait has,[49]

which you might think was Gautier's, like:

O thou I should have loved, O thou aware of it,[50]

which you might think was Sully Prudhomme's, like:

All those whom he would love set eyes on him with dread,[51]

which you might think was Racine's, like:

O lure of nothingness, crazily bedizened,[52]

which you might think was Mallarmé's, like so many others that you might think were Sainte-Beuve's, or Gérard de Nerval's—Gérard, who has so much in common with him, who was more tender-hearted, he who also has to contend with a family (O Stendhal, Baudelaire, Gérard!), but does it so affectionately, who like him was a neurotic, and like him wrote the most beautiful poetry—which we ought to turn to next—and like him was indolent, infallibly right over details and uncertain as to the whole. It is very interesting in the Baudelaire poems with those great lines, that his inspiration, swept on through the turning-point after the previous hemistich, is preparing itself in mid-career to replenish them for the whole length of their enormous course, and that this gives one the utmost impression of the wealth and eloquence and boundlessness of a genius:

> *Whose aspect would have loosed a flow, a flood of alms,*

(into)

> *But for the spitefulness which glittered in their eyes.*[53]

>   *that little river*
> *Scant, sorry looking-glass, wherein aforetime blazed*

(into)

> *The pomp and stature of your grieving widowhood,*[54]

and scores of other examples. Sometimes, though there is to be nothing magnificent in the line to follow, the preceding half-line still has this wonderful slowing-up that will swing the chariot into the course of the line to follow—that climb of the trapeze which gradually, almost idly, goes higher and higher to gather impetus:

> *None could tell them apart, from the same hell come*
>   *forth,*

(into)

> *That senile replica, and those fantastic wraiths.*[55]

And the way these poems end, suddenly halted, shorn of their wings, as if he who but a line before had sent his chariot thundering round the immense arena had not the energy to go further; the end of *Andromaque:*

> *Captives, and worsted men, and many others more,*[56]

the end of *Le Voyage:*

> *Through depths of the unknown to come upon the*
> *New,*[57]

the end of *Les Sept Vieillards:*

> *And then my soul, an old dismasted wherry tossed,*
> *Tossed on a monstrous sea with never sight of land.*[58]

Some of Baudelaire's repetitions certainly seem a matter of preference and can hardly be taken for stopgaps.

Alas, a day was to come that would bring on him what he had called the Punishment of Arrogance:

> *His reason quitted him,*
> *The brightness of that sun put on a cloudy pall,*
> *Primordial Chaos rolled through that intelligence—*
> *A living temple once, ordered and opulent,*
> *Whose lighted halls had seen such feasting and parade.*
> *Then silence and darkness came to keep house in him*
> *As in a closed cellar to which the key is lost.*
> *So he lived on, the like of some masterless cur,*
> *And when he took himself into the fields, where he*
> *Saw nothing, knew no change 'twixt summer and winter,*
> *Dirty, useless, ugly, a rubbish-heap object,*
> *He was the children's joy, their sport and laughing-*
> *stock.*[59]

When that day came, he who in his day and till but a few days before had wielded the greatest power of the word that had ever exploded from human lips could stammer out no more than the bare words, "rot it, God rot it"; and when he caught sight of himself in a looking-glass which a woman (one of those barbarous friends who fancy they do you good by compelling you to "look tidy," and are not afraid to hold a looking-glass before the face of a dying man who has no idea what he looks like and whose fast-closing eyes expect to see a living visage) had brought him so that he might comb his hair, not recognising who it was, he bowed!

All these things come into my mind, "and many others more," as he said; and I cannot think that he was really a great critic, that man who, having lavished so many words on so many nincompoops, being well-disposed moreover towards Baudelaire, and with a mind constantly drawn towards Baudelaire's work—which marched, so he claimed, with his own (*Joseph Delorme* was an earlier version of *Les Fleurs du Mal*)—wrote no more than a few lines about it where, except for a display of wit (the *literary Kamtschatka* and the *Baudelaire Folly*) there is nothing that might not be equally applicable to most dancing-masters: "nice fellow, improves on acquaintance, polite, makes a good impression."

But the fact remains that Sainte-Beuve, just because of his astonishing intellect, was one of those who best understood him. When Baudelaire, who throughout his life had struggled against poverty and calumny, was dead, his mother, to whom he had been so often represented as a madman and a pervert, was amazed and overjoyed when a letter from Sainte-Beuve spoke of her son as a man who was good and intelligent. Poor Baudelaire had had to struggle against contempt from everyone all his life long, but:

The vivid lightning flashed from his clear mind
Hid from his sight the raging populace.[60]

They raged against him till the end; where he lay paralysed on the charity bed where the negress who had been his only real passion came to importune him with requests for money, it must needs happen that his wretched syllables of impatience against suffering, distorted by his stricken lips, should be heard as impieties and blasphemies by the mother superior of the convent where he was looked after and which he had to leave. But like Gérard,[61] he

> *Played with the wind, talked to the cloud, sang of the*
> *road*
> *To Calvary in a rapture as he trod it*

—like Gérard, who asked that his parents should be told that he was no fool.[62] It was at that stage of his life that Baudelaire had that mop of white hair which, he said, made him "look like an Academician—to foreigners." He has, above all in that last photograph, a fantastic likeness to Hugo, to Vigny, and to Leconte de Lisle, as if all four of them were but slightly different proofs of the same portrait, the portrait of that great poet who since the world began is really one poet, whose intermittent existence, spanning all mankind's, had in this century its hours of torment and victimisation, that we call the life of Baudelaire, its hours of industry and serenity, that we call the life of Hugo, its hours of vagabondage and innocence, that we call Gérard's life, and Francis Jammes's, perhaps, its goings-astray and degradations into paths of vain ambition, that we call the lives of Chateaubriand and Balzac, its goings-astray and hyperbolic flights of idealism, that we call the second half of Tolstoi's life, and of Racine's, Pascal's, Ruskin's, and perhaps Maeterlinck's, too.

10

Gérard de Nerval

"Gérard de Nerval, who was like the Paris to Munich bagman. . . ."

In these days, when by common consent *Sylvie* is declared a masterpiece, this strikes one as an odd statement. For all that, I must say that *Sylvie* is now admired for what I consider such wrongheaded reasons that I would really prefer to see it left in the obscurity to which Sainte-Beuve consigned it, whence at least it may emerge with its marvellous freshness unfingered. Though indeed, a work of art will emerge even from that most injurious of obscurities, a false interpretation, as soon as a true interpretation gives it back its beauty. Academicism and neo-classicism probably did more to discredit Greek sculpture and Racine's tragedies than the completest neglect could have done. Better never to read Racine than to read him in the light of Campistron. But now, washed clean from those drawing-master's stipplings, he is as original and as startling as though he had sprung from the unknown. The same holds good for Greek sculpture; and it is to Rodin, in revolt against the classic manner, that we owe it.

It is a current article of faith that Gérard de Nerval was a belated master of the eighteenth century, and that the Romantic Movement had no influence upon a purely Gallic talent, rooted in tradition and regionalism, whose *Sylvie* is an artless, delicate picture of an idealised French way of life. This is what we have made out of the man who was translating Faust at the age of twenty, who travelled to Weimar to meet Goethe, fueled the Romantic Movement with all his trans-Rhenan inspiration, was from his youth up subject to fits of madness; was finally put under restraint, felt the call of the East and eventually set out for it, and was found hanged in the doorway of a squalid alley—though whether he killed himself in a fit of frenzy or was murdered by his boon companions must remain debateable, either hypothesis, considering the strange haunts and habits into which he was led by his innate eccentricity and disturbed mind, being equally plausible. Mad, but not of a madness which is in some way purely organic and without the slightest influence on the mental processes—like those madmen one has met who in between their attacks had rather too much common sense, whose minds were almost too rational, too trenchant, vexed only by a purely physical melancholy.

In Gérard de Nerval's case, the incipient brooding madness is no more than a kind of inordinate subjectivity, a greater importance, so to speak, attached to a dream, to a memory, to the personal impact of sensation, than to what in our general, straightforward apprehension of those sensations we call reality. And when that artist's temperament—the temperament that leads, according to Flaubert, to thinking of reality only as providing "illusions to be described" and to fostering illusions that, in return for being described, take on a kind of reality—crossed the threshold of madness, that madness is so much the development of what was the essential element in his originality as a writer that he describes it as and when he experiences it, insofar, at least, as it remains describable; just as a creative writer continues, while falling asleep, to make mental notes of the stages of consciousness that lead him on from waking to sleeping until the moment when sleep usurps the whole of his divided mind. And so it is in this epoch of his life that de Nerval wrote those exquisite poems, where there are lines, the loveliest, perhaps, in the French language but obscure as Mallarmé's—so obscure, said Théophile Gautier, that they make *Lycophron* seem transparent:

I am the man of shadows. . . .[1]

and so many others.

However, this in no way dissolves the continuity between Gérard the poet and the Gérard who wrote *Sylvie*. One might even say—and this is obviously one of the things that can be urged against him, one of the things that designate in him, after all, if not the second-rate writer, then at least the writer without that really predestined genius which simultaneously creates form and content—that his poems and his novels are merely different essays at expressing the same thing—as are Baudelaire's *Petits Poèmes en prose* and *Les Fleurs du Mal*, for instance. In the case of such geniuses the inward vision is very visible and very potent, but—from a sicklied resolution in which the predetermining instinct is lacking[2] and intellect, which is readier to point out different paths than to tread in one of them, predominates, the idea is first tried out in verse, then, rather than lose sight of it, in prose, etc.

There are lines in his poetry that say almost word for word what he has said in prose. Just as in Baudelaire the line:

A clear sky and the quiver of interminable heat,[3]

is matched in the *Petits Poèmes en prose* by

A clear sky in which the endless heat is lost,[4]

I need only quote the line

The trellis where roses are mixed with the wild vine,[5]

for you to recognise Sylvie's window *where the wild
vines twine round the rosebush.*[6] And besides, later on
we find roses and vines entwining on every house in
Sylvie. M. Jules Lemaître, with whom I have otherwise no quarrel (I will make myself plain presently)
quotes in his book on Racine the passage where Sylvie
first appears. "Girls were dancing in a ring on the
greensward, while singing the old songs handed down
to them by their mothers, and in such naturally pure
French that one could feel no doubt one was living in
that old kingdom of Valois, where the heart of France
has beaten for over a thousand years." Traditional?
France of the French? To me it seems nothing of the
sort. We must restore the passage to where it was taken
from and to its proper lighting. It occurs in a kind of
dream. "I went back to bed and could find no rest
there. As I lay between sleeping and waking, my
whole youth passed through my memory. That state of
mind where intellect still holds out against the fantastic contrivances of dreaming often lets one see the
most striking scenes of a long period in one's life hud-
dled into the space of a few minutes." You will have
recognised immediately that poem of Gérard's:

There is an air for which I would relinquish. . . .[7]

So what we have here is one of those rainbow-
painted pictures, never to be seen in real life, or even
called up by words, but sometimes brought before us
in a dream or called up by music. Sometimes in the
moment of falling asleep, we see them, and try to

seize and define them. Then we wake up and they are gone, we give up the pursuit, and before we can be sure of their nature we are asleep again as though the sight of them were forbidden to the waking mind. The inhabitants of these pictures are themselves of the stuff of dreams:

> *A woman that some other life, perhaps,*
> *Showed me, and whom I now remember. . . .*[8]

Could there be anything less like Racine? That de Nerval's dream and longing should be centred on precisely that charm of the France Racine was born into, and which, moreover, he expressed without being sensible of it, is likely enough; but this is just as if one were to suppose that a glass of cold water and a feverish man belong to exactly the same order of things because the man craves for the water, or to confound a young girl's innocence and an old man's lechery, because the former is the dream of the latter. M. Lemaître—I say it without in any way qualifying my deep admiration for him, without in any way depreciating his incomparably fine study of Racine—has, in these days so ill-supplied with inventors, invented a style of criticism all his own, a creation in itself; and in the passages which are most characteristically his and which stand out because they are so, he enjoys eliciting a great many things from a work of art, which then come raining forth in profusion, rather as if they were goblets he might have put there.[9]

But in fact there is absolutely nothing of this in *Phèdre* or in *Bajazet*. If for some reason or another one makes use of the name, Turkey, in a book but otherwise has no notion of Turkey, no impression of Turkey, and no wish to go there, the book cannot be said to have anything to do with Turkey. Racine a solar author, rays of the sun, etc. It is what a work of art expresses or conveys that counts: to say that Turkey is present in a book is as much as to say that an idea of Turkey, a feeling about Turkey, etc.

I know quite well that the love inspired by some particular place exists not only for those who write about it but for those others who love quite as deeply perhaps, but less explicitly. I know there are men with no artistry about them, chief clerks, professional men, shopkeepers, doctors, who instead of living in a good quarter of Paris, or keeping a carriage, or going to the theatre, allot some part of their income to keeping a cottage in Brittany, where they stroll out at evening, never thinking that what they feel, and at most express by saying from time to time, "It's a fine evening; lovely weather," or, "I always enjoy a walk at sunset," is an artistic pleasure. But there is nothing to suggest that this even existed in Racine's mind, and in any case it would not have had the wistfulness, the visionary colouring, of *Sylvie*. Today there is a school of writers who, being in rebellion—it must be said, to good purpose—against the bloodless Battle of Words now in vogue, have imposed a new manner, which they believe to be a revival of the old manner, on the art of letters; and these are their tenets; that in order not to overweight a sentence one will keep it from expressing anything whatsoever, that to sharpen the outline of a book one will exclude any impression, any thought, etc., that cannot be straightforwardly expressed, and, that to preserve the traditional mould of the language one will be ready at all times to accept existing turns of speech, without even troubling to think them over. If this results in a brisk style, a grammar of respectable coinage, a free and easy demeanour, there is no special merit about it. It is not difficult to cover one's journey at a canter if before starting one jettisons all the valuables one was charged to carry; but the speed of the transit, the graceful ease of the arrival, are of no great significance, since there is nothing to deliver.

They are mistaken who believe that such a literature can claim an affiliation with the past. In any case, Gérard de Nerval's is the last name they should invoke. Why they think he has given them a warrant for doing so is that they prefer to restrict themselves in their articles, and verses, and novels, to describing a French loveliness that is "temperate, with pale buildings under a fair sky, and low hills, and churches like Dammartin or Ermenonville." Nothing is further from *Sylvie*.

If we thrill with that troubled delight when M. Barrès writes about the countryside of Chantilly and Compiègne and Ermenonville, and tells of landing on the islets of the Valois or of walking in the forests of Chââlis or Pontarmé, it is because we have read those names in *Sylvie*, because they are composed, not of real hours that we can remember, but of that April mood of pleasure (but pleasure founded on uneasiness) felt by that "sweet fool," and made these woodland mornings, or rather, his "half-dreamed" recollection of them, cast a cloudy enchantment over him. Ile-de-France, land of the golden mean, of modest charm, etc.: Oh, it is a far cry from that to the inexpressible something, something beyond the freshness of the air, beyond the morning light, beyond the cloudless weather, beyond the conjuration of the past,

even, which made Gérard prance and hold up his head
and sing, but with a joy half out of its senses, and
which infects us with this boundless perplexity when
we think that these places exist, and that we can take
ourselves for a walk through the landscape of *Sylvie*.
And what does M. Barrès do to bring it before us? He
repeats these names to us, he tells of things—the holy
honey-scented candles flickering in broad daylight at
a graveside, bells sounding through the October mist—
which seem to come out of the past, though our feeling for such things, and the fact that we draw pleasure
from them, is altogether contemporary, and has very
little of the decorum, very little of the "modest grace,"
very little of the "Ile-de-France spirit" according to
the Gospels of M. Hallay and M. Boulanger. And
that this is how he does it is best proved by the fact
that a few pages further on we find the same spell being repeated, this time on behalf of M. de Vogüé, who
for his part is faithful to Touraine, to landscapes
"composed to our liking," to the blonde Loire. What
leagues lie between this and Gérard! We recall, to be
sure, the intoxication of those first winter's mornings,
the longing to be afoot, the spell of those sunlit dis-
tances. But our pleasure is full of perplexity. The
measured grace of the landscape is the substance of it,
but it goes beyond that. There is no defining that Beyond. One day, it will become Gérard's madness.
Meanwhile, there is nothing measured about it, nothing so very French; Gérard's genius has impregnated
these names and places. I think every man of a keen
sensibility can yield himself over to the instigations
of that daydreaming which leaves a sort of puncture in
us, "for there is no steelier point than the point of infinity." [10] But it is not by talking about love that people

bring home to us the anguish of mind we suffer on account of a mistress, but by mentioning some small thing that calls her before our eyes, a detail of her dress or her Christian name. So it is the names Chââlis, Pontarmé, the islands of the Ile-de-France, which make the thought that we might set out one fine winter's morning to see the dream-country that Gérard wandered in, so intoxicating; the rest is nothing.

That is why all that can be said in praise of places leaves us cold. And why we so long to have written those pages of *Sylvie*. But as Baudelaire said, one cannot both have heaven and be rich; one cannot have called a landscape out of the void by means of intellect and discrimination, even like Victor Hugo, even like Heredia, and have steeped a real countryside in that dream-like atmosphere which Gérard has left behind in the Valois; because it really is from his dream that he has spun it. We admire Victor Hugo's *Villequier*, we admire Heredia's *Loire*, but we can think of them and remain in our senses. A shiver runs down one's back when one reads the name, *Pontarmé*, in a railway guide. There is an indefinible something in Gérard that we respond to, that we would contrive to have if it could be got by contrivance but which is a birthright, present in the make-up of these geniuses, and absent from the make-up of others, which is something further, just as there is something further to the act of falling in love than finding a woman beautiful and to one's liking. It is what happens sometimes in the illumination of a dream, the light in which he saw the Louis XIII castle; and though one were as intelligent as Lemaître, if one put forward Gérard as a paragon of well-ordered grace, one would be wrong. He is a paragon of morbid obsession. . . . To bring back to the present how harmless he was in his madness, how nearly in the old ballad tradition, by calling him a "sweet fool," is a charming stroke of appreciation on the part of Barrès.

But Gérard revisited the Valois in order to write *Sylvie?* Certainly. Passion believes that what it loves is a reality, the man in love with a dream country wants to set eyes on it. Otherwise, it would be no true love. Gérard is simple-hearted, and starts off. Marcel Prévost says to himself: "It's a dream, so we'll stay at home." But when all is said, it is only the inexpressible, the thing one believes one cannot succeed in getting into a book, that remains in it. It is something vague and haunting, like a memory. It is atmospheric, the atmosphere of *Sylvie*, a colouring in the air like the bloom on a grape. If we have not felt it, this inexpressible thing, we flatter ourselves that our work is as good as the work of those who feel it, since the words are more or less the same. But it is not in the words, it is not said, it is all in among the words, like the morning mist at Chantilly.

If ever a writer at the furthest remove from the bright water-colour style sought and laboured to see for himself, and seize, and elucidate, the cloudy shifting hues, the deep laws, the almost imperceptible impressions of the soul of man, Gérard de Nerval did it in *Sylvie*. Remember, the story that you call an artless picture is a dream about a dream. Gérard tries to call back to mind a woman he loved while at the same time he loved another, and who thus dominates certain hours of this life, and repossesses him every evening at a certain hour. And calling up those days in a dream-picture, he is seized with desire to set off for that countryside, he leaves his room, goes downstairs, has the street-door opened for him, and takes a cab. And while he is jolted on towards Loisy, he remembers and goes over the past. He arrives after this sleepless night, and what he then sees, disconnected, so to speak, from reality by the sleepless night and by this return to a place which for him is more like a past existing at least as much in his heart as on a map, is so closely intermingled with the memories he continues to call up, that one is constantly obliged to turn back to an earlier page to see where one is, if it is the present or the past recalled.

The characters themselves are like the woman in the line I quoted, *That in some other life I knew and whom I remember.* That Adrienne whom he believes to be the actress, which makes him fall in love with the actress, and who was not she, those castles, those lords and ladies whom he seems to see living in the past rather than the present, that gala which was held on Saint Bartholomew's Day and about which he is not clear in his mind as to whether it took place or whether it was only a dream ("the keeper's son was tipsy," etc.), I can rightly say that in all this even the characters are only the shadow of a dream. That heavenly early morning on the road, the visit to Sylvie's grandmother's cottage—these are real. But remember: that night he had slept out of doors, and then only for a minute, and with a strange kind of slumber in which he never lost consciousness, since he wakes up with the sound of the Angelus in his ears which he had not heard.

One can say that such mornings are real, if you like. But one lives them in a state of exaltation when the slightest beauty flies to one's head and gives one, though in everyday reality it could do no such thing, an almost dreamlike pleasure. The befitting colour of everything moves one as though it were music, one is on the edge of tears to see that the roses are rose-coloured, or, if it be winter, lovely tints of almost mirroring green on the tree-trunks; and if a brief light falls on those colours, as for instance at sunset when the white lilac becomes a hymn to whiteness, one feels flooded with beauty. In dwellings where the lively open air still excites you, in cottages or castles, that exaltation is as lively as it was out of doors, and a relic of past days that gives you something to dream about adds force to it. How many matter-of-fact hosts must I thus have astonished by the intensity of my gratitude or my admiration, while doing no more than walk up a flight of stairs laid with a Turkish carpet, or seeing from the luncheon table the pale March sun brightening the transparent shades of green that encrust the treetrunks in the park, or gliding in to warm its pale beams on the carpet near the great fire, while the coachman came for his orders about where we would drive that afternoon. Such are the blessed mornings that a sleepless night, the tossed nerves of a journey, a physical exaltation, some event out of the common, will hollow out for us in the hard rock of our daily lives, mornings that miraculously retain the delicious feverish colours and the dreamlike charm which sets them apart in our memory like an Aladdin's cave, magical and prismatic in an atmosphere all its own.

The colouring of *Sylvie* is a purple colouring, from the purple of a rose to the purple or violet of velvet, and has nothing of the water-colour tints of their temperate France. Hints of red are continually brought in: the shooting-match, red handkerchiefs, etc. And

the very name is empurpled by its two *I* sounds—
Sylvie, the true Daughter of Fire.[11] Since I can number
them, those mysterious laws of thought which I have
often hoped to expound and which I find expounded
in *Sylvie*—I believe I could count up to five or six of
them—I have the right to say that whatever the distance a faultless execution—and that is all—sets between a mere intellectual fancy and a masterpiece, between the authors derisively called intellectuals and
Gérard, it is nevertheless the intellectuals who can
invoke his name, rather than those who can achieve a
faultless execution quite easily, since they execute
nothing. Certainly, the picture that Gérard paints is
beguilingly simple; and this is the unparalleled gift of
his genius. With these very subjective feelings, if we
describe the thing that aroused them in us, and do no
more than that, we do not convey exactly what gave it
its value for us. But if we try to convey these subjective values by analysing the impression they make on
us, then we obliterate the picture of what we saw. So
that from despair, we still find more food for our imagination in what gives a name to our dreams without
explaining them, in railway time-tables, travellers'
narratives, names of shopkeepers and village streets,
M. Bazin's memorandums in which every tree is mentioned, than in the over-subjective Pierre Loti. But
Gérard discovered how to give his picture the colouring of a dream by doing no more than just painting it.
Perhaps, even so, there is a little too much intellect in
his story. . . .

11

Sainte-Beuve and Balzac

One of the writers of his day that Sainte-Beuve was wrong about, is Balzac. You look down your nose. You don't care for him, I know. And there you have some right on your side. The vulgarity of his mind was so massive that a lifetime could not leaven it. It was not only when he was no older than was Rastignac at the outset of his career that he set before him as his goal in life the gratification of the most grovelling ambitions—or at least, confused these ambitions so thoroughly with other and better ones that it is almost impossible to disentangle them; but in the year before his death, when the fulfilment of the love of his life, the marriage to Mme. Hanska whom he had loved for sixteen years, was in sight, he writes to his sister like this: "Say what you like, Laure, in Paris it means something to be able, when one wants to, to throw open one's house and entertain the cream of society, who will meet a woman there who is polished, stately as a queen, of high descent, related to the grandest families, witty, well-educated and handsome. That's a great step towards becoming a power in the land. I can't help it, this business that's going on, quite apart from my feelings (failure would as good as kill me), means all or nothing to me, double or quits. Heart, soul, ambition, everything about me is set on just this one thing that I've been in pursuit of for the last sixteen years: if this stupendous happiness slips through my fingers, there's nothing else I want. Don't suppose that I love luxury. It's the luxury of the Rue Fortunée that I love, and all that goes with it: a beau-

tiful woman, well-born, comfortably off, and knowing
all the best people." Elsewhere he again speaks of
Mme. Hanska in like terms. "This person who brings
with her (apart from her money) inestimable social
advantages." After this, one can't feel surprised that
Mme. de Mortsauf in *Le Lys dans la Vallée*, his superlative ideal woman, his "angel," writing from her
deathbed to Félix de Vandenesse, whom she loves
both amorously and maternally, a letter so enshrined
in his memory that years later he will say of it: "*This
was the heavenly voice that suddenly spoke out of the
silence of night, this was the sublime figure that arose
to show me the true path*," should give him good advice as to how to get on in the world. To get on in the
world virtuously and in a Christian spirit; for Balzac
knew he ought to paint a saintly figure, but he could
not conceive how social success should not be the goal
of all goals, even in the eyes of a saint. And when he
enlarges to his sister and his nieces on the benefits to
be drawn from close acquaintance with such a wonderful being as the woman he loved, that *summum bonum*
she might impart to them is to be found in a particular aristocratic deportment that knows how to indicate
and preserve the distinctions due to age, rank, etc.,
with some theatre tickets thrown in: "a box at the *Ital-
iens*, and the *Opéra*, and the *Opéra-Comique*." And
Rastignac, when he falls in love with his aunt, Mme.
de Beauséant, confides in her quite seriously, "You
could do a lot for me." Mme. de Beauséant shows no
surprise[1] at this, and smiles.

I say nothing of the vulgarity of his language. It
was so inherent that it even contaminated his verbal
resources and made him use expressions that would
jar in the most careless conversation. *Quinola's Expe-*

dients he first intended to call *Quinola's Dodges.* "His
hair stood up on end" is how he paints d'Arthez's astonishment. To a worldly-wise reader these expressions sometimes seem primed with deep social observation: "Vandenesse's earlier loves, Mme. d'Espard,
Mme. de Manerville, Lady Dudley and others of less
note, felt serpents stirring in the depths of their
hearts; they envied Félix's happiness; gladly would
they have given *their prettiest slippers* to see some
misfortune befall him." And whenever he tries to hide
this vulgarity, he develops a vulgarian's refinement,
like those mawkish attitudes, those fingers affectedly
propping the brow, which frightful stock-jobbers put
on when they go for carriage rides in the Bois. So he
says, "Dear Lady," or rather, *"cara," "addio"* for
goodbye, etc.

You have sometimes thought Flaubert vulgar in the
light of some of his collected letters. But at least there
is no vulgarity in Flaubert himself, for he understood
that the writer's life is centred in his work, and that
the remainder only exists "to provide an illusion to
describe." Balzac puts the achievements of life and of
literature on exactly the same level. "If the *Comédie
Humaine* does not make a great man of me," he writes
to his sister, "this achievement will" (the achievement
of his marriage to Mme. Hanska). *

But if you come to think of it, the verisimilitude of
some of his pictures may be due to that same vulgar-

---

* But are we slightly surfeited with truth as conceived by Flaubert,
Mallarmé, etc., and beginning to crave for the infinitesimal amount
of truth that may lie in the antithetical falsehood (like someone
who will need salt after a long and beneficial "salt-free" treatment,
like those savages who feel "sick-mouthed," and, so M. Paul Adam
tells us, fall on other savages in order to consume the salt in their
skin)?

ity. Even in those of us whom high-mindedness specifically impels to reject vulgar motives, to condemn
and disinfect them, those motives may exist, fundamental though transfigured. In any case, though an
ambitiously-minded man should feel an ideal love—
even though his ambitious thoughts may not be transfigured by it—that love, alas! is not the whole of his
life and often is no more than the few best days of his
youth. It is with that part of himself alone that a
writer composes his book; but there is a whole part
which is left out. And so what force of truth we acknowledge when we see Vandenesse or Rastignac im-
pulsively falling in love, knowing that Vandenesse and
Rastignac are cold-hearted climbers whose whole lives
have been ambition and scheming; and again when
these youthful romances of theirs (yes, almost more
their romances than Balzac's) are forgotten things
which they only refer to with smiles, with the smiles
of those who have really forgotten, and the love-affair
with Mme. de Mortsauf is discussed by third parties,
or even by the hero himself, just as if it were any other
adventure, and without even a sense of grief that its
remembrance should not have filled their whole lives.
To reach such a degree of truth to life—life as the
worldly and the experienced know it, where it is
agreed that love is fleeting, a youthful vagary, that ambition and lust have more than a hand in it, that one
day all that kind of thing won't seem very important,
etc.—to show that the most romantic feelings may be
no more than a play of refracted light transfiguringly
directed on his ambitions by the ambitious man himself and to show this, consciously or unconsciously, in
the most compelling way, that is by showing objec-
tively as the bleakest of adventurers the man who

himself, subjectively, sees himself in his own eyes as a
romantic wooer; this, perhaps was a privilege granted
in return for, or even conditional on, the author precisely and quite naturally conceiving the noblest feelings in such a vulgar way that when he supposed he
was describing the fulfilment of a life-long dream of
happiness he actually told us about the social advantages of that marriage. Here there is no call to differ-
entiate between his letters and his novels. If it has
often been said that his characters were real people to
him, and that he seriously debated if so and so were a
better match for Mlle. de Grandlieu, or for Eugénie
Grandet, one can say that his life was a novel which he
set about in exactly the same spirit. There was no
dividing line between real life (which as you and I
think, is not real) and the life in his novels (which for
the writer is the only true life). In the letters to his
sister where he talks about the possibilities of this marriage to Mme. Hanska, not only is everything built up
like a novel, but those involved are placed, analysed,
described, seen as factors in the development of the
plot, as if in one of his books. Wishing to impress on
her how his mother writes to him as if he were a little
boy, and how the disclosure not only of his debts but
of the family insolvency might bring the marriage to
nothing and incline Mme. Hanska towards another
suitor, he writes exactly as he might write in *Le Curé
de Tours*: "Then you learn that being a sculptor is a
chancy business, that the government is cutting down
its commissions, that work is at a standstill, that the
sculptor has incurred debts, has settled them but for
all that still owes money to a marble-importer, to the
stone-masons, and reckons on his earnings to pay it off.
A letter from a married brother tells you that this

brother is battling to support a wife and family, and is in poor health; that a sister who has married a waster is living in abject poverty in Calcutta; then comes another revelation that the sculptor has an old mother, and has to make her a regular allowance.

"Suppose that at this juncture another suitor presents himself. He is a satisfactory young man, he is not burdened by any debts, he has thirty thousand francs a year, and is Solicitor-General. What do Mme. Surville and her husband do? On the one hand, they see a poor family, a dubious future; they find some excuse, and Sophie marries a *Procureur-Général* with thirty thousand francs a year.

"The dismayed sculptor says to himself, Why the devil did my mother write to me, why the devil must my sister in Calcutta write to me about the fix she was in! Why didn't my brother keep quiet? See where this has got us to! I had the chance of a marriage that would have made a rich man of me, and best of all, a happy man. Everything's gone to wrack and ruin for a lot of nonsense." Elsewhere, in *La Recherche de l'Absolu*, we can see his last-minute contrivances to recover some semblance of fiction.[2]

Just as his sister, his brother-in-law, his mother* (the mother for whom, much as he adores her, he feels none of that touching humility of those great men who always remain children where their mother is concerned and forget, as she does, that they are gen-

---

* He said: "the mother of a man like me," and when he speaks of how fond he is of her, how humble before her, it is the same as when he depicts the ideal angelic nature of Mme. de Mortsauf; he embosses and glorifies and overloads that ideal but the mean alloy is still there; his ideal woman is none the less a woman who enjoyed having her shoulders kissed by a strange man, who understood and could teach how to get on in the world. His angels are Rubens angels, winged, and showing a great deal of bosom.

iuses) interest us as characters in that novel of his life: *Un Grand Mariage*, so, in the same way, his pictures, whether those in his collection or those he saw at Wierschownia, most of which were to go to the Rue Fortunée—are "characters in fiction" too. Each of them calls forth those historical disquisitions,[3] those picture-lover's reviews, that admiration that turns quickly into illusion, exactly as if it hung not on Balzac's walls but in the collections of Pons, or of Claës, or in the Abbé Chapeloud's modest library, in those novels of his where there are pictures on the footing of people, and where the slightest Coypel "would not disfigure the finest collection"; just as Bianchon is the equal of Cuvier, of Lamarck, of Geoffroy Saint-Hilaire. And he does not describe the furniture of Cousin Pons or of Claës with more affection, more realism, more illusion, than he describes his pictures in the Rue Fortunée or those at Wierschownia. "I have received the table-cistern that Bernard Palissy made for Henry II or Charles IX. It is one of his best pieces, and one of the rarest, a priceless specimen, for it has a diameter of fifteen to twenty inches and stands twenty-seven inches high, etc." "The little house in the Rue Fortunée will soon receive some fine pictures, a charming head by Greuze which comes from the collection of the late king of Poland, two Canalettos that once belonged to Pope Clement XIII, two Van Huysums, one Van Dyke, three canvasses by Rotari—the Greuze of Italy, a *Judith* by Cranach which is a miracle, etc. These pictures are *di primo cartello*, and would not disfigure the finest collection." "How different is the Holbein in my collection, fresh and intact after three hundred years." "The Holbein *St. Peter* has been thought sublime; in a public auction it might reach three thousand francs." In Rome he bought "a Sebastian del Piombo, a Bronzino, and a Mirevelt of the utmost beauty." He has Sèvres vases "that must have been designed as a gift to Latreille," since one could not undertake such a piece of work "except for a very celebrated figure in entomology. It is a real find, I have never seen such a bargain." Elsewhere he speaks of his chandelier—"from the household goods of some German emperor, because it is surmounted by a two-headed eagle"; of his portrait of Queen Maria Leczinska "which is not a Coypel, but painted in his workshop by an apprentice, possibly Lancret, possibly another; one needs to be a connoisseur not to take it for a Coypel." "A charming Natoire, signed and very authentic, a trifle pretty-pretty, however, against the substantial specimens of painting in my collection." "A delicious sketch of the birth of Louis XIV, an *Adoration of the Shepherds* where the shepherds are bewigged in the fashion of the date and represent Louis XIV and his ministers." Of his *Knight of Malta*: "One of those radiant masterpieces which are, like the *Violin Player*, the sunshine of a collection. Everything about it is like a well-preserved original Titian; what excites the greatest admiration is the dress, which, as connoisseurs express it, contains a man. . . . Sebastian del Piombo is not capable of having painted it. In any case, it is one of the finest works of the Italian Renaissance, it is of the school of Raphael with improved colouring. But until you have seen my Greuze *Portrait of a Woman*, you can form no idea, believe me, of the French School. In a way it beats Rubens, Rembrandt, Raphael, Titian. Of its type, it is as fine as the *Knight of Malta*. An *Aurora* of Guido's in his powerful manner, when he was completely Caravaggio. It reminds me of Canaletto, but it is more grandiose. In short, it is incomparable, for me, at least." • "My Watteau tea-service, a milk-jug which is magnificent, and two tea-caddies." "The finest Greuze I have ever seen, done by Greuze for Mme. Geoffrin; two Watteaus done by Watteau for Mme. Geoffrin: these three pictures are worth eighty thousand francs. There are also two excellent Leslies—James II and his first wife; a Van Dyke, a Cranach, a Mignard, a Rigaud, every one of them superlative, three Canalettos purchased by the King, a Van Dyke bought from Van Dyke by Mme. Hanska's great-great-great-grandmother, a Rembrandt—what pictures! The Countess wishes the three Canalettos to go to my collection. There are two Van Huysums whose value could not be met though one covered them with diamonds. What treasures there are in these great Polish families!"

Because of this half-baked realism, too fabulous for life, too prosaic for literature, we often get very much the same kind of pleasure from Balzac's books that we get from life. It is not mere legerdemain when Balzac, wanting a list of eminent doctors or eminent artists, hotchpotches the names of real men with those of characters in his books, saying: "He had the genius of a Claude Bernard, a Bichat, a Desplein, a Bianchon," as panorama painters mingle figures in actual relief with painted urns and melons in their foregrounds. Quite often these real persons are but the more real for it. The livingness of his characters is due to Bal-

---

• He often said: "for me, at least"; he said of *Cousin Pons:* "It is, for me, at least, one of those fine works. . . ." It must have been his mother who told him: If you talk like that, you should say, for me, at least.

zac's art, but the satisfaction this affords him is non-artistic. He speaks about them as though they were real people, and really celebrated: "the distinguished late Minister de Marsay, the only great statesman produced by the July Revolution, the only man who could have saved France"—now with the bland conceit of a parvenu who, not content with owning fine pictures, must continually be proclaiming the name of the artist and the price he had been offered for the picture, now with the artlessness of a child who having christened its dolls thinks they have really come alive. He carries this to the point of calling them, all of a sudden, and when so far not much has been said of them, by their Christian names; be it Princesse de Cadignan ("Diane did not look twenty-five"), Mme. de Sérizy ("No one could have followed Léontine; she flew"), or Mme. de Bartas ("'Biblical?' replied Fifine, astonished"). We see this familiarity as slightly vulgar but quite without that snobbery which made Mme. de Nucingen refer to Mlle. de Grandlieu as Clothilde—"to give herself the quality," as Balzac says, "of being on terms of Christian names with her, as if she, born a Goriot, frequented that society."

Sainte-Beuve blames Balzac for having magnified the Abbé Troubert, who finally becomes a sort of Richelieu, etc. Balzac did the same thing with Vautrin and many others. This is not merely a way of adding splendour and stature to these characters and presenting them as the finest of their kind—as Bianchon and Desplein are peers of Claude Bernard and Laënnec, and M. de Grandville of d'Aguesseau: it is also the fault of one of Balzac's most cherished theories, the theory of the great man to whom greatness of circumstances has been denied, and because his real objective as a novelist is precisely that: to be the historian of the unhistoried, and to study certain characters of historic dimensions just as they manifest themselves while lacking the historical factor which would impel them to greatness. As long as this is how Balzac sees them, it does not disconcert us; but when Lucien de Rubempré, on the point of killing himself, writes to Vautrin, "If God wills it so, these mysterious beings are Moses, Attila, Charlemagne, Mahomet or Napoleon. But if he leaves these gigantic instruments to rust beneath the ocean of a generation they are no more than Pougatcheff, Fouché, Louvel, or the Abbé Carlos Herrera. Farewell, then, farewell to you, who on the right path could have been more than a Ximenes, more than a Richelieu, etc.," Lucien talks too much like Balzac, and leaves off being a real person, distinguishable from all others. And in spite of the amazing variety of Balzac's characters, and their amazing degree of personal identity, this, for one reason or another, sometimes happens. For instance, though there are more individuals in his books than there are types, one feels all the same that this individual and that are just different christenings of the same type. Mme. de Langeais seems at times to be Mme. de Cadignan, and M. de Mortsauf, M. de Bargeton.

We recognise Balzac in such passages, and we smile, not unkindly; but because he can be recognised, all the details that were intended to make the characters of his novels more like people in real life, have the opposite effect. The character lived; Balzac so plumes himself on it that he mentions, quite needlessly, the sum of her dowry, and her connections with other characters in *La Comédie Humaine*, who are thus put on the footing of living people—which seems to him to be killing two birds with one stone. "Mme. de Sérizy (though born a de Ronquerolles) was not on their visiting list." But because one sees Balzac's legerde-main one loses a little of one's faith in the reality of those Grandlieus who did not invite Mme. de Sérizy to their house. Though the impression made by the trickster's, or the artist's, vitality is deepened, it is at the expense of the impression made by the vitality of the work of art. A work of art, for all that; and though it is a trifle eked out with all these overconvincing de-tails, all this Musée Grévin business, they too are fuel to its fire, and something is made of them. And as all this relates to an epoch, records its outward habili-ments and judges very acutely on what lies beneath, when its interest as a novel is exhausted, it begins a new life as a historical document. As the *Aeneid*, just where poets find it boring, can be enthralling to myth-ologists, so when Peyrade, Félix de Vandenesse, and the like, don't seem to us to have much life in them, Albert Sorel tells us that it is in them we must study the police system of the Consulate or the politics of the Bourbon Restoration. The novel is itself a gainer by this. As with those people whom one makes friends with on a holiday and is about to take leave of when one learns that they are catching the same train and may be remet in Paris, so at the depressing moment when we must say goodbye to a Balzac character—a moment that Balzac had put off as long as he could by making him reappear in other novels—just when he is about to disappear and be no more than a dream, Sorel says to us: "Not at all. This isn't a dream. Study them, it's authentic, it's part of history."

So in reading Balzac we can still feel and almost gratify those cravings which great literature ought to allay in us. With Tolstoi, the account of an evening party in high society is dominated by the mind of the author, and, as Aristotle would say, we are purged of our worldliness while we read it; with Balzac, we feel almost a worldly satisfaction at taking part in it. His very titles carry the stamp of actuality. While with many writers the title is more or less of a symbol, an emblem that must be understood in a wider and more poetical sense than a reading of the book would warrant, with Balzac it is more apt to be the other way about. To read through that wonderful book called *Les Illusions Perdues*, clips the wings, rather than not, of that lovely title, *Lost Illusions*, and brings it to earth. The title means that on going to Paris Lucien de Rubempré discovered that Mme. de Bargeton was absurd and provincial, that journalists were rascals, that life was hard. They are quite personal, quite arbitrary illusions, and the loss of them can drive him to despair, while the nature of them gives the book a powerful stamp of reality, but they slightly abate the transcendentalism of the title. So each title should be taken literally: *Un Grand Homme de Province à Paris*, *Splendeurs et Misères des Courtisanes*, *A combien l'Amour revient aux Vieillards*, etc. In *La Recherche de l'Absolu*, the absolute has more the nature of a formula, an alchemical rather than a philosophic affair. Not much is made of it, anyhow. And the story is much more concerned with the havoc a ruling passion can wreak on an affectionate family that must put up with it, whatever the object of that passion may be. Balthasar Claës is brother to Hulot, and to Grandet. Anyone electing to write about a neurasthenic's family will have material for a picture on the same lines.

Style is so largely a record of the transformation imposed on reality by the writer's mind that Balzac's style, properly speaking, does not exist. Here Sainte-Beuve is completely off the scent. "This style which is often titillating and melting, enervated, flushed and streaked with all manner of hues, this delightfully corrupted style, thoroughly Asiatic, as our teachers used to say, and in places more dislocated and more pliable than the limbs of a Greek pantomimist." Nothing could be less accurate. In Flaubert's style, now, all the elements of reality are rendered down into one unanimous substance, into vast, unvaryingly polished surfaces. No flaw remains in it. It has been rubbed to looking-glass smoothness. Everything is shown there, but only in reflection, and without affecting its uniform substance. Everything at variance with it has been made over and absorbed. In Balzac, on the other hand, all the elements of a style which is still to come exist together, undigested and untransformed. It is a style that neither suggests, nor mirrors; it explains. It explains, moreover, by the aid of images which are intensely striking but do not fuse with the rest, and which convey what he wants to say as we convey something in course of conversation—if we happen to be conversational geniuses—without concerning ourselves as to whether what we say is out of keeping or an interruption. As he will say in a letter: "Good marriages are like cream; a mere nothing will turn them sour," it is by images of this sort—striking, that is, and apt, but discordant, explaining instead of suggesting, and refractory to any considerations of beauty or fitness—that he will get his effects: "M. de Bargeton's laugh which was like damp squibs going off, etc.," "Her complexion had taken on the warm tone of a porcelain vase with a light inside it," "Finally, to describe the man by a stroke the force of which will be appreciated by people accustomed to do business, he wore blue spectacles, whose object was to conceal his glance under a pretext of protecting his eyesight from the glare of the light."

In fact, he had such a ridiculous conception of the beauty of imagery that Mme. de Mortsauf can write to Félix Vandenesse: "To use an image *that will engrave itself on your poet's mind*, though the numeral be of measureless size, written in gold, written in pencil, it can never be more than a numeral."

If he is content to hit on a stroke that will make us see what the person is like without attempting to fuse it in a harmonious general effect, in the same way he gives concrete examples, instead of liberating what they may contain. He describes Mme. de Bargeton's state of mind like this: "She imagined the Pasha of Janina, she would have liked to struggle with him in the harem, and thought there was something splendid about being sewn up in a sack and thrown into the Bosporus. She was envious of Lady Hester Stanhope, that blue-stocking of the desert." So, not content with evoking the impression he wishes to leave us with, he immediately qualifies it. "His expression was appalling. At that moment, his glance was sublime." He will tell us about Mme. de Bargeton's natural talents which turn into affectations from dwelling on the petty affairs of provincial life; and he adds, as if he were the Comtesse d'Escarbagnas: "In truth, a sunset is a great poem, etc." Even in *Le Lys dans la Vallée*, "one of the most chiselled stones in my edifice," he himself said—and we know that he called it back in proof from the printers as many as seven or eight times—he is in such a hurry to state the facts that the sentence is left to shift for itself. It knew from him what it should tell the reader, for the rest it must manage as best it could: "Although it was so hot I walked down to the meadows to see once again the Indre and its islets, the valley and its hillsides, *of which I appeared a passionate admirer.*"

Balzac makes use of all the ideas that come into his head, and does not try to resolve them into a way of writing where they would be in keeping with each other and with what he intended them to suggest. No, he states them baldly, and however eccentric or however unlikely a simile may be, besides being unfailingly apt, in it goes: "M. du Châtelet was like one of those melons that ripen from green to yellow in a single night." "It was impossible not to compare M. X. . . . to a frozen viper."

As he had no conception that literary style is a particular medium where things that are topics for conversation, subjects for study, etc., should not be incorporated in a crude state, he dogs every word with what he thinks of it, and the ideas it calls up in him. If he mentions an artist, he immediately says what he knows about him, as though in a footnote. Speaking of the Séchard's printing-press, he says that it was necessary to adapt the paper to the requirements of French civilisation which threatened to extend the right of discussion to every subject and base its existence on a continual manifestation of individual thinking—a real misfortune, since nations which deliberate, seldom act, etc. And so he puts in all manner of reflections which because of that natural vulgarity of his are often commonplace, and take on a rather comic quality from being artlessly plumped down in the middle of a sentence; the more so, as terms such as "peculiar to," employed for the specific purpose of defining or elucidating something said in parenthesis, give them an added pomposity. In *Le Colonel Chabert*, for instance, there are several references to "the intrepidity natural to attorneys, the mistrust natural to attorneys." And when he has to supply an explanation, Balzac does not mince matters: he writes, "This is why;" and a chapter follows. Again, there are his recapitulations where, without allowing a moment's breathing-space, he tells us everything we ought to know: "From the second month after his marriage, David spent most of his time . . . etc." "Three months after his arrival in Angoulême, etc." "The nun accompanied the *Magnificat* with rich, graceful extemporisations where the rhythmical variety expressed a human happiness." "The themes had the brilliance of a prima-donna's warblings, her strains skipped like a bird, etc."

He hides nothing, he says everything. So one is amazed to find that there are nevertheless wonderful effects of silence in his works. Goncourt marvelled at *L'Éducation*. I marvel even more at the *implications* in Balzac's books. "You know Rastignac? Really? . . ."

Balzac is like those people who on hearing a gentleman say, in speaking of the Duc d'Aumale, *Le Prince*, in speaking to a duchess, *Madame la Duchesse*, and seeing him put his hat on the floor in a drawing-room, have enquired, not then having learned that a prince, whether he is called Comte de Paris, Prince de Joinville, Duc de Chartres, or by other titles, is referred to as *Le Prince*, "Why do you say Prince, when he is a duke? Why do you say, Madame la Duchesse, like a servant? etc." But no sooner do they know that it is customary than they believe they have always known it, or, if they remember their previous cavils, are no less ready to instruct others, and enjoy giving them lessons on the customs of good society, customs they have only just become aware of. Balzac has exactly their peremptory, Mr. Know-all tone of voice when he lays down what is done and what is not done. When d'Arthez is introduced to the Princesse de Cadignan: "The Princess did not pay the great man any of those compliments that common people would have overwhelmed him with. People of good taste, like the Princess, are chiefly to be recognised by the way they listen. At dinner, d'Arthez sat next to the Princess, who, far from the excessive daintiness that fine-lady ladies think proper, etc., etc." When Félix de Vandenesse is introduced to Mme. de Mortsauf: "Mme. de Mortsauf began a conversation about country life, the harvest—subjects where I was at sea. Such behaviour in a hostess testifies to a lack of education, etc. But a few months later on, I understood how significant it was, etc." Here, at least, the note of assurance is comprehensible, since he is dealing with customs only. But he still retains it when he passes moral judgments: "In society, no one has any feeling for suffering, or misfortune, everything is words," or supplies interpretations: "The Duc de Chaulieu found the Duc de Grandlieu waiting for him in his study. 'Tell me, Henry,' he said (these two Dukes addressed each other in the second person singular, and by Christian names: it is one of the fine distinctions invented for indicating degrees of friendship, beating back the invasions of French familiarity, and mortifying people's self-esteem)." Besides, I must point out that Balzac, like those neo-Christian writers who attribute to the Church a control over authorship that the most

austerely orthodox popes have never dreamed of, con-
ferred privileges on dukes that Saint-Simon, for all his
high opinion of dukedoms, would have been quite
dumbfounded to see bestowed on them. "The Duke
gave Mme. Camusot one of those swift glances by
which the lords of the land can analyse a whole lifetime, and often a soul itself. Oh, if the judge's wife
could have known about this ducal gift!" If the dukes
of Balzac's day indeed possessed this gift, it must be
admitted things have, as one says, somehow changed.

Balzac does not always directly express that wonder-
ment his slightest remarks inspired in him. He en-
trusts the expression of it to the characters engaged.
There is a very famous story of his called *Autre Étude
de Femme*. It is made up of two narratives which do
not call for a large cast of walking-on parts; but almost
all Balzac's characters are grouped round the narrator,
as in the "*à-propos*," those "command performances"
which the Comédie Française puts on for anniversa-
ries or centenaries. Each one chimes in with the ap-
propriate remark, as in those dialogues of the dead,
too, in which an author wants to parade a whole
epoch. At every minute another of them makes his
appearance. De Marsay begins his narrative by explaining that a statesman is a kind of monster of self-
possession. "Now you've explained why statesmen are
so rare in France," said old Lord Dudley. Marsay goes
on: "This monster became so, thanks to a woman."
"I fancied that in politics we were more destructive
than constructive," said Mme. de Montcornet, with a
smile. "If this is to be a love-story," said the Baronne
de Nucingen, "I beg that it will not be broken into by
any moralisings." "Moralising is so out of place there,"
exclaimed Joseph Bridau. "He wouldn't stay to sup-

per," said Mme. de Sérizy. "Now, none of your shocking aphorisms, pray," said Mme. de Camps with a smile. And each on his cue, the Princesse de Cadignan, Lady Barimore, the Marquise d'Espard, Mlle. des Touches, Mme. de Vandenesse, Blondet, Daniel d'Arthez, the Marquis de Montriveau, Count Adam Laginsky, etc., successively speak their lines, as when on Molière's birthday the members of the society file past his statue and lay a palm-leaf before it. However, this rather unconvincingly assembled public is exceedingly well-inclined towards Balzac, quite as well-inclined as Balzac himself, whose mouth-piece it is. When de Marsay had uttered the reflection: "True and only love gives rise to a kind of bodily apathy in tune with the contemplative state one sinks into. The mind tangles everything together, then sets itself to work, calls up fancies, makes realities and torments of them, and that jealousy which is as sweet as it is painful," a statement from abroad smiled at recalling in the light of memory the truth of this remark. A little further on de Marsay concludes a description of one of his mistresses by a comparison which is not a very pretty one but it must have pleased Balzac, for we find its fellow in *Les Secrets de la Princesse de Cadignan:* "There is always a first-rate monkey in the prettiest and most angelic of women." At these words, says Balzac, *all the women cast down their eyes, as if pricked by that cruel truth so cruelly observed.* "'I will tell you nothing about the night nor the week that I spent,'" de Marsay goes on. "'I knew myself once more as a statesman.' *At these well-chosen words we could not refrain from exhibiting our admiration.*" De Marsay then explains that his mistress pretended that he was her only love: " 'She could not live without me, etc.; in short, she made me into her God.' The women listening to de Marsay seemed offended at *seeing themselves made such game of.*" Further on de Marsay says, " 'A woman in society may give rise to calumny, but never to gossip.' 'All this is dreadfully true,' said the Princesse de Cadignan." (This last remark, incidentally, can be justified by the Princesse de Cadignan's reputation.) Besides, Balzac had not omitted to tell us before-hand what a feast we were going to enjoy. "It is in Paris alone that this type of wit abounds. Only Paris, the capital city of taste, understands this science that changes a conversation into a tourney. . . . Deft repartees, sharp observations, admirable witticisms, pictures sketched with brilliant precision, sparkled and jostled, and were appreciated with delight and enjoyed with discrimination." (We have seen that on this point Balzac was right.) We ourselves are not always so ready in our admiration as this public was. True, we do not share their observation of the narrator's mimicries, lacking which, Balzac tells us, "this ravishing improvisation" is untransmittable. In fact we have to take Balzac's word for it when he tells us that a repartee of de Marsay's "was accompanied by mimicking postures, tilts of the head, airs and graces," or that "the women could not help laughing at the airs and graces with which Blondet illustrated his banter."

Thus Balzac will have us know, down to the least detail, the admiration all these sayings aroused. "That cry of the heart which was echoed among the guests pricked their curiosity, already so skilfully aroused. . . ." "These words everywhere unloosed the stir which journalists in their reports of speeches in parliament describe as *Profound sensation.*" Does Balzac want us to construct from that triumph of de Marsay's narratives the triumph that he, Balzac, enjoyed in that evening party at which we were not present? Does he quite simply give way to the admiration that he felt for the lines that flowed from his pen? Perhaps it was a mingling of the two. I have a friend, one of the few authentic geniuses I have known, and endowed with a magnificent Balzacian arrogance. Retailing for my benefit a lecture he had given in a theatre at which I had not been present, he interrupted himself from time to time to clap his hands where the public had clapped theirs. But he put so much fervour into it, so much energy, and went on for so long that I really believe that instead of giving me a faithful version of what took place, he was applauding himself.

But this is exactly what Balzac lovers delight in. Smiling, they repeat to themselves: "The ignoble name of Amélie." " 'Biblical?' repeated Fifine, astonished." "The Princesse de Cadignan was one of the ablest women in matters of dress." To love Balzac! Sainte-Beuve, who was so fond of defining what it meant to love someone, would have had his work cut out for him here. For with the other novelists, one loves them in submitting oneself to them; one receives the truth from a Tolstoi as from someone of greater scope and stature than oneself. With Balzac, we know all his vulgarities, and at first were often repelled by them; then we began to love him, then we smiled at all those sillinesses which are so typical of him; we love him, with a little dash of irony mixed in our affection; we know his aberrations, his shabby little tricks, and because they are so like him we love them.

Because in some respects Balzac is a slapdash writer, one might suppose that he did not trouble to make his characters talk like themselves, or that if he had tried to, he would not have been able to resist drawing attention to it at every turn. However, it is quite the opposite: the man who artlessly reels out his views on history, art, and so forth, keeps the most deep-laid schemes under cover, and leaves the truth of the dialogue to speak for itself, without attempting to underline what he does so artfully that it might go unnoticed. When he makes the lovely Mme. de Roguin, that born Parisian whom Tours knew as the country prefect's wife, talk about how the Rogrons have furnished their house, how infallibly all those sallies are *hers*, not Balzac's! The jokes of the office-clerks, Vautrin's song of "Trim-là-là, trim-trim," the vapidity of the talk between the Duc de Grandlieu and the Vidame de Pamiers: " 'The Comte de Montriveau is dead,' said the Vidame; 'He was a stout man with an incredible passion for oysters.' 'Why, how many did he eat?' said the Duc de Grandlieu. 'Ten dozen every day.' 'And none the worse for it?' 'Not in the least.' 'Really! But that's extraordinary. Didn't all this oyster-eating bring on the stone?' 'No, he was perfectly healthy, he died from an accident.' 'From an accident! —his constitution must have told him to eat oysters, they were probably what he needed.' " Lucien de Rubempré has, even in his asides, exactly the animal high spirits, the aroma of raw youth, that Vautrin would be attracted by. " 'Aha!' thought Lucien, 'he plays *bouillote.*' 'I've caught him.' 'What an oriental nature,' Lucien said to himself. 'I'll make him show what he is.' 'This is a lascar who's no more a priest than I am.' " And as it happened, Vautrin was not the only one to love Lucien. Oscar Wilde, whom life, alas, would teach that there are sorrows more piercing than those we get from books, said in his first period (the period of his remark: "Before the Lake poets there were no fogs on the Thames"), "The greatest grief of my life? [4] The death of Lucien de Rubempré in *Splendeurs et Misères des Courtisanes*." There is besides something particularly dramatic about Oscar Wilde in his most brilliant days having been drawn to Lucien de Rubempré, and moved by his death. No doubt like every reader he grieved over it because he saw it from Vautrin's point of view, which was Balzac's. And it was a point of view, too, which he as a reader was peculiarly fitted and marked out to adopt more wholeheartedly than most readers could. But one can't help thinking how a few years later he was himself to be Lucien de Rubempré; and Lucien de Rubempré in the prison of the Conciergerie, seeing all his brilliant worldly career in ruins about him, brought down by the proof that he had been living in close friendship with a convict, was but a foreshadowing—though of course Wilde did not know it at the time—of just what was going to happen to Wilde.

In this last scene of the first part of Balzac's tetralogy (with Balzac, the novel is seldom a whole; the whole consists of a cycle in which the novel is a part),* every

---

* Make plain Balzac's slow approach (*La Fille aux Yeux d'or, Sarrazine, La Duchesse de Langeais*, etc.), the noose gradually tightening on the subject, then the devastating stranglehold at the end. And also the interpolation of *passages of time*, like geological formations where lava from different epochs lies intermingled (*La Duchesse de Langeais, Sarrazine*).

word, every incident, has an underlying significance
that Balzac gives the reader no hint of. These implications arise from such a specialised psychological
study, and one which no one, Balzac excepted, has carried out, that it is a delicate task to point them out. But
everything, from the way Vautrin stops Lucien on the
road, when he does not know him and so could only
be attracted to him by his good looks, to the involuntary gesture with which he takes his arm, doesn't it
betray the very different, very definite significance of
the theories about domination, about a pact of friendship, etc., by means of which the pretended Canon
glozes to Lucien's eyes, and to his own, maybe, an un-
admitted thought? And the interpolation of the man
who couldn't help eating paper, isn't that, too, ad-
mirably indicative of Vautrin's character, and of characters like him—one of their favourite lines of argument, the modicum of their secret that they will let
out? But indisputably the finest thing is the marvellous passage where the two travellers pass the tumble-
down manor-house where Rastignac was born. I call
that the *Tristesse d'Olympio* of homosexual love:
"*He would revisit all—the pool beside the spring.*"

We know from *Le Père Goriot* that Vautrin at the
Pension Vauquer had entertained—though to no purpose—the same designs for dominating Rastignac as
he now entertains about Lucien. It came to nothing,
but Rastignac had been none the less deeply involved
in Vautrin's life. It was that Rastignac might marry
Victorine that Vautrin contrived the murder of young
Taillefer. Later on, when Rastignac turns against
Lucien, Vautrin, wearing a mask, will remind him
about certain doings at the Pension Vauquer and com-

pel him to protect Lucien, and even after Lucien's
death Rastignac will often summon Vautrin into a
dark street.

Such effects would scarcely be possible if it were not
for Balzac's masterly invention of retaining the same
characters throughout his novels. And so a ray of light,
emerging from the depth of the whole sequence and
bridging a lifetime, can come to cast its turbid melancholy gleam on that little manor-house in the Dor-
dogne and the two travellers who halt there. Sainte-
Beuve completely failed to understand this business
of retaining names and characters: "This affectation
finally led him to take up a theory that could scarcely
have been falser or more thwarting to what makes a
book interesting; I mean the way he continually re-
introduces his characters from one novel to another,
like actors with walking-on parts. Nothing is more
damaging to the piquancy which depends on novelty
nor to that charm of the unexpected which gives a
novel its appeal. Wherever one turns, one encounters
the same faces." It is Balzac's stroke of genius that
Sainte-Beuve here fails to understand. It can be said,
of course, that Balzac did not hit on it immediately.
Some portions of his great sequences were not linked
up by its means till afterwards. What does that matter? Wagner had composed *The Good Friday Music*
before he thought of writing *Parsifal*, and put it into
the opera later on. But the additions Balzac made,
these lovely things that are brought in, the new relationships suddenly perceived by his genius between
separate parts of his work, which rejoin each other,
come to life, are henceforth inseparable, are they not
his finest creative intuitions? His sister has told us how

overjoyed he was, that day when he conceived this idea, and I think it is just as magnificent an idea as if he had conceived it before he began his great work. It is a light that dawned, that suddenly encompassed parts of his work that till then had lain scattered and wan, and which united them, brought them to life, illuminated them; but that light is none the less a part of his intention.

Sainte-Beuve's other criticisms are just as absurd. Having upbraided Balzac for those "refinements of style" which he unfortunately lacked, he then upbraided him for faults of taste which were only too really his; but for an example picks on a sentence that comes from one of those pieces of admirable writing which, when all is said, Balzac has in plenty, where the style is recast and unified by the idea, where the sentence is a whole; that about the old maids "living scattered about the town, where they might be looked on as so many capillary vessels of a plant, aspiring after tittle-tattle and the secrets of every household as leaves thirst for dew, mechanically sucking them up and transmitting them to the Abbé Troubert, as leaves transmit to the stalk the moisture they have breathed in." And a few pages later comes the sentence denounced by Sainte-Beuve: "Such was the substance of the remarks cast forth by the capillary tubes of the great female confabulation and obligingly repeated by the city of Tours." He dares to account for Balzac's success by saying that he flattered the failings of women, in particular those of them who were no longer in their first youth (*La Femme de trente Ans*): "My stern friend said: Henri IV conquered France town by town, M. de Balzac has conquered his sickly public by infirmities. Today, women of thirty, tomorrow those of fifty (there have even been those of sixty), the day after tomorrow the anaemic, in Claës the deformed, etc." And he dares add another reason for Balzac's rapid spread of popularity throughout France: "It is his cleverness in choosing the series of places where he will plant his successive novels. In a street in Saumur the traveller will be shown the house where Eugénie Grandet lived, and at Douai, Claës' house is probably already decided on. The owner of La Grenadière, easy-going man of Touraine that he is, must swell with modest pride. The author earns the submission of every town where he instals his characters by the compliments he pays it." That Sainte-Beuve, writing of Musset's admission that he loved both sweetmeats and roses, should add: "When one has loved so widely . . ." * one can accept. But that he should try to defame Balzac for the very vastness of his design, for the multiplicity of his portraits, that he should call this an intimidating jumble: "Subtract *La Femme de trente Ans, La Femme abandonnée, Le Réquisitionnaire, La Grenadière, Les Célibataires*, from his stories; subtract from his novels the story of *Louis Lambert* and his masterpiece *Eugénie Grandet*, what a mob of volumes, what a swarm of stories, novels of all kinds, drolatic, economic, philosophic, magnetic and theosophic, still remain!"—Well, but that was the very greatness of Balzac's achievement. Sainte-Beuve said of him that he cast himself on the nineteenth century as on his subject, that society is a thing of the female gender, that society wanted a portrait, that he was that painter, that he

* One of the things he liked saying, and he said it about Chateaubriand too.

painted it without any regard to tradition, that he brought the methods and expedients of painting up-to-date in order to comply with the ambition and coquetry of a society that was resolved to be its own precedent and to resemble nothing but itself. But Balzac did not have such a straightforward portraiture in mind, at any rate in the plain sense of painting exact likenesses. His books resulted from splendid ideas, ideas of splendid pictures, if you like (for he often thought of one art in terms of another), but in that case from a splendid artistic effect, from a splendid pictorial idea. As he saw an artistic effect as a splendid idea, in the same way he could see the idea of a book as an artistic effect. His mind's eye showed him a picture where there was something strikingly original and compelling. Imagine a writer nowadays who would have the idea of treating the same theme twenty times over in different lights, and who would feel that he was doing something as deep, as subtle, as powerful, overwhelming, original, and striking as Monet's fifty cathedrals or forty water lilies. An ardent picture-lover, Balzac at times delighted in the thought that he too had a splendid idea for a picture, for a picture that people would rave about; but it was always an idea, a ruling idea, not unpremeditated portraiture, as Sainte-Beuve took it to be. From that point of view even Flaubert worked with less of the preconceived idea than he. Colour of *Salammbô*, *Bovary*. Beginning on a subject that doesn't appeal to him. Takes whatever's handy to get to work on. But all the great writers coalesce somewhere, and are like different moments, sometimes incompatible, of a single man of genius whose life is coterminous with the story of mankind. Where Flaubert coalesces with Balzac is where he said: "I've got to have a glorious finish for Félicité."

Because of this true-to-life reality in Balzac's novels, by knowing them we come to see a sort of literary quality in a hundred everyday occurrences which till then we should have looked on as too accidental for it. But it is just the law of such accidents that emerges from his books. Don't let us hark back to his characters and events in their lives. We needn't repeat between ourselves what others have said. But suppose we take a prostitute who has read Balzac and who, in some place where she is unknown, feels a genuine love which is returned; or go further, take a man who has a scoundrelly past, or a bad name in politics, for instance, and who in some place where he is unknown makes delightful friendships, gathers a pleasant circle about him, reflects that when, as soon they will, these people begin to find out who he is, they may turn away from him, and casts about for some means to avert the storm. Driving alone through the lanes of that holiday landscape which he will go away from, and where disagreeable stories about him will soon be current, he nurses an uneasy melancholy that is not without its charms, because he has read *Les Secrets de la Princesse de Cadignan*, he knows he is a participant in a situation which is in some way literary and derives a certain beauty from this. While the carriage bears him through the autumnal lanes towards friends who still trust him, his uneasiness is tempered by a charm which would not possess the sadness of love if there were no such thing as poetry. If the crimes attributed to him are only imaginary, he has even more reason to count the hours until his cronies d'Arthez,

Rastignac and de Marsay are dragged through the
mire.[5] The truth of Balzac's situations—a truth somehow contingent and personal, so that one remembers
so many of the situations in terms of those who take
part in them, as for instance, that of Rastignac mar-
rying the daughter of his mistress Delphine de Nucingen, or Lucien arrested on the eve of his marriage
with Mlle. de Grandlieu, or Vautrin inheriting from
Lucien de Rubempré whose fortune he had tried to
make, like the Lanty's fortune, founded on a cardinal's
love for a eunuch, the little old man to whom all pay
their respects—is here striking. And there are those
subtle truths, gathered from the surface of fashionable
life and all with enough general applicability for one to
be able to say long afterwards: How true that is! (The
two sisters in *Une Fille d'Ève*, Mme. de Vandenesse
and Mme. du Tillet, who have married into such different ranks and yet adore each other, and through
political upheavals du Tillet, the commoner brother-
in-law, getting a title of office when Félix de Vandenesse has lost his—and the two sisters-in-law, the Comtesse and the Marquise de Vandenesse, being an-
noyed because they bear the same name.) And there
are truths that go deeper, like Paquita Valdès loving
precisely the man who resembles the woman she lives
with, like Vautrin keeping the woman who can see
his son, Sallenauve, every day; like Sallenauve marry-
ing the daughter of Mme. de l'Estorade. There, beneath the patent external action of the plot, run the
mysterious laws of feeling and of flesh and blood.

The only thing that is rather worrying about this
interpretation of his works is that these are just the
things he never mentions in his letters; where he says
of his slightest works that they are sublime, where he

dismisses *La Fille aux Yeux d'or* with the utmost disdain, and doesn't mention the close of *Les Illusions perdues* or that marvellous scene I have been talking about. The character of Ève, which to us seems trivial, seemed to him, so he says, another great find. But all this may depend on the chance of which letters have survived, and even of which letters he wrote. About Balzac, Sainte-Beuve does as he always does. Instead of discussing Balzac's *Femme de trente Ans*, he discusses women of thirty in general, and after a few words about Balthazar Claës (in *La Recherche de l'Absolu*) he talks about a real-life Claës who actually left a book about his own searchings for the absolute, and gives long quotations from this production—of no literary value, needless to say. Looking down from the height of his false and baleful ideal of the gentleman of letters, he misjudges Balzac's harshness towards Steinbock (in *La Cousine Bette*), that mere amateur who conceives nothing, who produces nothing, who does not understand that to be an artist one must devote the whole of oneself to art. Here Sainte-Beuve rears up with ruffled dignity against the phrase that Balzac uses: "Homer . . . cohabited with his Muse." It is not, perhaps, very happily expressed. But really there can be no interpreting the masterpieces of the past unless one judges them from the standpoint of those who wrote them, and not from the outside, from a respectful distance, and with all academic deference. That the outward conditions of literary production should have changed during the course of the last century, that the calling of the man of letters should have become a more absorbing and excluding affair, is quite possible. But the inward, mental laws of that production cannot have changed. That a writer should be a genius occasionally, *so that* for the rest of his time he may lead the pleasant life of a cultured social dilettante, is as false and silly a notion as that of a saint pursuing a life of the austerest contemplation so that in Paradise he may lead a life of vulgar enjoyment. One is nearer to understanding the great writers of the ancient world if one understands them as Balzac did, than as Sainte-Beuve did. Dilettantism has never created anything. Even Horace was certainly closer to Balzac than to M. Daru or M. Molé.

12

Monsieur de Guermantes's Balzac[1]

Balzac, of course, like other novelists and more so than they, has had a faithful public, which reads the novels merely on the score of finding them thrilling and lifelike, regardless of whether or no they might be works of art. It was not the defects of his style that these readers boggled at, but rather his gifts, and his searching mind. In the small library on the second floor, where on Sundays at the first ring of the doorbell M. de Guermantes hurriedly took refuge from his wife's visitors, and where his *sirop* and biscuits were brought up to him at five o'clock, were the complete works of Balzac, bound in gilded calf with green labels, and published by Bechet, or Werdet, publishers to whom Balzac wrote word of the superhuman effort he would make to send them ten pages instead of six of a book the public were clamouring for, and from whom he demanded a correspondingly greater payment. Often, when I had gone to see Mme. de Guermantes, if she felt that her visitors were boring me, she would say to me: "Won't you go up and see Henri? He says he isn't there, but you are different, he'll be delighted to see you!"—thus demolishing at one blow all M. de Guermantes's precautions not to have it known that he was in the house lest he should be thought uncivil if he did not put in an appearance—"Just find someone to take you up to the library on the second floor and there you'll find him, reading Balzac." She often said, with a look of congratulatory consternation: "Oh—if you get my husband on to Balzac—" as if Balzac were an untoward event that

made one unpunctual and upset one's plans for going
out, and at the same time a sort of personal favour on
M. de Guermantes's part, a favour he did not grant
to all and sundry, and which I should count myself
very fortunate to have bestowed on me.

To those who were uninformed, Mme. de Guermantes would explain: "Because if my husband gets
on to Balzac, you know, it's like the stereoscope, he can
tell you about every photograph, where it was taken,
what country it is. I don't know how he remembers it
all, and really, it's not in the least like Balzac. I can't
think how he can keep two such different things going
at once." At this point, the Baronne des Taupes, a
disagreeable relation, always put on an icy expression, as though she weren't listening, hadn't been at-
tending, and yet disapproved; for she considered that
Pauline made a fool of herself by saying this and
showed no tact, since, as it happened, M. de Guermantes "kept going" a great many affairs which were
possibly more taxing and of a nature which his wife
should have felt more call to attend to, than reading
Balzac and handling the stereoscope. I was, I must admit, one of the chosen few, since I had but to be there
for a display of the stereoscope to be vouchsafed.
The stereoscope contained photographs of Australia,
brought back to M. de Guermantes by I know not
whom; but if he himself had taken them in places
which he had been the first to explore, and clear, and
colonise, the act of "showing the stereoscope" could
not have seemed a more precious, immediate, hard-
won communication of M. de Guermantes's scientific
attainments. If a guest at Victor Hugo's table had, at
the close of dinner, expressed a hope that the poet
would give a reading of a still unpublished play, he

certainly would not have felt as much intimidated by
the audacity of his suggestion as the daredevil who at
the Guermantes's asked if after dinner the Count
would show the stereoscope. Mme. de Guermantes
would hold up her hands as if to say: "What will you
ask next?" And on special occasions when a guest was
to be signally honoured or some unforgettable good
office acknowledged, she would whisper in an awed,
confidential, marvelling way, as if not daring to raise
such high hopes unwarrantably, while yet making one
feel that she must be sure of her facts even to speak
conditionally of them: "I believe that after dinner M.
de Guermantes is going to show the stereoscope." And
if M. de Guermantes showed it for me, she said: "Well,
but there you are, I don't know what my husband
wouldn't do for that young man." People who were
there looked enviously at me, and one impoverished
Villeparisis cousin who made it her business to flatter
the Guermantes said in an affectedly wounded voice:
"But M. Marcel isn't the only one. I haven't forgotten
that my cousin showed me the stereoscope—it was the
year before last, don't you remember? Oh, I'm not
likely to forget a thing like that, I'm very proud of
it." But the cousin was not on a footing to visit the
library on the second floor.

It was a cool room, the wooden blinds were kept
closed, the window too if it was very hot outside. If it
was raining, the window stood open; one could hear
the rain falling on the trees, but even when it left off
the Count did not open the blinds, for he was afraid
he might be seen from below and his whereabouts
disclosed. If I went anywhere near the window he
hurriedly pulled me back. "Take care no one sees
you, they'll guess I'm here," he said, not knowing

that his wife had said in front of everybody: "Do go up to the second floor and see my husband." I do not think that in him the sound of rain falling outside the window unskeined that tenuous, frozen perfume, that rare frail substance which Chopin stretched to its full extent in his famous prelude, *The Rain on the Roof*. Chopin—that ailing, sensitive, self-centred, dandified great artist, who in his music, momentarily and sweetly, unfolds the successive contrasting aspects of an inward frame of mind which is constantly changing and after a moment's even tenor is always checked, collided with, broken in on, by something altogether different; but always with a note of being sick at heart, and introspective amid its frenzies of activity, always full of sensibility and never spontaneous, often achieving the wildest transports, never the relaxation, the sweetness, the fusion with something other than himself that Schumann knew. A music whose sweetness is like a woman's glance when she sees that the weather will be overcast all day, a music that has no impulsion other than that with which, in the damp room, she lifts her hand and barely gathers a priceless fur about her shoulders, lacking resolution, amid this general anaesthesia that she partakes in, to get up, to walk into the next room and say the word that would reconcile, set going, warm, bring to life—but moment by moment letting her will turn to water and her body freeze, as though every tear she gulps down, every moment that passes, every drop of rain that falls, were a drop of her blood trickling from her, leaving her weaker, more frozen, more susceptible to the day's sickly-sweet contagion.

Besides, the rain that falls on trees whose outdoor flowers and foliage seem like the assurance and in-

destructible blossoming promise of the sunshine and
warm airs which are soon going to return, such a
rain is no more than the noise of a rather prolonged
hosing of the garden which one can watch unsad-
dened. But whether the noise of rain came in by the
opened window or whether on afternoons of scorching
sunlight one heard, like a tinsel margin to the dusty
heat, the distant strains of a military band, or a fair-
ground, M. de Guermantes certainly enjoyed his so-
journs in the library, from the moment when on entering it, and closing the wooden blinds, he drove out
the sunlight from its repose on his couch and on the
old royal map of Anjou that hung above, much as
though he were saying to it: "Take yourself off, my
boy, to make room for me," till the moment when he
sent for his things, and gave orders that the carriage
should be got ready.

If this was the hour when my father went out to his
work, the Count, as he knew him slightly and often
had some neighbourly requests to make of him, would
hurry up to him, settle the collar of his overcoat, and,
not content with shaking him by the hand, but still
retaining that hand in his own, lead him, as on a
leash, from the house door to the porter's lodge. For in
their flattering anxiety to seem unaware of any distinction between themselves and you, some great persons
become as obliging as footmen and almost as brazen
as harlots. The Count had the disadvantage of having
perpetually moist hands, so that my father would pretend not to see him, not to hear what he said, and even
went so far as not to answer when he was spoken to.
The Count was not disconcerted, saying only: "He
must be deep in thought," and went back to his
horses.

These had more than once lashed out at the florist's little shop, breaking window panes and flowerpots. The Count did not admit liability till he was threatened with legal proceedings, and thought that the florist had behaved abominably, "when everyone knew how much Mme. la Comtesse had done for the place and for the neighbourhood." But the florist, who seemed on the contrary to have no notion of what the Countess "did for the place and for the neighbourhood," and who even thought it very odd that when she gave her parties, she never bought her flowers from him, saw the matter in another light, which was why the Count thought his behaviour abominable. What was more, the florist always said, *Monsieur*, never *Monsieur le Comte*. The Count suffered this in silence, but one day when the Vicomte de Praus, who had newly moved into the flat on the fourth floor and was talking to the Count, asked for a boutonnière, the florist, who was still uncertain how to address him, said "Monsieur Praus." In kindness to the Vicomte, the Count burst out laughing. "Monsieur Praus, that's it! And with things going the way they do, you can consider yourself lucky that it hasn't come to Citizen Praus."

On weekdays the Count lunched at his club, but on Sundays he lunched with his wife. During the season, the Countess was at home to her friends every afternoon between two and three. Going into the garden to smoke a cigar, the Count would ask the gardener, "What flower is this? Shall we have any apples this year?" and the old gardener, as much moved as if he had never seen the Count there before, replied in tones that were even more grateful than they were respectful as though to this mark of the Count's interest in the flowers he ought to return thanks on their behalf. When the first ring of the doorbell told of the arrival of the Countess's first visitor, the Count hurried upstairs to his study, the servants meanwhile getting ready to carry the blackcurrant cup and the soda water into the garden.

The Duke of X . . . and the Marquis of Y . . . , who came several days a week, could often be seen in the evening, sitting in the narrow little garden; elderly men, they did not flinch from the effort of changing into evening dress, of sitting the evening through, on chairs that were far from comfortable, in that really minute scrap of garden with nothing to look forward to but the blackcurrant cup, when in so many luxurious homes of financial magnates they would have been made so welcome in their day clothes to cushioned sofas and a wealth of drinks and cigars. But evidently the kind of pleasure they sought there was the beefsteak and the cup of coffee, uncontaminated by any suggestion of low company. They were men of education, and when from time to time the Count, at the dictates of his heart, brought in some young man whom "nobody had heard of," they knew how to make themselves charming to him by talking about subjects he would be familiar with ("You are an architect, Monsieur?"), with considerable knowledge and taste, and even affability—the dated nature of which was indicated by an exceedingly chilly goodnight. The newcomer once departed, however, they spoke of him with the utmost goodwill, as though to justify the whim which had brought him among them, praising his intelligence and his good manners, and repeating his name several times as if to practice themselves in some new, strange, far-fetched word

that they had just got hold of. They talked about projected family marriages, the young man always being
an excellent young man, they were glad for Isabelle's
sake, they discussed whether it was her daughter who
was the better match in the matter of pedigree. These
people, all of whom were well-born and rich, dwelt
on the good birth and riches of people who were certainly no better-born or richer than they as if they
would have been very glad to equal them. The Count
said: "But it is an enormous fortune," or, "But it's
quite one of the oldest titles, connections with the best
people, all the grandest, that is," although he was certainly as well-born and as splendidly intermarried.

If the Countess had done something they disapproved of, they never found fault with her, they never
expressed an opinion on anything that the Count or
she might do; this was part of a good upbringing.
Conversation moreover was carried on very slowly,
and in rather hushed tones. Only when there was a
question of relationship did the Count blaze into animation. At the utterance of some name he would cry
out: "But she's my cousin!" as if this were some unhoped-for stroke of luck, and in a voice that made one
long to reply: "But I never said she wasn't." It was
mainly to strangers, though, that he said it, since on
this subject the Duke of X . . . and the Marquis of
Y . . . needed no tutoring from him. Sometimes they
forestalled him, saying: "But she's your cousin, Astolphe, through the Montmorencies." "But of course
she is," exclaimed Astolphe, apparently afraid that the
Duke of X . . . 's statement might not be absolutely
categorical.

The Countess affected a pretty, "countrified" manner of speech, saying: "She's a cousin of our Astolphe's

and the stoopidest creature. We were goin' to the races,
the Duchesse de *Rouen*"—for Rohan. But her diction
was charming. The Count's conversation on the other
hand, the vulgarest imaginable, offered a choice of almost every kind of linguistic vermin, as some beaches
present zoologists with a wonderful assortment of mol-
luscs. "My aunt Villeparisis, who's a good sort," or
"who can tell you something," or "who's a sharp one,"
or "who's a holy terror." "Believe me, he didn't stop
for more. He's still running." If a world could be vul-
garised just by leaving out its demonstrative article,
or by transferring it from the singular to the plural,
one could feel sure this was how he would deal with
it. Normally, we would say of a coachman that he had
worked for one of the Rothschilds. The Count said:
"He worked for a Rothschild," not meaning by this
a particular known Rothschild, but voicing the man
in the street—and man in the street he was, for all he
was well-born and educated by the Jesuits—and saying: "a Rothschild." Where the word *moustache* is
more correctly used in the singular, he said: "He has
moustaches." If he were asked to take a lady down to
dinner and the Duke of X . . . happened to be
among those present, he said: "I don't like to go
down *in front* of the Duke." This was intensified in
his letters; words to him never meaning just what
they said, he always yoked them to a word from a different grouping. "Come and see me at the Agricul-
tural, it's a place I joined last year"; "I am sorry I
could not meet M. Bourget, I would have been glad to
shake hands with that distinguished mind"; "Your
letter charmed me, above all the peroration"; "I am
sorry I could not lend my applause at the interesting
recital"—true, he added, as if pulling silver-grey

gloves over dirty hands—"of that lovely musick." For he thought it very clever to spell music with a "k," and to write "sincerely—yours" instead of "yours sincerely."

But besides this, his conversation consisted much less of words than of names. He knew so many people that by swivelling on an *actually* he could immediately bring in what in society is called an anecdote, which was usually somewhat like this: "Well, actually, in 186- ——let me see, yes, it was in 1867, I was dining with the Grand Duchess of Baden, actually, she is the sister of the Prince, Prince of Weimar he was then, and afterwards Crown Prince, who married my Villeparisis niece; I definitely remember that the Grand Duchess, who was the soul of kindness and who had been good enough to ask me to sit beside her, was even willing to tell me that the only way to keep furs from getting mothy, please don't take exception to my rather low way of putting it, there were times when she didn't hesitate to go the whole hog, was to put in, not naphthaline, but the peelings off peeled radishes. I didn't turn a deaf ear to that, I can tell you. What's more, we handed on the recipe to Ketty de Dreux-Brezé and to Loulou de la Chapelle-Marinière-sur-Avre, and they were fascinated by it, weren't they, Floriane?" And like any good housewife the Countess said: "Yes, it's wonderful. Do try it for your furs, Juliette, and you'll see. Would you like me to send you a little? The servants here do all the preliminaries very nicely, and they could teach yours. It's nothing, once one knows how to set about it."

Sometimes the Marquis came to see his brother; when this happened, they were very apt to "get on to

Balzac," for Balzac was much read when they were
young and in their father's library they had read
these very same volumes, which the Count had inherited and which now stood on his shelves. Their taste
for Balzac still unsophisticatedly reflected the prefer-
ences of readers of that time, before Balzac had become a classic and subject as such to the fluctuations of
literary opinion. If someone, someone who was not
an outsider, mentioned Balzac, the Count cited various titles, which were not the titles of the Balzac
novels we now most admire. "Balzac! Balzac!" said he.
"He takes some reading. The *Bal de Sceaux*, for instance. Have you read the *Bal de Sceaux?* It's capital." It is true that he said the same thing of *Le Lys
dans la Vallée:* "Mme. de Mortsauf! None of you
have read all that, I suppose. Charles!"—calling in his
brother—"Mme. de Mortsauf, *Le Lys dans la Vallée*,
—capital, isn't it?" He spoke in the same way of *Le
Contrat de Mariage*, which he called by its first title,
La Fleur des Pois, and of *La Maison du Chat-qui-
pelote*. On days when he had really got going on Balzac he also referred to books which to speak truth are
not by Balzac but by Roger de Beauvoir or Céleste de
Chabrillan. But it must be pleaded for him that the
small library to which the *sirop* and the biscuits were
brought up to him, and where on rainy days, if there
was no one below who might catch sight of him he
was saluted through the open window by the wind-
lashed poplar tree, curtseying three times a minute,
contained together with the works of Balzac, those of
Alphonse Karr, Céleste de Chabrillan, Roger de Beauvoir, and Alexandre Duval, all bound alike. When one
opened them, and the same thin paper printed in

large type brought the heroine's name before you, exactly as if it were she herself who had come before you in this convenient portable guise, accompanied by a slight odour of glue, dust, and old age which seemed the very breath of her charm, it went against the grain to classify these books by a pseudo-literary canon, arbitrarily based on ideas that were equally foreign both to the theme of the book and the look of the volume. And to talk to you Blanche de Mortsauf and the others made use of such beguilingly clear print (the only effort required of you in order to follow them was to turn over those pages that old age had gilded and made transparent, but which were still as pliable as a fine muslin) that it was impossible not to believe the narrators had been one and the same, and that there had not been a much closer kinship between Eugénie Grandet and the Duchesse de Mers than there was between the *Eugénie Grandet* in one's hand and a Balzac novel in a shilling edition.

I must admit that I can understand M. de Guermantes, I who throughout my childhood read in the same fashion, I, for whom *Colomba* was for so long "the book where they said I must not read the story *La Vénus d'Ille*" (*they* meant you, Mamma). Those copies in which we read a book for the first time, they are like the dress a woman was wearing when we first saw her—they tell how the book came to us then, and how we came to the book. Hunting for these is my only form of bibliography. The edition in which I read a book for the first time, the edition in which it made its original impression on me, these are the only "first" editions, "original" editions, that are dear to me. Besides, all I really want to do is to recall them.

Their old pages are so porous, so ready to take in a memory, that I am afraid they might absorb today's impressions too, so that I should find my impressions of the past were no longer there. I want them to open, whenever I think about them, at the page where I closed them as I sat under the lamp, or on the wickerwork garden chair, when Papa would say to me: "Sit up straight."

And there are times when I wonder whether even today my way of reading is not more like M. de Guermantes's than contemporary critics'. To me, a book is still a living entity, which I begin to know from the first line, which I listen to with deference, and which, while we remain together, I unreservedly and undemurringly agree with. When I find M. Faguet saying in his *Critical Essays* that the first volume of *Le Capitaine Fracasse* is splendid and the second volume tame, or that in *Le Père Goriot* everything to do with Goriot is first-rate and everything to do with Rastignac shoddy, I am quite as surprised as if I heard someone saying that the country round Combray is ugly on the Méséglise side, but on the Guermantes side, beautiful. When M. Faguet goes on to say that lovers of Gautier do not read beyond the first volume of *Le Capitaine Fracasse*, I, who took so much pleasure in the second, can only feel sorry for the lovers of Gautier, but when he adds that the first volume was written for the lovers and the second for schoolboys, my pity for the lovers turns to scorn of myself, since I realise how schoolboyish I still am. Finally, when he declares that Gautier wrote the second volume in a state of intense boredom, I am amazed that what was so boring to write should later on become so entertaining to read.

So, too, with Balzac, where Sainte-Beuve and Faguet
pick and choose and analyse, and think that the beginning is wonderful and the end worthless.* The only
advance I have achieved towards this outlook since
my childhood, and the sole point on which, if I may
say so, I claim to differ from M. de Guermantes, is that
I have slightly extended the bounds of this unalterable world, this mass from which nothing can be sub-
tracted, this quantitative reality, so that I no longer
think of it in terms of single books, but as the works
of an author. I see but little difference between the
various books. I am as much perplexed by critics who
think, as does M. Faguet, that in *Un Ménage de Garçon* Balzac wrote a masterpiece, and in *Le Lys dans la
Vallée* the worst of all bad books, as I was by Mme. de
Guermantes when she thought that on such an evening the Duke of X . . . had been intelligent and on
some other occasion stupid. My own opinion of people's intelligence may vary from time to time, but I
know quite well that it is my opinion that varies, not
their intelligence. Nor do I believe it true that intelligence is a variable force, which at the will of God is
sometimes powerful, sometimes feeble. I believe that
the mental level to which it rises is always the same, and
that it is precisely on that level that it syphons into
those vessels which communicate with the past and

* What is rather odd and rather comforting is that Sainte-Beuve
said: "Who has ever drawn the duchesses of the Restoration better
than he?" M. Faguet laughs uproariously at his duchesses, and invokes M. Feuillet. Finally, M. Blum, who likes making distinctions,
admires his duchesses, but not in so far as they claim to represent
duchesses of the Restoration. Here, I admit, I feel inclined to say
with Sainte-Beuve: "Who told you so, what do you know about
it?" and "On this point I prefer to rely on persons who knew
them, and" . . . above all, on Sainte-Beuve.

which, whether it be *Un Ménage de Garçon* or *Le Lys dans la Vallée*, are the Works of Balzac.

However, if M. de Guermantes thought the "vicissitudes," the careers of René Longueville or Félix de Vandenesse "delightful," by which he really meant, diverting and make-believe, on the other hand he often dwelt admiringly on Balzac's powers of observation: "Life in a solicitor's office, it's the very thing; I've had my dealings with people of that sort; it's the very thing. *César Birotteau* and *Les Employés!*"

A person who did not agree with him and whom I tell you about because she represents another type of Balzac reader, was the Marquise de Villeparisis. She refused to believe that Balzac's portraits were true to life. "The man says: I will show you how a solicitor talks. No solicitor ever talked like that in his life." But what, above all, she could not stomach was that he should have laid claim to describe good society. "To begin with, he never set foot in it, he was invited nowhere, what could he have known about it? Towards the end he knew Mme. de Castries, but he could not have seen anything of it in her house, she was a nobody. I once saw him there, just after I married, he was a very common sort of man, with nothing in particular to say, and I wouldn't have him introduced to me. Somehow or other in the end he contrived to marry a Pole, she came of a good family, distant relations of our Czartoryski cousins. The whole family was appalled at it, and I can assure you they don't look any too pleased if one talks to them about it. Besides, it all ended very badly. He died almost immediately." Then, looking censoriously down at her knitting: "And I *have* heard some very nasty stories about that.

Do you really mean to say that he ought to have been *at* the Académie?" (as one might say, *at the Opéra*). "To begin with, he hadn't the wherewithal for it. Besides, the Académie is 'a chosen few'. Sainte-Beuve, yes! Now there was a charming man, so witty, such a gentleman, he never put himself forward, and one never had to meet him unless one wanted to. Not like Balzac. And then, he had been to Champlâtreux; so he, at least, would have been able to write about society. But he took care not to, because he was a gentleman. Besides, that Balzac, he was a bad man. There's no good feeling in what he wrote, there are no nice people. It's always unpleasant reading, he always sees the seamy side of everything. It's all he ever sees. Even if he describes a poor parish priest, he has to make him unfortunate, every one's hand has to be against him." "You can't say—" said the Count before the assembled listeners, who were thrilled to be present at such an absorbing tilting-match, and dug each other in the ribs to draw attention to the Marquise "taking the bit between her teeth"—"Aunt, you can't say that the *Curé de Tours*, which is the one you mean, isn't well drawn. That country town, could anything be more like the real thing?" "Precisely," said the Marquise, proceeding to what was one of her favourite gambits, and the universal test that she applied to literary productions, "and in what way can it interest me to read a treatise about things I know quite as much about as he? People say, It's so like a country town. By all means; but I know all about that, I've lived in the country, so why should I be interested in it?" And so proud was she of this line of argument, a favourite one of hers, that a smile of arrogrance brightened her eyes as she glanced towards her audience, adding, to pour oil on the troubled waters: "You may think it very silly of me, but I must admit that when I read a book, I am weak-minded enough to want to learn something new." For the next two months, it was retailed, even among the Countess's remotest cousins, that this particular At Home at the Guermantes's had been quite the most interesting affair imaginable.

For when a writer reads a book, the closeness of social observation, the slant towards pessimism or optimism, are accepted conditions which he does not dispute, which he does not even begin to see. But for "intelligent" readers the fact that something may be "untrue" or "dismal" is a defect in the author himself, which they are astonished and rather pleased to find recurring, and even being made more of, in each of his books, as if he had not been able to get the better of it, and which finally makes them see him in the disagreeable light of a person who is always wrong-headed or who has a depressing effect on one, so much so that whenever the book-seller hands them a Balzac or a George Eliot, they push it away, saying: "No, thank you! It's bound to be untrue, or gloomy, this new one will be worse than all the rest, I don't want any more of it."

As for the Countess, when the Count said: "Ah, Balzac, Balzac! He takes some reading. Have you read *La Duchesse de Mers?*" she remarked: "I don't care for Balzac myself, I think he exaggerates." In general, she disliked people who "exaggerated," and were thus an implied rebuke to those who, like herself, did not; people who gave "exaggerated" tips, which made hers look exceedingly stingy, people who felt a more than ordinary degree of sorrow at the death of a rela-

tion, people who did more than is usually done for a
friend in distress, or went to an exhibition expressly
to see any picture that was not a portrait of someone
they knew or "the thing to see." She herself, who
did not exaggerate, when someone asked her if she
had seen this or that picture at an exhibition, simply replied: "If it's on show, I saw it."

The member of the family who was most influenced
by Balzac was the Marquis. . . .

Of these readers of Balzac, it was the young Marquise de Cardaillec, by birth a de Forcheville, who was
the most susceptible to his influence. Among her husband's properties was the old mansion of Forcheville
at Alençon, with an imposing front on the town's
main square, as in *Le Cabinet des Antiques,* and a
garden stretching down to the Gracieuse, as in *La
Vieille Fille.* The Comte de Forcheville, who saw no
point in going to "bury himself" in Alençon, had
abandoned it to the garden staff. But the young Marquise had it done up, and every year she spent several
weeks there, finding it full of a charm which she herself described as Balzacian. She had some old furniture
brought from the castle of Forcheville, where it had
been stowed away in the attics as out of date, pieces
that had belonged to the Comte de Forcheville's
grandmother, together with various objects that were
interesting historically or for reasons, at once senti-
mental and aristocratic, of family piety. In Paris she
had in fact become one of those young women of the
aristocracy who cherish their rank with a sort of artistic appreciation, and who stand in relation to the old
nobility as do the shrewd hotel-keepers of Mont Saint-
Michel or the "William the Conqueror" to the com-

mon people of Brittany or Normandy—young women who had realised that their charm (a charm of retrospect which they were first made aware of by literary men whom their own personal charms had attracted) rested specifically under the protection of that antiquity, a compound reflection of both literature and contemporary (though lineaged) beauty being thus thrown over this aestheticism.

In the house at Alençon photographs of the loveliest of the great ladies of today stood on bracket-tables of old oak, such as had belonged to Mlle. Cormon. But the ladies had posed in those old-fashioned, Book of Beauty attitudes which through masterpieces of painting and literature have become so evocative of the grace of bygone days, so the photographs only added a further artistic touch to the period effect—which in other respects, alas, from one's first sight of the servants in the lobby to the conversation of their employers in the drawing-room, was inevitably of today. So much so, that the little conjuration of Balzac in the house at Alençon worked best on people with more taste than imagination, who knew what to look for but needed to set eyes on it, and who came away in raptures. For my part, I found it rather disappointing. When I heard that at Alençon Mme. de Cardaillec lived in the very house of Mlle. Cormon or Mme. de Bargeton, the knowledge that something I had so often pictured in my mind really existed made too deep an impression on me for it to be possible for the disparities of real life to live up to it.

I ought to say, however, before I wash my hands of Balzac, that Mme. de Cardaillec did the honours of her house like a most accomplished Balzacian. "If you like, I'll take you to Forcheville tomorrow," she said to me. "You'll see what a to-do it will make in the town—like the day when Mlle. Cormon had her mare harnessed for the drive to Prébaudet. Meanwhile, let us have lunch. And if you feel strong enough to stay on over Monday—I am 'at home to company' that evening—you won't leave my part of the world without having seen M. du Bousquier and Mme. de Bargeton with your own eyes, and you'll see the cut-glass chandelier lit up in honour of all these good people, which Lucien de Rubempré, you remember, found so overwhelming."

Well-informed persons who witnessed this pious reconstruction of a bygone provincial aristocracy put it down to her Forcheville blood. I myself knew that it was attributable to her Swann blood, which she had forgotten about, but whose intelligence and good taste she had retained, and even a sufficiency of that intellectual detachment from the world of aristocracy (howsoever she might be attached to it for practical motives) to find in it, as in something alien, useless, and extinct, an artistic charm.

13

A *race accursed*

Early every afternoon there appeared a tall stout gentleman with a strutting gait; his moustache was dyed, and he always wore a flower in his buttonhole: this was the Marquis de Quercy. He walked through the courtyard and went to call on his sister, Mme. de Guermantes. I doubt if he knew we had a flat in the house; in any case, I did not have occasion to meet him. At the time he came, I was often at the window, but he could not have seen me because of the shutters; besides, he never looked up. I never went out at that time of day, and he never came at any other. His life was extremely methodical; he saw the Guermantes daily from one till two, spent the next hour with Mme. de Villeparisis whose flat was overhead, then went on to his club where he did various things, and in the evening went to the play or sometimes into society—though never to the Guermantes unless they were giving a formal party, which was but seldom, and then he came late and did not stay long.

The light of poetry in which I no longer beheld the Comte and Comtesse de Guermantes because I had seen too much of them, now rested upon the Prince and Princesse de Guermantes. As I did not know them, though they were quite near relations, it was they who represented the name of Guermantes for me. I had occasionally seen them at the Guermantes's, and they gave me the vaguely acknowledging bows of people who have not any cause to know who you are. My father, who passed their house in the Rue Solférino every day, said: "It's a palace, a palace out of a fairy-tale," so that I had come to think of it as part of the fairy-land secreted in the name of Guermantes, along with Geneviève de Brabant, and Charles the Bad in the stained glass window, and the tapestry with a portrait of Charles VIII. The idea that at some time I might have anything to do with them had not even entered my mind when one day I opened an envelope: "At Home. The Prince and Princesse de Guermantes request the pleasure. . . ."

It seemed as though an untouched pleasure, undegraded by any human idea, any concrete remembrance of the use and wont which make things comparable to others of their kind, had been tendered to me on that card. It was a name, a transparent name, still full of its lovely pictures that no earthly memory had debased, it was a fairy-tale palace which by the fact of that pasteboard in my hand and through a sort of flattering predilection felt for me by the mysterious name, had turned into something potentially at my disposal. I felt this was too good to be true. Between the intention it conveyed, the offer the address on the envelope made manifest, and the melodious stately syllables of that name, the contrast was too great.

The fairy-palace spontaneously opening its doors to me, myself an invited guest and mingling with those legendary, magic-lantern, painted-window, tapestry beings with their ninth-century feudalities of pit and gallows, that proud name of Guermantes seeming to come to life, to acknowledge me, to reach out to me—since, after all, it really was my name on the envelope, and in imposing calligraphy—all this seemed too good to be true, and I was afraid it might be a practical joke that someone had played on me. The only people

who could have settled my doubts were our neighbouring Guermantes, who were away, and being
in doubt, I preferred not to resort to them. The invitation did not require a written answer, I had only to
leave my card. But I was afraid that even this would be
going too far, if, as I thought, I were the victim of a
practical joke. I consulted my parents, who did not
understand my doubt (or thought it ridiculous). Having that kind of arrogance which comes of a total
lack of conceit or snobbery, they thought it was the
most natural thing in the world that the Guermantes
should have invited me. They did not care in the least
as to whether I did or did not go, but they did not
want me to get into a way of thinking people would
play jokes on me. They thought it would be "nicer of
me" if I went; but in other respects they were unconcerned, saying that one should not be self-important,
and that my absence would pass unnoticed, but on
the other hand, that these people had no cause to invite me unless they would be glad to see me. Besides,
my grandfather, having learned that the Princess was
the granddaughter of the most eminent statesman of
the reign of Louis XVIII, was not unwilling that I
should tell him what it had been like at the Guermantes, nor Papa to know if he was right in supposing
that it must be "splendid inside."

To cut a long story short, I did not make up my
mind till that same evening. The household had been
at particular pains to supervise my preparations. I had
wanted to order my boutonnière from the florist, but
my grandmother thought a rose out of the garden
would be more "natural." Having scrambled up a steep
bank I cut the best one, catching my clothes on the
thorns of other roses meanwhile, and then boarded

the omnibus that passed the door, where I found it even more agreeable than usual to be friendly to the conductor and to give up my seat on the lower deck to an old lady, telling myself that this gentleman who was being so charming to them, and whose request: "Put me down at the Pont de Solférino, please," had given no intimation that he was on his way to the Princesse de Guermantes's, had a beautiful rose beneath his overcoat, whose perfume climbed unseen to his nostrils and wooed him like a love-philtre. But no sooner had we reached the Pont de Solférino, where the whole embankment was obstructed by a line of carriages, moving up and stopping to put down, with now and then a carriage coming away, and footmen hurrying with pale silken evening wraps over their arms, than my terror returned. Of course it was a practical joke! And when I mounted the stairs, and heard that the guests were being announced as they went in, I wanted to turn back. But I was caught in the stream, and was helpless; besides, I was distracted by having to deposit my overcoat, get a ticket for it, and throw away my rose, which had lost its petals beneath the overcoat and whose enormous green stalk was really too "natural." I murmured my name in the usher's ear in a hope that he would announce me in equally subdued tones, but at the same moment I heard it resounding like a thunderclap through the Guermantes drawing-rooms which opened before me, and felt that the crack of doom was now at hand. Huxley tells of an old lady who suffered from delusions and had left off going into society because never knowing whether the object before her eyes was a delusion or was really there, she did not know how to behave. At last, after twelve years, her doctor compelled her

to go to a ball. When she was offered an armchair
she saw an old gentleman sitting in it. She said to herself: It's out of the question that I should be asked to
sit down on top of this old gentleman; so either the
old gentleman is a delusion and I must sit down on
this chair which is unoccupied, or it is a delusion that
the lady of the house is offering me a chair, and I must
not sit down on the old gentleman. With but a moment to decide in, she compared the old gentleman's
face with the face of the lady, and both seeming to
her equally substantial she could form no conclusion
as to which of them was the delusion. At last, when the
moment of decision was nearly up, something or other
made her opine that probably the old gentleman was
the delusion. She sat down, there was no old gentleman
there, she heaved a great sigh of relief, and was cured
for ever after. Painful as that afflicted old lady's moment of decision before the armchair must undoubtedly
have been, it was probably no worse than mine when,
on the outskirts of the Guermantes drawing-rooms, I
heard my name, launched by an usher with the
stature of Jupiter, ring through the air like some unil-
lustrious, catastrophic peal of thunder, and when, in
the act of going forward with a matter-of-course demeanour, so that through no hesitation on my part
should it be supposed—if this were someone's practical joke—that I was feeling out of my depth, I
looked round for my host and hostess to ascertain if
they were going to have me turned out. In the hubbub
of conversation they could not have heard my name.
The Princess, in a mauve "princess" dress and wearing a magnificent pearl and sapphire tiara, sat talking
on a sofa, and held out her hand to newcomers without getting up. As for the Prince, I could not see where

he was. As yet, she had not seen me. I went towards her, still looking at her as intently as the old lady must have looked at the old gentleman she was about to sit down on—for I suppose she would have been on her guard not to persist in sitting down if once she felt the solidity of his knees beneath her. In the same way, from the moment the Princesse de Guermantes became aware of me I would scrutinize her face for the first signs of stupefaction and indignation, in order to cut short the scandal and beat a speedy retreat. I see her catch sight of me, I see her get up, although she had not got up for any other guest, I see her come towards me. My courage wavers, but is renewed, for her blue eyes are lit with the most charming of smiles and her long suede glove extends toward me in a graceful curve. "How nice of you to have come, I am so delighted to see you. What a pity that our cousins should be away just now—but it is all the kinder of you to have come like this, we can feel sure it is just for ourselves. Look, there is M. de Guermantes in the small drawing-room, he will be delighted to see you." I made a deep bow and the Princess did not hear my sigh of relief; but it was the sigh of the old lady when she sat down on the chair and found there was no old gentleman in it. From that day forward I was forever cured of my shyness. I have perhaps almost certainly received invitations more unexpected or more flattering than that from the Prince and Princesse de Guermantes; but the Combray tapestries, the magic-lantern, the walks along the Guermantes Way, did not lend them enchantment. I have always expected the smile of welcome and never the practical joke; and had the practical joke come uppermost, it would have been one and the same to me.

M. de Guermantes was very welcoming—too welcoming; for at these evening parties when he played host to all the small-fry nobility, the lesser or provincial lordlings in whose eyes he was a Lord indeed, he thought himself constrained to assume an openhearted, easy-going manner, to pat shoulders and say affably: "I hope you're not feeling bored" or "I'm proud to see you here," in order to dispel from every bosom the bashfulness and trembling awe which were not quite so prevalent as he supposed.

Not far from him, the Marquis de Quercy was talking to a lady. He was not looking in my direction, yet I felt his barrow-boy's eyes had not missed me. He was talking to a lady I had met at the Guermantes; I bowed and began to talk to her,[1] which obliged him to break off; but in spite of that, dislodged and interrupted, he looked in another direction, exactly as if he had not seen me. Not only had he seen me, but he continued to see me, for I had no sooner turned towards him to bow, trying to attract the attention of his smiling face and police-prospecting eyes from the other side of the room than he put out his hand, and without further movement had only to make use of his available smile and tenantless gaze for my benefit, which I could take, since he how-do'ed me with his disengaged hand, as intending to be affable, which, if I had not spoken to him, I could have taken as intending to quiz me, or as the expression of no matter what intention, affable or quizzical, towards someone else, or of a mere mood of gaiety, had I thought he had not seen me. I had clasped the fourth finger which seemed by its melancholy droop to be languishing for an archiepiscopal ring, I had made a forced entry, so to speak, into his state of sustained unidentifying How-

do-you-doing; I could not claim that he had said
How-do-you-do to me. At a pinch, I could have supposed that he had not seen me or did not recognise me. He went on talking to the lady, and I moved
away. A little operetta was performed, for which
young ladies had not been invited. They came later,
and we danced.

The Comte de Quercy had begun to doze, or at
least had closed his eyes. For some time he had been
looking tired and very pale; in spite of his black moustache and curly grey hair, one felt that he was old,
though still very handsome. Seen thus, with his noble,
sculptural, white face stilled and sightless, I saw him as
he would look after his death, carved in stone on his
tomb in the church at Guermantes. I felt that he was
his own effigy, that his individuality was snuffed out,
and that all I saw was the family face, that face which
the personality of each wearer had changed and
adapted to its own requirements, intellectualised by
some, coarsened by others, like the room in a castle
which has been, according to the inheritor's taste, now
a study, now a gymnasium. I saw it, this family face,
looking very fragile, very noble, very beautiful; his
eyes opened, a faint smile that he was not in time to
sophisticate wandered over his visage where at that
moment I was studying the oval of the brow beneath
the scattered locks of hair, and the set of the eyes; his
lips parted, his glance shone above the classical line
of his nose, his delicate hand pushed back the locks of
hair, and I said to myself: "Poor M. de Quercy, setting
such store on everything manly—if he but knew what
that weary smiling creature I'm looking at reminds
me of. One would take him for a woman!"

But even as I said this to myself, I seemed to see a magical reversal taking place in M. de Quercy. He had not moved, but all of a sudden he was illuminated by a light from within, in which everything about him that I had found startling, perplexing, contradictory, had been harmoniously resolved as soon as I said those words to myself: "One would take him for a woman." I had understood, he *was* one. He was one of them. He belonged to that race of beings who are in effect, since it is precisely because their temperament is feminine that they worship manliness, at cross-purposes with themselves, who go through life apparently in step with other men, but bearing about with them, on that little disk of the eye's pupil, through which we look at the world and on which our desire is engraved, the body, not of a nymph but of a youth, who casts his shadow, virile and erect, over all they see and all they do. A race accursed, since the thing which for it is the ideal of beauty and the food of love is also the embodiment of shame and the dread of punishment, a race compelled to live in falsehood and perjury, even when it comes to defend itself before the seat of justice and in the sight of Christ;[2] since its desire, if it knew how to comprehend it, would be in some way unadmittable; since loving only those men who are completely manly, men who are single-sexed, it is only with such a man that it can appease a desire it ought not to feel for him, and which he ought not to feel in return—if the need for love were not an arch-cheat, and did not make it see in the most ignominious pansy the likeness of a man, of a real man like other men who by a miracle would feel love for it, or stoop to it; since like criminals it must perforce hide its secret from those it holds dearest, dreading the grief of a family, the scorn of friends, the criminal code of a country; a race accursed, persecuted like Israel, and finally, like Israel, under a mass opprobrium of undeserved abhorrence, taking on mass characteristics, the physiognomy of a nation; all with certain characteristic features, physical features that are often repulsive, that sometimes are beautiful, all with a woman's loving, breakable heart, but with a woman's suspicions, her wilful, coquettish, tale-bearing nature, a woman's knack for being clever at everything, a woman's incapacity to do anything supremely well; cut off from family life, where they can never be quite open, from national life, where they would be regarded as undisclosed criminals, cut off even from their fellows, in whom they inspire the chagrin of discovering in themselves the warning that the thing they believe to be a natural love is a sickly madness, as well as that womanliness which offends them; yet for all that, loving hearts cut off from friendship because when a simple friendliness is all they feel, their friends may suspect an intention of something other than friendship and, if they should own to feeling something else, would not understand it; now the object of a blind incomprehension which can only love them by not understanding them, now of an aversion which condemns them for what is purest in them, now of a curiosity which wants to account for them and sees them all askew, working out a barrack-room broadmindedness towards them which even when it supposes itself impartial is still biased, and admits *a priori*—like those judges for whom to be a Jew is to be a traitor—that homosexuality can easily lead to murder; like Israel, still aspiring towards what they are not, what they never could be, and yet feeling for one

another, under a show of slander and rivalry and a contempt of the least perverted for the most perverted
like that of the most desemitised Jew for the little
Jew in the slop-shop, a profound solidarity—a kind of
freemasonry which is wider than that of the ghetto
because nothing is known about it and no bounds can
be set to it, and inherently more powerful than real
freemasonry because it rests on a natural conformity,
on identity of taste, of need, of theory and practice, so
to speak, between the man in the cab and the gutter-
snipe who opens the cab door, or sometimes more
painfully between him and his daughter's suitor, or
again with bitter irony between him and the doctor
to whom he goes to be cured of his perversion, or the
man of the world who blackballs him at the club, or
the priest who hears his confession, or the advocate
who cross-examines him in a court or court-martial, or
the sovereign in whose name he is prosecuted; endlessly harping with persevering (or exasperating) satisfaction on the theme that Cato was a homosexual,
as Jews harp on the theme that Christ was a Jew, never
understanding that just as there were no Jews before
the death of Christ there was no such thing as homosexuality in an epoch when it was as customary and
befitting to live with a young man as nowadays it is
to keep a ballet-dancer, when Socrates, the most virtuous man there ever was, cracked jokes about two
youths sitting side by side, as we might do about a
nephew and niece who make eyes at each other,
jokes that came quite naturally and which are clearer
evidence of a way of society than opinions, which
might have been merely personal to him—so that
original as it may be, the sin of homosexuality dates
its historical origin from when, having lost its good

name, it did not conform; but thenceforward by its
resistance to exhortation, example, contempt, the punishment of the law, gave proof of a disposition that
other men know to be so strong and so ingrained that
they are more repelled by it than by crimes which
drive a coach and horses through the ten command-
ments—for a crime can be a momentary thing, and
theft or murder everyone can understand, but not
homosexuality; the reprobate tribe of humankind, yes,
but for all that, essentially, indivisibly, innumerably, a
branch of the human family, suspected where it does
not exist, flaunting insolent and unpunished where it
is not recognised, and everywhere, in the streets, in the
ranks, in the house of God, at the theatre, in the prison,
on the throne, mutually rending and supporting itself,
unwilling to recognise itself yet recognising itself, and
divining a fellow in one whom it would be most loth to
admit to itself—still less have others know—it is in fel-
lowship with; living on terms of household intimacy
with those who at the sight of its offence, should a scandal break out, would turn savage as wild animals do at
the sight of blood, but seeing them at peace with it in
daily life, accustomed to play with them like a lion-
tamer, to talk homosexuality, to provoke their growls
(so that nowhere does one talk homosexuality so
freely as before a homosexual) till that day comes, as
soon or late it will, when it will be torn to pieces—like
the poet to whom every London drawing-room was
open—it and its works prosecuted, it not able to find a
roof to shelter it, they, a theatre to perform them—
and after expiation and death seeing its statue put
up above its grave; compelled to travesty its feelings,
to alter its words, to put she for he, to find pretexts
in its own eyes for its friendships and its angers, more

hampered by compliance with the inner need, and the imperious command of its vice that it should not believe itself a prey to vice, than by the social obligation to keep its inclinations out of sight; a race whose pride is set on not being a race, on not differing from the rest of the world, lest its desires should seem like a sickness and their very fulfilment like an impossibility, its pleasures like illusions, its characteristics like blemishes, so that the first pages (so I believe), since there have been men and men have written, that have been dedicated to it in a spirit of justice towards its virtues of soul and mind—which are not disfigured by it, as people say, and in a spirit of pity for its innate ill-starredness and its undeserved sufferings, will be those that will make it angriest to hear, and most reluctant to read, because if in the depth of almost every Jew there is an anti-Semite whom we best flatter when we attribute every kind of fault to him but treat him as a Christian, so in the depth of every homosexual there is an anti-homosexual to whom we cannot offer a greater insult than acknowledging that he has talents, virtues, intellect, heart, and in sum, like all human characters, the right to enjoy love in the form that nature allows us to conceive of it, though respect for truth meanwhile compels us to confess that this form of love is strange, and that these men are not like other men.

You have seen them, now and then, at a station, in a theatre, these delicate, sickly-faced, fantastically-attired creatures whose glances, travelling with ostentatious indifference over a negligible crowd, are really seeking whether they may not light on one of those recondite specialists in the singular pleasure they have to offer, and who would already have recognised as a flag of muster the mute enquiry they hide beneath that air of remote indolence. Nature, as in the case of certain animals, certain flowers, in whom the mechanism of love is so ill-contrived that they can scarcely ever feel pleasure, has not been over-indulgent to them where love is concerned. Of course, there are no beings for whom love is perfectly easy, and it often exacts the encounter of beings who are set on different paths; but for this being towards whom Nature was so [step-motherly] it is a hundred times harder. His species is so thinly distributed over the world that he may pass his whole life without ever meeting the matched being whom he could love. It must be another of his species, with a woman's nature in order to comply with his desire, and yet with the aspect of a man in order to inspire it. One would think that his temperament, so fragile, and so rigorously limited, had been fashioned in such a way that love under such conditions, and apart from the unanimous conspiracy of all the social forces that threaten it, even to the scruples and the sense of sin within him, must be an impossible wager. Yet they lay it. But for the most part, contenting themselves with gross imitations, and failing to find, not the man-woman but the woman-man that they need, they hire a woman's embraces from a man, or led by the mirage with which pleasure finally embellishes what it feeds on, discover some manly charm in the wholly effeminate beings that love them.

Some of them, taciturn and marvellously handsome, beautiful Andromedas chained to a sex that vows them to solitude, have eyes where the anguish of unattainable Paradise is reflected with a splendour to which women flutter like moths, and kill themselves for love; hateful to those whose love they seek, they cannot satisfy the love their beauty awakens. And in others again, the woman is almost half-declared. Her breasts emerge from them, they seize every opportunity of fancy dress to show them off, they are as fond of dancing and dress and cosmetics as girls are, and at the most sedate gatherings break into giggling fits, or start singing.

I remember seeing at Querqueville a young man, much laughed at by his brothers and friends, who used to take solitary walks on the beach; he had a charming, thoughtful, melancholy face, and long black hair, whose raven hue he burnished in secret by dusting a sort of blue powder over it. He reddened his lips a little, though he pretended their colour was natural. He spent hours alone on the beach, walking or sitting on the rocks, searching the blue horizon with sad eyes, anxious and insistent even then, asking himself if this expanse of sea and pale blue sky, the same bright sky that looked down on Marathon and Salamis, would not show him, borne on the swiftly advancing boat and coming to carry him away, that Antinoüs of whom he dreamed all day and every night, sitting at the window of the holiday villa, where the belated passer-by saw him in the light of the moon, staring out at the night, and quickly moving back when someone noticed him. Still too innocent to suppose that such a desire as his could exist elsewhere than in books, never thinking that it could have any sort of bearing on the scenes of debauchery we associate with it, putting them on the same level as theft or murder, always going back to his rock to look at the sky and the sea, and ignoring the port where the seamen ask no better than to pick up a wage, however they may earn it. But his unacknowledged desire was plainly to be seen in his aloofness from his friends, or in the oddity of his talk and behaviour when he was with them. They sampled his rouge, laughed at his blue powder and his melancholy; and wearing blue trousers and a sailor's cap, he went for his sad, solitary walks, consumed by lassitude and self-reproach.

When M. de Quercy was a little boy, when his playmates told him about the pleasures of going with a woman, he pressed up against them, supposing he only partook in a common wish for the same excitements. Later on, he felt that they would not be the same; he felt it, but did not say so, nor say so to himself. On moonless nights he went out of his castle in Poitou and followed the lane into the road that goes to the castle of his cousin, Guy de Gressac. Here, at the crossroads, they met, and on the grass bank they renewed what had been the games of their childhood, and parted from each other without having spoken a word, nor ever spoke a word about it during the daytime when they met and talked, maintaining rather a sort of enmity against each other, but from time to time meeting again in darkness, silently, as if it were an encounter between the ghosts of their childish selves. But his cousin who had become Prince de Guermantes took mistresses, and was only occasionally re-assailed by the fantastic recollection. And after waiting for hours on the grass bank at the crossroad, M. de Quercy often went home heavy-hearted. Then his cousin married, and from that time forward he only saw him as a laughing talking man, on rather cool terms with him, for all that, and he never felt the ghost's embrace again.

Meanwhile, Hubert de Quercy lived on in his castle, lonelier than any mediaeval lady in her bower. When he went to catch the train at the railway station, for all that he had never spoken to him, he regretted that the whimsicality of the legal code did not allow him to make the station-master his bride; infatuated though he was about noble lineage, perhaps he could have put up with the misalliance. And when the lieutenant-colonel whom he had eyed during the manoeuvres went off to another garrison town, he would have liked to be able to move house. His pleasures consisted of coming down from time to time from the tower-room, where he felt as dull as patient Grizel, and, after innumerable falterings, going into the kitchen to tell the butcher that the last leg of mutton was rather tough, or to collect his letters from the postman. Then he went up into his tower again, and studied his ancestors' pedigrees. One evening, he went so far as to put a drunk man back on the right road, on another occasion, meeting a blind man whose shirt was undone, he buttoned it up for him.

He went to Paris. He was in his twenty-fifth year, extremely good-looking, and for a man of fashion, witty, while his peculiar tastes had not as yet encompassed his person with that vexed aura which later would mark it out. But an Andromeda fettered to a sex he was in no way designed for, his eyes were filled with a nostalgia that made women fall in love with him, and while he was a thing of loathing to those he was attracted to, he could not wholeheartedly share the passions he inspired. He had mistresses. A woman killed herself for him. He began to go about with various young men of the aristocracy whose tastes were the same as his.

Who, seeing those elegant young people grouped round a table, and knowing them to be loved by women, could suspect that they were talking of pleasures incomprehensible to the rest of mankind? They hate and pour scorn on others of their race, and never go near them. They snobbishly cultivate the society of men who only love women, and frequent no other. But they like to make merry with one or two others as well-whitened as themselves, and to feel a racial bond. Sometimes, when no one else is there, a tribal word or a ritual gesture escapes them, launched on an impulse of deliberate mockery, but from an unconscious solidarity and a deep-lying pleasure. Such a group in a café will draw apprehensive glances from those bearded Levites who, in their dread of contumely, will only associate with those of their own race, who are the bureaucracy of perversion, overdo the correct thing, daren't go out except in a black tie, and look coldly on these handsome young people whom they could never suspect of being like themselves—since though one easily believes in what one wishes, one does not dare put too much belief in it either. And of these, some whom bashfulness forbids, are afraid to reply to a young man's civil greeting by more than a rude stammer, like those country-bred young girls who think it immoral to smile or shake hands. And a young man's affability sows the seed of perennial love in their hearts, since the alms of a smile is enough to give rise to hope, and then they know themselves to be so criminal, so disgraced, that they cannot conceive of a forthcomingness that would not be a sign of complicity. But in ten years' time the handsome unsuspected young men and the bearded Levites will recognise each other, for the secret thoughts they share in common will have expanded around their persons that unmistakable halo amidst which one discerns what seems the visionary form of an Antinoüs; the inward growth of their incurable sickness will have played havoc with their bearing; at the end of the street where one meets them, belligerently tautening feminine hips as if making ready for combat, forestalling a conjectural scorn by a show of impertinence, masking—and underlining—by a sham indifference their dread of losing that quarry, which they delayingly approach and pretend not to see, there will always be a schoolboy's blazer, or a military headgear, and in the one and the other alike one can see the sharp eye and the uninterested demeanour of spies prowling round barracks. But in the café where they still ignore each other, the one and the other shrink back from the dregs of their race, the braceletted sect, those who are not afraid to sit hugging another man in public, and continually push back their cuffs to reveal a string of pearls on the wrist, until the normal young men whom they pester —now with ogles, now with glares—and the Levites and dandies whom they indicate with girlish giggles and ambiguous malicious gestures, are driven, as if by some intolerable stink, to get up and go away, while the waiter—indignant but philosophic, as one who knows life—serves them with exacerbated politeness, or wonders if he should send for the police, though still continuing to pocket their tips.

But there were times when, just as the desire for a perverse pleasure may blossom for once in a normal being, he was haunted by a desire that the body he clasped to his own might have had the breasts of a woman, breasts like tea-roses, and other more sequestered characteristics. He fell in love with a girl of high breeding whom he married and for fifteen years all his desires were contained in his desire for her, like a deep river in a blue-tinted bathing-pool. He marvelled at himself, like the former dyspeptic who for twenty years could take nothing but milk and who lunches and dines every day at the Café Anglais, like the idler turned industrious, like the reformed drunkard. She died; and the knowledge that he had found the cure for his sickness made him less afraid to relapse into it. So little by little he became like those who had once been most abhorrent to him. But his rank and standing saved him from the worst. On his way to the club he would pause for a moment outside the Lycée Condorcet, and then console himself with the thought that it was his yacht that would take the Duke of Parma and the Grand Duke of Genoa to Cowes, since after all there was no one in the peerage of France who held so splendid a position as he, and that because of this the King of England would probably come to lunch with him there.

14

Names

If with a light hand I could extricate from the swaddlings of habit and see again in its first freshness that name, Guermantes, coloured as then it was by the light of my fancy alone, and contrast with the Mme. de Guermantes that I have known, and with what her name means to me now, the imagined being whom acquaintance brought to reality—in other words, destroyed—the town of Pont-Aven was no more built of the entirely imaginary components that the ring of its name calls up than Mme. de Guermantes was composed of the stuff of legend and romance that I beheld when I uttered her name. She was thus a contemporary person, while her name made me see her in the present and at the same time in the thirteenth century, inhabiting simultaneously a town house that was like a glass showcase and, at the same time the tower of a lonely castle on which the last gleam of sunset perpetually rested and where her rank impeded her from speaking to anyone. In Paris, in the glass-case town house, she conversed, I thought, with other persons who also simultaneously belonged to the thirteenth century and the present day, who also possessed gloomy castles, and equally did not converse with the rest of the world. But I felt it incumbent on these mysterious grandees that they should bear names I had never heard; La Rochefoucauld, La Trémoille, celebrated names of the nobility which have become names of streets, names of books, seemed to me too public, too nearly household words to enter her company.

The various Guermantes were always identifiable
in the precious matrix of aristocratic society, where
they were to be seen to this side or that, like those
threads of a lighter-hued rarer substance which vein
a piece of jasper. One could pick them out, one could
trace the flexible ripple of their golden manes
through this mineral deposit in which they are embedded, as though tracing that almost luminous tress
of hair that flows unbraided through a moss agate.
And on many occasions my life, too, on its surface, in
its depth, had been crossed by their trail of light, or
grazed by its passage. I had forgotten, to be sure,
that among the ballads my old servant had sung to me
there had been a *Gloire à la Dame de Guermantes* that
my mother had remembered; but afterwards, year
after year, these Guermantes rose into view on one
side or another of my life's haphazard winding course
like the castle reappearing now on one's right, now
on one's left, that one sees from a railway train.

And for the very reason that the windings of my
own career never brought me before the same aspect
of them twice over, on no one of these occasions, perhaps, did I think about that race of Guermantes, but
only about the old lady to whom my grandmother introduced me and whom I must not forget to bow to,
of what Mlle. de Quimperlé might think on seeing
me with her, etc. With each Guermantes my acquaintance was so much a matter of accident, and each
Guermantes impinged on me with such massive actuality because of some quite physical impression
registered by my eyes or my ears, the pimples on an
old lady's face, the way she said: "I am always at home
before dinner," that I had not been able to develop
the sense of contact with their mysterious race, mys-

terious in rather the same way that a race descended from an animal or a deity might have seemed to our forefathers, though for this very reason, when I thought about it, and reflected that circumstances alone had already and so often and on such a variety of pretexts brought me into contact with what had been the dream of my childhood, perhaps making life rather more poetical for me. One day at Querqueville, when we were talking about Mlle. de Saint-Étienne, Montargis said to me, "Oh, she is a regular Guermantes, just like my Aunt Septimie—they're Dresden, Dresden china figures." As these words entered my ears they conveyed such an ineffaceable picture that I felt a resulting obligation, beyond the scope of the most fatuous simple-mindedness, to take them literally. Since that day I can never think of Mlle. de Saint-Étienne's sisters or of Aunt Septimie except as Dresden china figures arranged in a glass showcase reserved for precious objects, and whenever a Guermantes town house in Paris or in Poitiers was mentioned, I always saw it as a square crystal box, fragile and flawless, interpolated among houses like a Gothic spire among rooftops, behind whose glass panes, and unapproachable by those unlicensed persons who make up the rest of the world, the Guermantes ladies sparkled in the most delicate hues of little Dresden china figures.

When I met Mme. de Guermantes I had the same slight disappointment in finding that the Dresden china figure of my imagination had plump cheeks and wore a tailor-made coat and skirt, as when I saw the façade of Saint Mark's, that Ruskin had said was all of pearls, sapphires, and rubies. But I still imagined her house as a show-case and what I saw was indeed rather

like one, and besides could only be thought of as a
sort of protective casing. I thought that even the
neighbourhood where she lived must be as different
from the rest of the world, as cloistered, as impossible
for mortal foot to tread, as the show-case's glass
shelves. To tell the truth, although the real Guermantes differed essentially from those of my fancy,
they were nevertheless, even when judged as men and
women, quite odd enough. I do not know what myth-
ical race it was which sprang from the mating of a goddess and a bird, but I feel sure the Guermantes belonged to it.

Though tall, the Guermantes, alas! were as a rule
tall without being shapely; and as if to establish a
fixed mean, a sort of ideal order, a harmony which,
as in violin-playing, one must constantly adjust for
oneself, between their shoulders which were too wide,
their necks, which were too long, and which they
shrugged apprehensively into their shoulders as if
someone had kissed them under the opposite ear,
their ill-matched eyebrows, and their legs which
through accidents in the hunting field were often ill-
matched too, they were always getting up and down,
always wriggling, never to be seen otherwise than
askew or straightening up, stooping to pick up a mono-
cle, raising it to an eyebrow, or winding a right hand
round a left knee.

The Guermantes nose—among those of them at least
who had remained true to type—was pronouncedly
hooked (although with nothing of the Jewish hook),
and too long, which in the women of the family, especially the pretty ones, and above all in the case of
Mme. de Guermantes, immediately bit into the memory like an etcher's acid as something at first sight al-

most disagreeable; beneath this sharp nose, lips that were too thin, too rudimentary, gave a kind of gauntness to the mouth, from which proceeded a harsh voice like the cry of a bird, rather shrill but intoxicating to the ear. Their eyes were of an intense blue, which at a distance glittered like sparks of light, and surveyed you sternly and unwaveringly, seeming to bring the point of some unbluntable sapphire to bear on you with an air not so much of domination as of penetration, as though wishing to scrutinize rather than bully you. The stupidest members of the family inherited through the female line and perfected by education this air of a divine right to inspect and dominate mankind, but their stupidity or their poor vitality would have made this rather comic if this glance had not been in itself so ineffably beautiful. The Guermantes hair was almost always blond and inclining to sandy, but of a nature all its own, a sort of golden moss, half tufted silk, half cat-fur. Their complexion, which was already a byword by the seventeenth century, was a mauvish pink (there is a cyclamen of that same shade), and often roughened at the angle of the nose and the left cheekbone with small dry pimples, always in the same place and sometimes inflamed by fatigue; and in certain branches of the family where cousins had always married cousins, this family complexion had been deepened and empurpled. There were some Guermantes who seldom came to Paris, and who, wriggling, as every Guermantes did, beneath their beaks that jutted between garnet chops and amethyst cheekbones, looked like some kind of swan, majestically plumed with purple feathers, which battens ill-temperedly on irises and heliotrope.

The Guermantes manner was that of the highly-bred, but nevertheless this manner evinced the independent spirit of nobles who had always liked being at odds with the throne rather than the consequentiality of other nobles, quite as noble as they, who liked to feel favoured by kings and serviceable to them. Thus, when these others said by choice, even when talking amongst themselves, "I have been to visit Mme. la Duchesse de Chartres," the Guermantes, even to their servants, would say, "Call up the Duchess of Chartres's carriage." In short, the Guermantes frame of mind was governed by two traits. In the field of morality, by the prime importance they attached to goodheartedness. From Mme. de Villeparisis down to the least little Guermantes, they all put on the same tone of voice to remark of a coachman who had once driven them somewhere, "One can tell that his heart is in the right place, honest by nature, all the right instincts." And for all that among the Guermantes, no less than with any human family, there might be hateful specimens—liars, thieves, sadists, libertines, swindlers, killers—these, who incidentally were more engaging than the rest, patently more intelligent, more likable, kept, apart from the bodily aspect, the searching blue eye, the unbluntable sapphire, only one trait in common with the rest, which was that in those moments of bedrock, when the permanent Guermantes came out, when they were most themselves, they said: "One can tell his heart is in the right place, an honest fellow, a good sort, every inch of him."

The two other governing traits in the Guermantes mentality were less universally maintained. Being purely intellectual, these only cropped up in the intelligent Guermantes, the Guermantes, that is to say, who believed themselves to be intelligent and consequently believed themselves intelligent to an extraordinary degree, for they had an extremely good conceit of themselves. One of these traits was the belief that intelligence—goodness and piety too—consisted in outward acquirements, in being well informed. Books treating of things they knew about they considered beneath their attention—"This man only talks about living in the country and country houses. Anyone who has lived in the country knows all that. Odd as it may seem, we like books that tell us something new. Life is short, one can't waste precious time over *L'Orme du Mail*, and Anatole France telling us things about the country life that we know as well as he does."

But this Guermantes singularity which life brought me in compensation, like a non-voting share, was not the singularity they lost for me from the moment I knew them, and which had made them poetical and gilded as their name, legendary and disembodied as the pictures cast by a magic lantern, inaccessible as their castle, sparkling with colour in a clear transparent house, in a glass show-case, like Dresden figures. For that matter, many territorial titles share this charm of being names of castles, names of railway stations where, reading them in a timetable, one has imagined oneself getting out at the close of a summer afternoon—when in the north of France, the dense, unfrequented hornbeam plantations, amongst which the station is tucked away out of sight, are already browned by the moist chill air, like trees elsewhere at the oncome of winter.

Today it is still part of the glamour of the nobility
that the titled families seem to be ensconced in some
particular part of the world, so that their title, which
is always the name of a place or the name of their
castle (in some cases, one and the same) immediately
fills the imagination with the impression of their
dwelling and the wish to travel. Within its span of
coloured syllables every such title contains a castle,
where after a tedious approach it is sweet to arrive on
some festive winter evening, and all around it the
poetry of its lake and its church, which in its turn
reiterates, on tombstones, on the bases of painted an-
cestral effigies, in the rose of armorial windows, the
name and the coat of arms. That family, you tell me,
for the last two hundred years inhabiting a castle near
Bayeux that looks as though the spindrift beat on it
throughout winter afternoons, and fogs imprisoned it,
and laces and tapestries hung on its inner walls—their
name really originates in Provence. This does not prevent it from reminding me of Normandy, just as many
trees, native to India or the Cape, are so well acclima-
tised in our country that nothing seems less exotic to
us, more French, than their leaves and blossoms. If during three centuries the name of this Italian family has
towered haughtily above a deep Normandy valley, if
from there, through a dip in the landscape, one catches
sight of the castle front, red stone and weathered
ashlar, against the same distance as the slated belfry[1]
of Saint-Pierre-sur-Dives, it is as Norman as the apple
trees that [   ] and were not brought from the
Cape until [   ]. If the town house of that Provençal family at the corner of the main square of
Falaise has been theirs for two hundred years; if the

guests who have spent an evening at their card-table
risk waking up the citizens of Falaise if they should
leave after ten p.m., and their footsteps, as in a novel
by Barbey d'Aurevilly, can be heard interminably re-
echoing through the night as far as the dungeon-keep;
if one sees the roof of their house framed between
two church spires, like a pebble on a Normandy beach
between two eyeletted shells, between the rose-tinted
ribbed turrets of two hermit-crab shells; if the guests
who have arrived too soon for dinner, leaving a drawing-room full of curiosities brought back from China
during the heyday of trading between Norman sea-
captains and the Far East, can go down to stroll about
with members of the various titled families with estates between Coutances and Caen, between Thury-
Harcourt and Falaise, in a garden whose slopes, bor-
dered by the old walls of the town, extend as far as
the running brook where, while waiting for the din-
ner-hour, one can fish from the grounds, as in a story
by Balzac, what does it signify that the family should
have come from Provence to settle here, and should
bear a Provençal name? It has become as Norman as
those lovely pink hydrangeas one sees from Honfleur
to Valognes, from Pont-L'Évêque to Saint-Vaast—an
imported bush, but now it characterises the landscape
it embellishes, and enamels a Norman manor with
the delicious old, fresh tints of a piece of Chinese pottery brought (but brought by Jacques Cartier[2]) from
Pekin.

Others have a castle deep in the forest, and to get
there entails a long journey. In the Middle Ages only
the sounding of a horn and the baying of hounds
broke the surrounding silence. Now when a journey-
ing visitor arrives at dusk, the motor-horn replaces the

one and the other, as much in harmony as the first with the damp air, smelling of woodlands, then steeped in the rose-scent of the garden-court that it traverses, and like the second, with touching, almost human cries, telling the lady of the house who has gone to her window that she will not be alone this evening, sitting opposite the Count at dinner and then at picquet. No doubt when I hear the name of a splendid Gothic castle near Ploërmel, and think of the long galleries of the cloisters and the paths where one walks amid broom and roses over the graves of the abbots who from the eighth century onwards lived there, walking in those cloisters, looking out over that valley, when Charlemagne was still unborn, when Chartres had no towers, nor Vézelay an abbey on the hill above the deep fishy pools of the river Cousin; no doubt, if in one of those moments for which even the language of poetry is too explicit, too overburdened with words and consequently with familiar images not to cloud that mysterious current which the *Name*, that prior existence to the known, sets flowing, and which is incompatible, as now and then our dreams are, with anything we could have experienced; no doubt, after I have rung the bell at the foot of the terrace and seen two or three servants come out, one whose melancholy swoops, long curvilinear nose, and harsh, scattered cries prompt the thought that when the lake was drained one of the swans was reincarnated in him, another whose frightened eyes reeling in a muddied face suggest a deft and harried mole— I shall find in the great hall the same coat-racks, the same coats, as everywhere else, and in the same drawing-room the same *Revue de Paris* and *Comœdia*. And even if everything still breathed of the thirteenth century, the hosts, however intelligent, above all if intelligent, would be making the intelligent remarks of the present day. (Perhaps they ought to have been dullards and their conversation limited to local information, as with those accounts of places that only come to life when they deal in exact descriptions and avoid the abstract.)

The same thing holds good for the nobility of other countries. In the title of one German nobleman a breath of fantastic poetry seems to be making its way through the smell of a stuffy room, and the humdrum iteration of its first syllables might make one think of comfits eaten in a little grocery shop of some old German market place, while the old painted window by Aldgrever in the old church across the way darkens in the parti-coloured sonority of its last syllable. Another German title is the name of a brook, that rises in the Black Forest under the legendary Wartburg, flows through all the gnome-haunted valleys, and is frowned down on by all the castles where the old barons held sway, and Luther meditated afterwards; all these are in this noble person's domain and inhabit his title. But I dined with him last night, his face is today's, his clothes are today's, his words and his ideas are today's. And if one refers to blue blood or to the Wartburg, he says with the broadmindedness of one quite above such things, "Oh, there are no more princes nowadays."

And of course, there never were any. But in their one possible existence of being imaginable, it is only nowadays that a long-accumulated past has filled up the names with dreams (Clermont-Tonnerre, Latour and P . . . , the Dukes of C. T.). There is a Duchess in Debrett[3] whose castle in Scotland, with a name that occurs in Shakespeare and in Walter Scott, dates

from the thirteenth century. The marvellous abbey
that Turner painted so often is on her estate, her ancestors lie beneath the ranked tombs in the ruined
cathedral, where the cattle graze among broken arches
and flowering brambles and which we feel to be dou-
bly a cathedral because we are obliged to fasten its
abstract being upon things that otherwise would be
something else, to call that paddock the floor of the
nave, and that thicket the entrance to the chancel.
Her ancestors had it built, and now it is hers, and
through her estate runs that heavenly stream, flowing, all coolness and mystery, beneath two bridges,[4]
with the boundless stretch of plain and the sun setting
in a great patch of blue sky framed between two
orchards that indicate, as a sundial does, by the slope
of light falling upon them the blissful hour of late
afternoon, and the town in the distance all laid out in
tiers, and the man fishing so contentedly—we know it
through Turner, and we would travel the world over
to find it, to be assured that the beauty and charm of
nature, the happiness of living, the supreme beauty
of that hour and that place exist, if it were not for
the thought that in choosing to present a certain
place as inherently and incomparably entrancing,
Turner—and Stevenson after him—did no more than
they would have done for any other place that happened to call out the entrancing beauty and incom-
parability of their minds. But the Duchess has invited
me to dinner where I shall meet Marcel Prévost, and
Melba is going to sing, and I shall not cross the chan-
nel.

But were she to summon me to the company of
mediæval barons, I should feel the same disappointment, since there can be no identity between the un-

known poetry that a name—an urn of unknowabilities, that is—may hold, and the things we arrive at by experience and can match to words and by other experiences. From the inevitable disappointment of our encounter with things that we knew as names, the bearer of some great landed and historic title, for instance, or—a better instance still—every place we have gone to see, we might conclude that this imaginary charm which reality belies is a poetic convention. But beyond the fact that I do not believe this and intend one day to establish quite the contrary, merely on grounds of realism, this psychological reality, this detailed clairvoyance of our fancy, is worth quite as much as the other, since of the two it is concerned with a far more living reality which tends perpetually to reshape itself within us, and which while forsaking the countries we have visited spreads out over all the others and flows back over those we have known as soon as we have begun to forget them, as soon as they have once again become *names* to us; since it haunts us even in our dreaming, where it clothes landscapes, churches seen in childhood, castles seen in fancy, with the appearance that is *akin to the name*, the appearance woven by imagination and wish, that eludes us when we wake up, or in that moment when as we catch sight of it we fall asleep; since it brings us far more pleasure than the other reality, which bores and disappoints us, and is a reason for action, and keeps the traveller—that fond lover who is forever disappointed, forever setting out with higher hopes—travelling still; and since the pages that succeed in giving us an impression of it are the only pages that give us an impression of genius.

Nor is it only that an earl or a duke has a title that

sets us dreaming; in the case of many noble families, the names of parents, grandparents, and so forth, are beautiful too, so that nothing prosaic breaks the sequence of that continual grafting-in of names—vivid, and yet transparent, since no base matter clings to them —by means of which we go climbing on from one coloured crystal sprig to another, as on a Tree of Jesse in a stained glass window. In our minds the people take on the purity of their immaterial nomenclature. To the left, a clove pink, then the tree ascends; on the right, a wild rose, and the tree ascends, on the left, a lily, still the stem of the tree goes up, on the right, a blue love-in-a-mist; his father married a Montmorency, a damask rose, his father's mother was a Montmorency-Luxembourg, a fringed pink and a Provence rose, whose father married a Choiseul, blue love-in-a-mist, and then a Charost, a clove pink. From time to time an old purely local name like some rare flower which now one only sees in Van Huysum's pictures seems a duskier colour because we have not observed it so often. But presently our attention is called off by discovering on either side of the Jesse window a further series of painted windows which narrate the lives of persons who were at first no more than a lily or a love-in-a-mist; but as the narratives are also old and painted on glass, it all fits in wonderfully. "Prince of Wurtemberg, his mother was born Marie de France, whose mother was of the royal house of the Two Sicilies." But then his mother must have been that daughter of Louis Philippe and Marie-Amélie who married the Duke of Wurtemberg? And then to the right in the little window of our memory, we see the Princess wearing a cotton dress at the wedding of her brother the

Duc d'Orléans, to manifest her annoyance at the rebuff received by the ambassadors who had asked on her behalf for the hand of the Prince of Syracuse. Next comes a handsome young man, the Duke of Wurtemberg, who has asked for her in marriage, and she is so delighted to go with him that she smiles as she kisses her weeping parents goodbye, which is thought badly of by the motionless servants in the background. Soon she reappears, she is ill, she gives birth to a child (no other than this Prince of Wurtemberg, a yellow marigold, who has led us up his Tree of Jesse to his mother, a white rose, whence we jumped sideways to the window on the left) without having seen her husband's nonpareil palace, Fantaisie, the mere name of which had made her decide to marry him. Whereupon, without sparing time for the window's four bottom lights which show us the poor Princess dying in Italy and her brother Nemours hurrying to her side while the Queen of France has a fleet made ready to carry her to her daughter, we look at this castle of Fantaisie, where she thought to shelter her ill-guided life, and in the window that follows—for places, like races, have a story—we see in this same Fantaisie another princely figure, himself vowed to fantasies and destined, too, to die young and after loves as erratic, Ludwig II of Bavaria; and indeed at the base of the first window we had read without giving them a thought the words of the Queen of France: "a castle near Bayreuth." But we must go back to the Tree of Jesse, to the Prince of Wurtemberg, a yellow marigold, son of Louise de France, a blue love-in-a-mist. What! He is still alive, this son of hers whom she scarcely knew? For having asked her brother how she was getting on, when he said, "Not too badly, but the doctors are worried," she answered, "Nemours, I understand," and thereafter was affectionate towards everyone but never again asked to see her child for fear she would betray herself by weeping. What! He is still alive, this child, he is alive and the Prince Royal of Wurtemberg? Perhaps he takes after her, perhaps he has inherited something of her taste for painting, for dreaming, for fantasy, which she thought she would house so well in her castle of Fantaisie. With what different eyes do we see his face in the little window when we know he is the son of Louise de France! For either these lovely lineaged names are storyless and obscure as a forest, or they are historic; and the mother's eyes, that are familiar to us, shed a light that still illumines her son from head to foot. The countenance of a living son, that monstrance to which a high-minded dead mother committed all her trust is like a profanation of that hallowed memory; because it is the countenance towards which those pleading eyes directed a farewell he ought not to be able to forget for a moment; because his nose is modelled from the lovely line of his mother's profile; because it is with his mother's smile that he inflames loose women to debauchery, because it is with the lifted eyebrows of her tenderest glances at him that he lies, because that tranquil expression she wore when speaking of things that left her unconcerned—of everything, that is, but him—it is he who now wears it when he speaks of her, when he says unconcernedly, "my poor mother."

In line with these windows, subsidiary windows come into play where we light on a name formerly obscure, the name of the captain of the guards who saves the Prince's life, of the master of a vessel who puts to sea so that the Princess may escape—an honourable name but an obscure one, and which has become known since, born in a cranny of tragic circumstances like a flower between two paving-stones, and for ever after secreting the reflected gleam of the fidelity that made it illustrious and still keeps it spell-bound. These honourable names touch my heart beyond all others, I want beyond all else to wind my way into the soul of the heir, who is enlightened only by the solitary ray of this tradition, and sees everything in the absurd distorted aspect cast on it by that tragic gleam. I remember laughing at that grizzled man who forbade his children to speak to a Jew, said Grace at meals, was so conventional, so avaricious, so ridiculous, so hostile to democracy. And now when I see him again, I see him lit up by his name, the name of his father who contrived the Duchesse de Berri's escape by sea, a soul for which that gleam of life ablaze that we see reddening the water at the moment when she, leaning on his arm, is about to set sail, has remained the only light. Soul of shipwreck, of burning torches, of unquestioning fidelity, soul of the stained glass window . . . perhaps in such names I shall find something so different from myself that in truth it will be almost consubstantial with the stuff that Names are made of. But how nature makes sport of us all! Behold, I meet a young man of the utmost intelligence, who is more like a great man of tomorrow than of today, having not merely mastered and understood the philosophy of Nietzsche, socialism, etc., but gone beyond them and given them new meaning. And I learn that he is the son of the man I saw in the dining-room —so bare in its English style of decoration that it seemed like the room in the *Dream of Saint Ursula*, or the room where the Queen, in the window before her

embarkation, is receiving the ambassadors who im-
plore her to make haste—the man whose silhouette
that reflection of tragedy lit up for me as no doubt
from his innermost thought it lit up the world for
him.

15

The return

They have ceased to be a name; what we see in them is inevitably less than what we imagined. Less? —and also perhaps more. It's the same with a historic building as with a person; our first impression of it is determined by a feature which the descriptions we've heard beforehand generally say nothing about. As what strikes us at first sight in a celebrity known by hearsay will be the way his face crinkles when he laughs, or something slightly silly about his mouth, or a clumsy nose or sloping shoulders, so in Venice when we see Saint Mark's for the first time our predominant impression will be of a broad squat building with Venetian masts, like an Exhibition pavilion; or at Jumièges, of the cathedral towers standing like giants in the forecourt of some genteel little property on the outskirts of Rouen; or at Saint-Wandrille, of the rococo casing of a Romanesque missal, like a Rameau opera with its peruked and befeathered treatment of a classical theme. Things are not so beautiful as we imagined them to be, but they have more personality than our preconception allowed for. Do you remember how pleased you were by my artless rapturous postcards from Guermantes? You have often said to me since: "Tell me something about how you enjoyed yourself." But children don't like to let it appear that they have enjoyed themselves for fear of jeopardising their parents' compassion.

Neither, I assure you, do they like to let it appear that they have been unhappy for fear their parents should compassionate them too much. I have never told you about Guermantes. Since everything I saw, everything you felt sure would please me, proved a disappointment, how came it, you asked, that I was not disappointed in Guermantes? Well, what I went to find at Guermantes, wasn't there. But I found something else. What is beautiful at Guermantes is that dead and gone centuries try to maintain themselves in it. Time has assumed a dimension of space. But that doesn't really disguise it. As one goes into the church by the north door there are three or four round-headed arches, quite out of keeping with the Gothic arches elsewhere, which merge into the masonry of a wall where the newer building embedded them. It is the eleventh century with its heavy round shoulders that is still going on there, furtive and walled-up, and gaping with amazement at the thirteenth and fifteenth centuries which interpose themselves between us and that lout and smilingly conceal it. But it reappears, baser and more emboldened, in the shadowy crypt where between two blocks of stone a couple of massive uncouth vaulting-ribs of Chilperic's time [   ] like old bloodstains denouncing his murder of Clothair's children. One feels oneself swept back through time, as when an ancient memory comes back to mind. Here it is no longer a personal memory, it comes out of the remembrance of centuries. As one enters the abbey refectory on the way to the castle one walks over the graves of abbots who ruled this monastery from the eighth century onward, and who are under our tread, stretched out beneath engraved tombstones; crozier in hand they lie, with the fine latinity of their epitaphs at their feet.

And if Guermantes does not disappoint one as all imagined things do when reduced to reality, this is un-

doubtedly because at no time is it a real place, because even when one is walking about in it, one feels
that the things one sees there are merely the wrap-
pings of other things, that reality lies, not in this present but far elsewhere, that the stone under one's
hand is no more than a metaphor of Time; and the
imagination feeds on Guermantes visited as it fed on
Guermantes described because all these things are
still only words, everything is a splendid figure of
speech that means something else. Take that great refectory paved with the abbots of Guermantes—ten,
twenty, and on to fifty of them, each stone as long as a
man and representing the body that lies beneath. It is
as if a graveyard of ten centuries had been turned
over to make a flagged walk. The forest that slopes
down and away from the castle is none of those forests that pertain to castles—game-preserves, mere ac-
cumulations of trees. It is the old forest of Guermantes where Childebert hunted the deer: "To the
left, a Forest"—exactly as in Shakespeare or Maeterlinck or my magic lantern. It colours the hill of Guermantes, mantling the western slope with its tragic
green velvet, as though an illuminator had painted it
in a Merovingian chronicle; far as it stretches, this
long perspective contains it. It is the *Forest* of the
play, *to the left* and below, on the other side, runs the
river where the Crippled Men of Jumièges[1] were cast
ashore. As for the castle towers, I tell you they are not
only *of* that date, they are still *in* it. This is what stirs
one's heart when one looks at them. People always account for the emotional quality of old buildings by
saying how much they must have seen in their time.
Nothing could be more untrue. Look at the towers
of Guermantes; they still look down on Queen Ma-

tilda's cavalcade, on their dedication by Charles the Bad. They have seen nothing since. The moment when things exist is determined by the consciousness that reflects them; at that moment, they become ideas and are given their form; and their form, in its perpetuity, prolongs one century through the midst of others. Think to yourself that those towers of Guermantes rose up, rearing the thirteenth century there for all time, at a date when for all their great field of vision they could not have sent a look of greeting, a friendly smile, towards the towers of Chartres or Amiens or Paris, which had still to come into being. Think of that immaterial fabric, abbatial Guermantes, older than they, going back further than its buildings, a long-established thing when William the Conqueror sailed to invade England, when the towers of Beauvais and Bourges had yet to be raised, and the traveller looked back from a distance and saw only the low hills of Beauvaisie outlined against the evening sky; at a date when the families of La Rochefoucauld, de Noailles, d'Uzès, that were to grow in might as towers do, rising aloft stage by stage, century by century, had scarcely raised themselves above the common level; when Harcourt with its vaunting golden name, the Butter Tower of lusty Normandy, still had no ducal coronet of seven sprigs on the summit of its sculptured granite tower; before Luynes, a peel-tower that housed a family, and, destined to become the greatest castle of France, had beckoned up from French soil all those lordships, all those princely castles and castles of defence, the princedom of Joinville, the battlemented ramparts of Châteaudun and Montfort, the forest shades of Chevreuse with its hinds and weasels, all those landed estates scattered throughout France in a mysterious unity, a castle in the Midi, a forest in the west, a northern city, all united by alliances and held together by a mailed hand, all those glittering territorial possessions assembled cheek by jowl, abstract emblems of power as in a heraldic achievement, castle *or*, tower *argent*, star *sable*, which during the course of centuries conquests and marriages had emblazoned in the quarterings of a field *azur*.

"But if you were so happy, why did you come back?"

I'll tell you. One day we had gone for a mid-day walk, a thing we did not usually do. On the way back, we came to a place—we had passed by it already, some days earlier—where there was a view of a great stretch of fields and woods and hamlets; and suddenly a layer of sky just above a little stretch of this view, to the left, seemed to grow darker and to take on a kind of breathing, sparkling substantiality, as no cloud could, and then it crystallised into an architectural design, and was a little blue-grey city dominated by a couple of bell-towers. I recognised it at once, that unsymmetrical, unforgettable, cherished, dreaded visage. It was Chartres. How had it got there, that apparition of a city on the sky-line—like some lofty symbolic shape appearing on the eve of battle to ancient heroes, as Carthage appeared to [   ] as Aeneas [   ]? But though the hazy geometrical structure that wavered and sparkled as if it were imperceptibly shaken by the breeze was like something appearing supernaturally, it was familiar too, it decked the horizon with the friendly outline of the town of one's childhood, as Ruysdael in some of his landscapes liked to show a glimpse of his dear Haarlem steeple against his distant blue or grey skies. . . .

Whenever we travelled with my grandmother to Combray she always made us break the journey at Chartres. Without being too sure why, she thought its two bell-towers had that absence of vulgarity and affectation which she found in nature when the hand of man does not smarten it up, and in those books which, subject to two provisoes—nothing vulgar, and nothing shoddy—she thought harmless to children, those beings who have nothing vulgar or shoddy about them. I think she would have said that they "looked natural" and looked "distinguished." In any case, she loved them, and thought we should be the better for seeing them. As she knew nothing at all about architecture, she had not learned that she ought to admire them, and said: "My dears, you'll laugh at me—they don't match, they may not be beautiful 'according to the rules,' but their unsymmetrical old faces please me. There is something about their ruggedness that I like very much. I feel that if they played the piano they would make it sing." And she looked at them so wholeheartedly that her head and her glance strained upward, one would have said she was longing to soar up in company with them, while she continued to smile tenderly at the old weather-beaten stonework.

I even think that she who was not "a believer" had nevertheless an implicit belief that the kind of beauty which she divined in certain historic buildings set it, past reasoning why, on another plane of being, less accidental than the plane we live on. During the year in which she died of a sickness whose nature she realised and whose outcome she was well aware of, she went for the first time in her life to Venice, where the one thing she really loved was the Doges' palace. It always made her happy when, coming back from an out-

ing, she saw it appear in the distance across the la-
goon, and she would smile at the grey and pink masonry with that abstracted look she wore when she was
trying to piece together some noble shadowy dream.
She said several times how glad she was to have seen it
before she died—just think, she might never have
seen it. Now I believe that at a time when the pleasures that are merely pleasurable cease to count, since
the being that found them pleasant has ceased to exist,
and when the fleeting spirit has outstayed the fleeting
sense, she would not have attached so much importance to that joy she got from the Doges' palace if she
had not felt it to be one of those joys which, in a way
we but imperfectly understand, outlive the act of dying, and appeal to some portion of us which at any
rate is not under the dominion of death. Is the poet
who devotes his life to a work which will not be appreciated until he is dead and gone, really governed by
a longing for the fame he will not know?—is there not,
rather, a deathless particle in him which labours as
long as he is spared, and even if it can only labour
while it is in that dated dwelling, at a work which is
deathless too? And if what we know of physiology is at
variance with the doctrine of the immortality of the
soul, are not certain instincts of ours at variance with
the doctrine of total extinction? Or may they not
both perhaps be equally erroneous, and the truth altogether different—as for instance two people who
fifty years before had been told about the telephone,
if one had believed it was all a fraud and the other
that it was something to do with acoustics, and that
the voice could be endlessly maintained in tubes, both
would be equally mistaken.

I myself, on the other hand, never saw the bell-towers of Chartres without a sense of grief, because when
Mamma left Combray before the rest of us we often
went with her as far as Chartres; and the fatal shape of
the two bell-towers was as dreadful in my sight as the
railway station. I walked towards them as towards the
moment when I would have to say goodbye to Mamma,
feel my heart give a stagger in my breast and break
away to follow her—and go back alone. I remember
one particular sad day. . . .

As Mme. de Z . . . had invited us to spend a few
days with her, it had been decided that Mamma
should go off with my brother and that my father and
I should follow a few days later on. So that I should not
make myself too unhappy beforehand I had not been
told of this. I have never been able to understand how
it is that when people try to keep something from us,
the secret, however well-kept it may be, automatically
affects us and works us up into a sort of exasperation,
a feeling of being persecuted, a frenzy to investigate. It
is so with children when, while still too young to have
the slightest notion of the method of procreation, they
feel that they are being deceived, and have an inkling
of the truth. I don't know what cloudy portents
gathered in my mind. When Mamma on the morning
of her departure came lightly into my bedroom—but
hiding an equally heavy heart, I know—and said with
a smile, and quoting Plutarch: " 'Leonidas knew how
to confront great calamities with [   ].' I
hope my threepenny-bit is going to be a match for Leonidas," I replied: "You're going away," with such
desolation in my voice that I saw her blench, and began to hope that I might manage to keep her back or

make her take me with her; I think this was what she
went to ask my father, but no doubt he said No, so she
told me that she had still a little time before she
needed to get ready, and that she had kept it to spend
with me.

She was to travel, as I said, with my little brother;
and as he was not coming back, my uncle had taken
him to Évreux to be photographed. They had set his
hair with curling-tongs, after the fashion of servants'
children when they are taken to the photographer's;
bosses of black hair, stuck with large bows like the
"roses" of a Velasquez Infanta, framed and helmeted
his broad face. I had surveyed him with the smile of an
affectionate elder brother—and whether admiration,
ironic superiority or tenderness was uppermost in it,
it would be hard to say. Mamma and I now went to look
for him, so that I might bid him goodbye, but he was
nowhere to be found. He had been told that the kid
someone had given him, and which, together with the
splendid toy cart which he trailed after him wherever
he went and sometimes "lent" to my father as a favour, was all the world to him, must be left behind. As
he was returning to Paris after the visit to Mme. de
Z . . . , the kid was to be sent to a neighbouring
farmer. Plunged into the depths of woe, my brother
made up his mind to spend these last hours with his kid,
with a further view, I daresay, of hiding himself so
that he could be revenged on Mamma by making her
miss the train. Be that as it may, we had looked everywhere for him when, nearing the little plantation that
screened the circular track where the horse was harnessed to the well-sweep that raised water, and where
no one ever went, we overheard a conversing voice
broken by sobs and moans. It was my brother's voice,

and we soon saw him, though he could not see us; seated on the ground beside his kid, fondling its head and kissing it on its innocent reddish nose, the nose of a mottled, insignificant fop with horns, he and his pet bore but a scant resemblance to that popular theme of English painters, a child fondling an animal. For if my brother, wearing his best little frock and his lace petticoat, and clutching as well as the inseparable toy cart, several small satin bags into which had been put his biscuits, his travelling brush and comb, and two or three pocket looking-glasses, looked as sumptuous as any English child beside its animal friend, his face gainsaid this by an expression of ravaging despair, which these contrasting splendours only enforced, by reddened eyes, and a bosom heaving under its furbelows like that of some rhetorical tragedy queen. From time to time he raised a hand burdened with the cart and the satin bags that he wouldn't let go of, the other hand being wholly engaged in clasping and fondling the kid, and pushed back the curls off his forehead with the impatient gesture of a Phèdre.

What hand importunate took pains to twine
In ringlets on my brow these locks of mine?[2]

"My little kid," he cried, as though the kid partook in his entirely personal grief, "You'll be miserable without your little master, you'll never, never see me again"—and tears swamped his words. "No one will be kind to you, no one will pet you like I do; and you love it so, my little baby, my little darling." Then feeling his tears choke him, he was suddenly inspired to put the finishing touch to his despair by singing a song he had picked up from Mamma, whose fitness to the circumstances made him sob the more:

Farewell! mysterious voices bid me flee
Mild sister of the angels, far from thee.

But my brother's temper, even at this age of five
and a half, was by no means mild, and passing from the
melting consideration of his and the kid's sorrows to
rage against the persecutors, after a moment's hesitation he proceeded to shatter his looking-glasses by
dashing them against the ground, to trample on the
satin bags, to tear out, if not his hair, the bows in it,
and to rend his frock of Indian embroidery, meanwhile screaming at the top of his voice and exclaiming
through his tears: "Why should I be all dressed up if
I am never going to see you again?" When she saw the
lace being ripped off, my mother, who so far had witnessed these goings-on rather tenderly, felt she must
intervene. She took a step forward; my brother, hearing a movement, instantly fell silent, saw her, did not
know if she had seen him or not, and with the look of
one plunged in thought, retreated, and hid himself
behind the kid. She went up to him. He submitted to
being led away, but made it a condition that the kid
should accompany him to the station. Time was growing short; my father, standing in the hall, was wondering why we hadn't reappeared. My mother had
sent me to tell him that for fear of missing the train
we would take the short cut at the back of the garden
and meet him where it crossed the railway track, and
my brother walked on, leading the kid with one hand
as though to a sacrificial altar and in the other holding the bags which had been picked up, the fragments
of looking-glass, the brush and comb, and the cart,
which trailed after him. From time to time, without
venturing to look at Mamma, in the midst of caressing
the kid, he let fly words whose reproachful import she

could not fail to understand. "My poor little kid,
you're not the one that wants to make me miserable,
you don't want to cut me off from what I love. You
mayn't be a human being, but all the same you've
got a kind heart, you're not unkind, like some people," he said, casting a glance towards Mamma as if
to ascertain the effect of his words, and whether
they had not gone too far. "You've never made me
miserable!"—then he began to sob. But when we
came to the railway track, where he asked me to
hold the kid for a minute, in his rage against her
he rushed ahead and sat himself down on the rail
where looking defiantly at us he remained. This was
an ungated crossing. A train might pass at any moment. Frantic with terror Mamma rushed after him;
but tug as she might, she could not detach him from
the rail, to which he clave with the unsurmisable
muscularity of a bottom on which, in happier days,
he was accustomed to slide all round the garden,
singing the while. She was pale with terror; luckily,
just then my father appeared, with two servants who
had come along in case they were needed. He hurried
forward, snatched up my brother, gave him a couple
of slaps, and ordered the kid to be taken back. Cowed,
my brother had to walk on, but he fixed a long glare of
concentrated fury at my father, and exclaimed: "I'll
never lend you my cart again." After that, realising
that no words could carry more sting than these, he
said no more. Mamma drew me aside, and said: "You
are older, so please do behave sensibly, don't look unhappy when I have to leave you. As it is, your father is
vexed that I'm going away, try to avoid making him
think that we are both of us insupportable." To show
myself worthy of the faith she placed in me, the task

she entrusted to me, I spoke no word of complaint. Waves of irresistible fury against her and my father, wild thoughts of making them miss the train, of frustrating the plot they had hatched to sever us, swept over me; they broke against my fear of grieving her, and I put a smiling face on my frozen misery.

We went back to have lunch. Because we were "going travelling" lunch was on the scale of dinner, with a main dish, a fowl, a salad, and pudding. Still brooding over his injuries, my brother ate in silence, sitting dumped on his high chair, an embodied woe. We talked of this and that; we had eaten our pudding, the meal was over, when there was a piercing cry: "Marcel had more chocolate shape than I did," he burst out. Only righteous indignation at such injustice could have made him forget the sorrow of being torn away from his kid. Yet, so my mother told me, he never again spoke about this friend whom the limitations of a flat in Paris had obliged him to leave behind in the country, and it is believed that he never thought of it again, either.

We set off for the station. Mamma had asked me not to go with her, but gave way before my entreaties. Since the evening before, she had seemed to admit that my sorrow was legitimate, to understand it, and only to ask of me that I should not make much of it. Once or twice as we were going along I was possessed by a sort of madness; I saw myself as persecuted by her and by my father who would not let me accompany her, I would have liked to avenge myself by making her miss the train, by preventing her from going, by setting fire to the house; but such thoughts lasted no longer than a moment. I startled her once by saying something rather unkind, but I quickly resumed my passionate gentleness towards her, and if I did not kiss her as much as I wanted to, it was to spare her feelings. When we came to the church we began to walk faster—that quickening march towards the thing we dread, one's feet going forward, one's heart in flight. . . . We turned another corner. "We shall be five minutes too early," my father said. Then the station came in sight. Mamma gave my hand a little squeeze to remind me that I must not give way. We went on to the platform, she got into her carriage and talked to us out of the window. We were told to stand back, as the train was due to leave. " 'In painful circumstances Regulus showed amazing fortitude,' " she said, and smiled at me. It was the smile she put on whenever she quoted anything she thought pedantic, and to be forearmed against being laughed at if she made mistakes. And she meant it, too, as a hint that I was making a mountain out of a molehill. But for all that, she felt my profound unhappiness, and when she said goodbye to us all she waited till my father had turned away, beckoned me back for an instant, and said, "We understand each other's feelings, don't we, my lamb? If my dear boy behaves sensibly, he will get a little letter from his Mamma tomorrow. *Sursum corda*," she added, with that guesswork air she kept for any Latin quotations, in order not to seem sure of them. The train went off and I stayed behind, but it was as though some part of me had gone too.

That was how I had seen [the belfry of Combray] when I came back from walks along the Guermantes Way with no hope that you would come and say goodnight to me in my bed; that was how I saw it when we had put you into the train and I knew that the town

where I must go on living was a town that held you no
longer. In just such a way, I felt that need to be close to
you, my precious Mamma, and to kiss you, which I had
felt in those days and could speak of to no one, and as
grown men are not so brave as children and life is less
merciless to them, I did what if I had dared I would
have done when you had left Combray: I took a train.
All the ways and means of departure jostled in my
mind: how to catch the train that same evening, the
objections I might perhaps have to overcome since my
hosts would not understand that I was wild to go, that
I was bent on getting to you as a stifling man is bent
on drawing breath. Mme. de Villeparisis, who had
sensed, without understanding why, that the view of
Chartres had upset me,[3] said nothing. I still had no
idea of what I ought to say to her. I did not want to
speak until I was sure of my ground, and knew the
time of the train, and had ordered the carriage, so
that no material obstacles could be put in my way. I
walked on beside her and we discussed plans for the
next day, though I knew well enough I should have no
part in them. At last we got back; I no longer saw the
village and the castle as something in my life but as in
a life that was already going on without me, like the
lives of those fellow-passengers who get out of the
train and go off to follow their country pursuits without us. I found an unimportant telegram from Montargis awaiting me. I said it was from you, that I must
go away, that you needed me on a matter of business.
Mme. de Villeparisis was very sorry and extremely kind,
took me to the station, made me those speeches that
the graces of a hostess and the traditions of hospitality
polish into a resemblance of concern and friendliness;
but later on in Paris she told me, truly or no: "I

didn't need to see your telegram. I told my husband so. On the way back, as we were walking along, you were different, and I thought at once, 'Here's a young man with something on his mind. He is talking about our plans for tomorrow, but he'll be on his way to Paris tonight.' "

Mamma said in a shaken voice: "My poor lamb, it grieves me to think that you were as unhappy as that when I left Combray. But we must learn to be more hard-hearted, my darling. What would you have done if I had gone away on a real journey?"

"I should have counted the hours."

"But suppose I had gone away for months, for years, for. . . ."

We both fell silent. There had never been any question between us of proving that each loved the other beyond anything else in the world; we had never doubted it. It was a question of mutually letting it be assumed that our loves were less than they seemed, and that whichever of us were left to live on alone would not find life unendurable. I felt I must put an end to this silence that was enforcing such anguish on my mother—an anguish that she must have known so often that now when I remember that she knew it in her dying hour, I turn for strength to the thought that it was no new thing to her. I took her hand, almost with composure, and said, kissing her: "You know, you've seen it for yourself, how wretched I am without you at first. And then, you know, my life shapes itself differently, and though I don't forget the people I love, I don't depend on them any more, I manage very well without them. For the first week, I am demented. After that, I can go on by myself for months, for years, for ever."

For ever, I said; but that same evening, arising out of something quite different, I told her that contrary to what I had previously believed, the latest scientific discoveries and the most advanced philosophic enquiries demolished materialism and made out death to be something merely phenomenal; that souls were immortal and eventually met again. . . .

16

The return to the present[1]

When I began to read an author I very soon caught the tune of the song beneath the words, which in each author is distinct from that of every other; and while I was reading, and without knowing what I was doing, I hummed it over, hurrying the words,[2] or slowing them down, or suspending them, in order to keep time with the rhythm of the notes, as one does in singing, where in compliance with the shape of the tune one often delays for a long time before coming to the last syllable of a word.

I knew quite well that, if never having been able to work I was no good as a writer, my ear for this sort of thing was sharper and truer than is common, which was what had enabled me to produce literary imitations; since when one picks up the tune the words soon follow. But I have not put this gift to use; and at different periods of my life I feel it, as likewise that other gift for discovering a profound affinity between two ideas or two feelings, still intermittently alive in me— but it is vacillating, and will soon dwindle and die out. For all that, it will die hard, because it is often when I am sickest, with neither strength nor an idea in my head left, that this intermittently acknowledged self perceives these affinities between two ideas, as often it is in autumn, when neither flower nor leaf is left, that one feels the deepest harmonies in a landscape. And this young man who thus plays among my ruins lives on air, the pleasure he draws from the sight of the idea he has discovered is all the food he needs, he creates the idea and is created by it, he dies, but an idea survives him—like those seeds which suspend the process of germination in too dry an atmosphere, and are lifeless; but a little moisture and warmth is enough to bring them back to life.

And I think the young man who amuses himself in me like this must be the same as he whose sharp true ear can likewise distinguish a subtle harmony that others are deaf to between two impressions or two ideas. Who this being is, I cannot say. But if in some way he creates these concords, he lives on them, he springs up there and then, he sprouts and waxes from whatever vital provision they may afford him, and then dies, unable to live except by their means. But however long he may lie (like M. Becquerel's grains of corn) in the ensuing slumber, he does not die, or rather he but dies in order to revive if another concord comes his way, even if in two pictures by the same artist he sees no more than a similar undulation of profile, or a similar piece of drapery, a similar chair, manifesting something in common between the two pictures: the artist's predilection and private mind. He cannot be fed by what there is in a picture by an artist, or a book by a writer, nor by a second picture by the artist, a second book by the writer. But if in the second picture or the second book he perceives something which is in neither the first nor the second but in some way exists between them, in a sort of ideal picture which he sees projecting itself in spiritual substantiality out of the picture, he has been given his meat, and begins to live and be happy again. Because to live and to be happy are one and the same for him. And if between this ideal picture and this ideal book, either of which is enough to make him happy, he finds an even more rarefied affinity, his joy grows the more.

Because he dies at once in what is particular, and immediately becomes buoyant and living again in what is universal. He can only live by the universal, it is life and meat to him and he dies at once in the particular. But while he is alive, his life is all rapture and felicity. He, and no other, should write my books. But would they be the better for it?

No matter if they should say: You're wasting your skill on this. What we are doing is making our way back to life, shattering with all our force the ice of the habitual and the rational which instantly congeals over reality and keeps us from ever seing it, is finding a passage back into the open sea. Why is reality brought back to us by this coincidence of two impressions? Perhaps because then it is resurrected along with what it *leaves out*, while if we apply our reason about it, or tax our memories, we add or take away.

Great literature is written in a sort of foreign tongue. To each sentence we each attach a meaning, or at any rate a mental image, which is often a mistranslation. But in great literature all our mistranslations result in beauty. When I read of the shepherd in *L'Ensorcelée*, I see a man like a figure by Mantegna with the colouring of Botticelli's T. . . . Perhaps this is not in the least what Barbey saw; but in Barbey's description there is a consort of statements, which, given the false premise of my mistranslation, leads to an equally beautiful shepherd.[3]

It would seem that the originality of a man of genius is no more than a flower-head, a blossoming crest superposed on a self similar to those of the merely clever men of his generation; but this same self exists, and this same mere cleverness, in the men of genius.

We think of Musset, Loti, Régnier, as belonging to a race apart; but when Musset vamps up an art criticism we are horrified to see Villemain's dreariest claptrap coming from his pen, we are aghast to find a Brisson in Régnier. When Loti has to compose an address for the Académie, or Musset to supply a hack article for some insignificant magazine without having had time to break the surface of his everyday self and release that other self which would emerge from it, we see that his thinking and his style are full [   ].

The part of us that comes into play when we are writing and making up as we go along is something so personal, so much a law to itself, that in the same generation minds of the same type, breeding, cultural background, creative intention, circle, walk of life, put pen to paper to describe the same thing in almost the same language, and each one of them adds the particular amplification which could proceed only from him and which turns the same thing into something quite new where all the relative merits of the others would be out of place. And the genus of writers of originality follows a corresponding course, each of them voicing a dominant note which is nevertheless by some fractional interval irreducibly distinct from the note that precedes it and the note that follows. Look at all our writers, one after the other; those of originality, that is, and the great writers of the past too, who were also originating writers, which for this purpose puts them on the same footing. See how close they are to each other, and how they differ. Follow them through, one beside another, as in a garland woven out of souls, made up of a myriad flowers, but all different—along one strand, Anatole France, Henri de Régnier, Boylesve, Francis Jammes, in the same stretch of garland, while in another you will see Barrès, and in another, Loti.

No doubt, when Régnier and France began to write, both of them had the same background, the same notion of art, the same artistic intention. And in those pictures they tried to paint, they had almost the same idea about the reality of what they were painting; for France, life is an illusion about an illusion, for Régnier, all things are coloured by our dreams. But from the outset, Régnier's meticulous and searching mind is more harassed by the obligation to examine this analogy between thoughts and things, and to show how they concur; his thinking permeates his writing, his sentences elongate, twist, sharpen to a point, are dark and detailed like a columbine, while those of Anatole France are smooth, shining and expanded, like the petals of a damask rose.

And because this true reality is subjective and can be won from a commonplace impression, a frivolous or worldly one even, if it has gone deep enough and discarded these associations—for that reason I make no distinction between High Art, which deals only with love and lofty conceptions, befitting a saint or a scholar rather than a man of the world, and the art which has no morality or purpose about it. Besides, in everything having to do with character, emotions, reactions, there is no call to distinguish. Character, like lungs or bones, is the same in both cases, just as it makes no matter to the physiologist whether the organs he uses for demonstrating the principle of the circulation of the blood were taken from the body of an artist or a shop-keeper. If we have to deal with a true artist, one who has

broken through the surface and made his way into the
underlying truth of life, then, perhaps, as a work of
art is involved, we favour the book that raises questions of wider import.[4] But first, there must be depth,
the book must have come from that region of the inner
life where the creation of works of art becomes possible. Now, when we find an author who, page after
page, through every event that happens to his hero,
never goes below the surface, never thinks it out in
terms of his own heart, but avails himself of the ready-
made phrases which whatever we take at second-hand
—and from such hands!—will prompt us to when we
want to talk about a thing, if we do not go down into
that deep inner quietude where thought chooses the
words which will completely reflect it; an author who
does not look at what he, himself, thinks—at that time,
imperceptible to him—but rests content with the
coarse veil of appearances which disguises our thoughts
from us at every turn, and which the mob in perpetual ignorance remains content with, and the writer,
trying to see what lies behind it, thrusts aside; when
the choice—or rather, the total absence of choice—of
wording and phraseology, the hackneyed flatness of all
his similes, the superficial rendering of every incident,
makes us feel that such a book, even if on every page it
pours scorn on affected art, immoral art, materialistic
art, is itself far more materialistic, since it has not
come even from that region of the inner life out of
which have come writings, limited, may be, to describing the material world, but doing it with a talent
which irrefutably proves them born of the spirit. It is
waste of breath for him to tell us that the other art is
an art for the few, not for the many; we shall go on
thinking that the boot is on the other leg, since there

is only one way of writing for the many, and that is to
write without respect of persons and for the sake of
what is deep and essential in oneself; whereas he
writes with his mind's eye dwelling on the few, on
those so-called "mannered" writers, and not with any
attempt to see where they go wrong, or to get down to
discovering what is permanent in the impression they
give him, a permanence as implicitly contained in
that impression as in a whiff of hawthorn-scent, or
anything else that one knows how to explore, but here,
as in everything else, ignoring his genuine reactions,
and contenting himself with hackneyed formulae and
his ill-humour, without trying to get down to the
truth. "*Canti fermi alla capella*, get out with you! Cassock or no cassock, what difference does it make? It's
revolting, such women ought to be thrashed. So then,
the sun never shines in France. So then, you can't compose light opera. You must needs dirty everything, etc."
This dishonesty and superficiality is to some extent
enforced on him, moreover, since his chosen hero is a
cross-grained genius whose dreadfully trite tirades get
on one's nerves, but might be met with in a man of
genius. Unfortunately, when Jean-Christophe—for it
is he I speak of—leaves off talking, M. Romain Rolland goes on heaping twaddle on twaddle; and when
he tries for some more arresting figure of speech, it is
never a happy stroke, but a studied contrivance, which
of all living authors he is worst at. His belfries like
great arms are worse than anything that M. Renard,
or M. Adam, or possibly even M. Leblond, could
have hit on.

Besides, this art, eminently superficial, eminently
insincere, eminently materialistic (even though it
deals with things of the spirit, since the only means by

which these can enter a book is that not the subject but the approach to it should be spiritual: there is more of the spirit in Balzac's *Curé de Tours* than in his portrait of the artist Steinbock), is also eminently worldly. For it is only the people who have no conception of what is profound and who, with platitudes, fallacies, monstrosities, continually before their eyes, don't notice them, but bawl out praises of profundity, and say: "Ah! Now that book goes deep!"—just as when someone says all the time, "Yes, I'm one for speaking out, I never mince my words, all these clever folk are flatterers, but I'm a John Blunt," and takes in people who know no better, a fastidious man knows that these assertions have nothing to do with the honest truth of the artist. As with morality, one cannot take the word for the deed. At bottom, all my philosophy, like all true philosophy, comes back to vindicating and re-establishing the actual. (In morality, in art, one does not only judge a picture by its claims to be High Art, or a man's moral worth by the speeches he makes.)

The artist's good sense, the only criterion of a work of art's spirituality, is talent.

Talent is the criterion of originality, originality is the criterion of sincerity, pleasure (the pleasure of the writer) is perhaps the criterion of true talent.

It is almost as stupid to say in speaking of a book, "It is very clever," as, "He was very fond of his mother." But the former still remains to be brought to light.

Books are the work of solitude and the *children of silence*. The children of silence should have no portion with the children of the word—thoughts that owe their being to a wish to say something, to a disapproval, or an opinion; that is, to an obscure idea. The stuff of our books, the substance of our sentences, should be drawn from our imaginations, not taken just as it comes from real life; but our actual style, and the episodes too, should be made out of the transparent substance of our best moments, those in which we transcend reality and the present. It is from those consolidated drops of light that the style and the story of a book are made.

Moreover, it is just as futile to write expressly for the working class as for children. It is not nursery books that children grow by. Why suppose that unless you write badly and talk about the French Revolution an electrician can't understand you? For one thing, it's just the other way round. As Parisians like to read about voyages in the Pacific and the wealthy like to read life-stories of Russian miners, so the working class likes to read about things that have no bearing on their lives. And further, why put up this barrier? A workman (see Halévy) can be a confirmed reader of Baudelaire.

That ill-temper which refuses to see itself for what it is (and which in the world of art is the counterpart of the man who tries to scrape acquaintance with some one, and having met with a snub, says, "What's the fellow to me? Why should I want to know him, I think he's revolting") is, on a much coarser scale, what I complain of in Sainte-Beuve; it is (for all that the author talks of Ideals, etc.) a materialistic criticism—sayings that roll off the tongue, and gratify pursed lips, raised eyebrows, shrugging shoulders, and whose adverse current daunts the mind from exploring furthur. But Sainte-Beuve, for all his faults, was a much better thinker, he proves it by being a much better writer.

The neo-classic style is made up of a great many insincerities, one of which is the assumption that the magic of the old masters can be assimilated by making use of their turns of speech, turns of speech that can do wonders in a fake, but which these old masters themselves were quite unaware of, since to them their style did not sound antique. There is a contemporary poet who believes that the music of Virgil and Ronsard is reborn on his lips because, like Ronsard, he calls Virgil "the learnèd Mantuan." His *Ériphyle* is graceful, since he was one of the first to realise that charm must have existed at all periods; his heroine has the engaging lisp of a girl-wife: "My husband, he was a hero, but his chin was prickly," and at the end she tosses her head in a pet like a little mare (the author having noted perhaps how Renaissance and seventeenth-century narratives are spiced by their involuntary anachronisms). Her lover addresses her as "Noble Lady" (the sect of Seekers after Grace, a gentleman of the Peloponnesus). He links up with the school of (Boulanger?)—and Barrès—the school of the implied statement—in his use of the indicative word. This is the exact opposite to Romain Rolland. But it is no more than a good quality, and this does not prevail against the basic nullity and absence of anything to say. His well-known *Stances* are only saved because the incompleteness, the effect of panting out commonplaces, is deliberate, and as this would otherwise be involuntary, the poet's failing abets his purpose. But as soon as he forgets himself and wants to say something, as soon as he opens his lips, he writes things like this:

> Do not say, life is a joyous banquet; it is
> A dullard mind or grovelling soul says so.
> Above all, do not say, life is woe unending;
> So says a coward heart, and one too quick to tire.
>
> Laugh as the reeds quiver in the winds of April,
> Lament like the north wind or the waves on the beach,
> Taste every pleasure, suffer every ill,
> And say, 'tis much, for 'tis the shadow of a dream.[5]

Since, like the compass needle or like carrier pigeons, we have an inner sense of our direction, we cannot take writers we admire as guides. But while directed by that inner sense we fly straight onward and follow our course, if we cast a momentary glance to left or right on a new book by Francis Jammes or Maeterlinck, or on a page of Emerson or Joubert that we have not read before, the reminiscences we are already expecting to find there of just such thoughts, impressions, artistic problems, as we are then engaged with, are as welcome as if they were friendly signposts showing us we are not out of our way; or while we rest for a minute in a wood, the nearby whirr of wings as our fellow pigeons who have not seen us go over in full flight puts new heart into us for our journey. Superfluous, I daresay; but not altogether useless. Such things show us that what [is valid for] that admittedly rather subjective self, the self busied in creation, extends, with a more generalized validity to selves of the same nature, and to that more objective self, the cultural group we belong to when we read; is valid not only for our private world but for our universal world. . . .

The fine things we shall write if we have talent enough, are within us, dimly, like the remembrance of a tune which charms us though we cannot recall its outline, or hum it, nor even sketch its metrical form, say if there are pauses in it, or runs of rapid notes. Those who are haunted by this confused remembrance of truths they have never known are the men who are gifted; but if they never go beyond saying that they can hear a ravishing tune, they convey nothing to others, they are without talent. Talent is like a kind of memory, which in the end enables them to call back this confused music, to hear it distinctly, to write it down, to reproduce it, to sing it. There comes a time in life when talent, like memory, fails, and the muscle in the mind which brings inward memories before one like memories of the outer world, loses its power. Sometimes, from lack of exercise or because of a too ready self-approval, this time of life extends over a whole lifetime; and no one, not your own self even, will ever know the tune that beset you with its intangible delightful rhythm.

MISCELLANEOUS
Writings

PROUST THE CRITIC

1

Against *the young writers of the day*[1]

The electorate of the rising generation is neither much more intelligent nor much less venal than that of the present. So it is quite natural to see a number of writers not only flattering the young as if they were voters, but even canvassing them with programmes cleverly rehashed to fall in with their tastes. Like the Republic, symbolism still has its opportunist adherents, who would as willingly adhere to anything else rather than submit to being neither re-elected nor re-read. Far from claiming to become our teachers on the grounds of being our elders, they assert that they must learn from us, and pass off their hatred of us as successors by exclaiming over us like courtiers. But these practices are confined to writers whose conception of art is so temporal, who are so artlessly sure that its kingdom is of this world, that we can only half sigh for the lessons they don't give us. There are some, more's the pity, who behave in the same way from higher motives, and instead of talking to the young listen to them, feeling certain—certainty is the word they use for the most arbitrary of hopes—that the words they wish to hear will be forthcoming, and meanwhile leave off giving us the teaching we have a right to expect from them.

But there is one thing even stranger: that although this has been going on for several years, not one young man has so far had the courage to say: "We have nothing to say, because we find nothing to think about. There has never been such a cheating younger generation as ours. And if we seem exceptionally full of

promise, it is as infant prodigies do, and such promises will not be kept. If, as everyone goes on saying,
there has never been so much talent, that is because
there are certain graces of style which are contagious,
and because a journalist with a little aptitude for it
can learn his trade in a few years, just as a harlot learns
hers. You are old enough to be through with her. How
much longer are you going to be fooled by the others?"
And he could have supplied some arguments in support of this. Never has there been such a knock-kneed
sense of duty, nor such a total contempt for tradition.
Giving no thought to things of the spirit, not working,
reading nothing but the current short stories, the
clever young men study for their semi-finals under
Mendès or Moréas, and take on a polish as superficial
as the classical polish that used to be given to schoolboys and now deceives no one. Will the fashion for
prize pupils in contemporary literature last much
longer? It would be a great pity.

2

On taste[1]

There are people for whom it is enough to enjoy the books that please them, as they enjoy flowers, fine days, or women. Others, tormented by an inordinate regard for truth, spoil their pleasure by wanting to make sure of its depth and justification. They are forever asking themselves: Is it really my mind which is so delighted by this book, or just my taste for what is in fashion, the copy-cat instinct which makes for so much unanimity in the tastes of a generation, or some other contemptible preference? So, driven by the pitiless wind of anxiety, they are tossed from one book to another, unable either to fasten on a blameless happiness or to enjoy it. Yet one day they seem to have found their anchorage, a happy haven where they see unwavering reflections of beauty on every side. Flaubert, or Leconte de Lisle, has brought them to this serene country, and the beauty it shows them is so manifest, and its origins are so patent, that sure at last of being in the presence of true beauty, they settle down to enjoy themselves. Then a doubt visits them, arising doubtless from the pale memory of true beauty, gazed at perhaps before soul put on body: true beauty could not be so outward, one ought to sense it and love it through an infinity of shadows, like a soul, rather than grasp it as matter—so directly, so perfectly, that one could indeed make tantamount counterfeits of it. And once again, the savage wind of anxiety has brushed them with its unpitying wing. The haven no longer complies with the demands of their dream of blest repose, they leave it, and resume their journey, they grope painfully on in quest of beauty, the mock of those who enjoy books as they enjoy flowers, fine days, women, and call these anxious migrants lunatics and neurotics. A neurosis that packs off all the poets and novelists as so many cheats and honey-tongued poisoners, an anxiety quite as taxing as a high fever to these souls athirst for what heaven alone, perhaps, can grant, for what here below only artless simple-mindedness can lend.

3

A history of French satire[1]

The French spirit being by nature and definition academic, flippant, ironical, and sharp-tongued, its history lies almost entirely in the history of French satire. So for a moment, seeing in the genius of our race only what those who write text-books and give lectures see in it—a genius for flippant perspicacity and bantering wit—let us examine how satire has always been its mouthpiece, and complied with changes, if not in that mocking genius, at any rate in the conditions which transformed its method of practice and scope of expression. To study the history of satire in this light could not be misleading; for if the French spirit is something other than the spirit of the satirists or even the spirit of the euphuist—for all that M. Gustave Larroumet may have said of it recently—that spirit certainly has its part in the French genius; though that genius may have other facets, even a great many others, it is certainly one of them. It is even a considerable factor of the French genius, and if the textbook definition which makes so much of it has become trite, that is apparently because it was true. Besides, this spirit of satire was present almost from the inception of our literature, of that genuinely French literature, at least, which had cut free from the Latin model; and today, in a literature Byzantinised by artful decadents and "euphuistic barbarians"—as M. Jules Lemaître calls them—it is still highly tenacious in the novel, in verse, and in journalism. This very persistence of the satiric spirit in France would make a history of French satire very lengthy. One can however, while not sketch-

ing it in broad outline, very quickly give an idea of it
at some of its most curious epochs.

One must begin by shelving two periods which
just because they are very interesting would take too
long to investigate: the present day and the Middle
Ages. To begin with contemporary writers—one likes
them too much and knows them too well not to give
more prominence to them than to the old masters, of
whom only a few have withstood the hand of time. It
is obvious, for instance, that in a very brief survey
where there would be little more than a mention of
Gringoire,[2] M. Jacques Normand's *Les Moineaux* could
not be included, nor even M. Dionys Ordinaire's *Les
Repues franches*. Apart from being on friendly terms
with one's contemporaries, friendly terms which make
it awkward to leave many real literary friends out of a
book, in decadent epochs one chooses badly and un-
easily. For one thing, extreme technical dexterity is so
general that one deludes oneself about the artist; and to
tell the truth, the most mediocre Parnassian, the most
mediocre Symbolist even, puts a sonnet together better than the great Corneille. For another, the vast
quantity of ideas, acquired, renovated, or even past
mark of mouth, and the plethora of "conscious styl-
ists," makes a just assessment almost out of the question. With the Middle Ages, it is otherwise; the labour would be light, the forest is still bushy, even
though time has thinned it, and one could gather a
full measure of fruit and flowers. But it would take
too long; besides, the journey from Régnier to Gilbert[3] is quite far enough to make it possible to describe French satire from notes taken on the way.

A very remarkable thing about satire in the Middle

Ages had been that it was at once moral, social, and political; and above all that the author had been so placed that his work is neither that of a noble, nor a commoner, nor a churchman, but that of a being apart, who cannot be grouped with the Troubador or the household Jester. In a word (at least this is what one gathers from reading various excerpts habitually cited), the Man of Letters, that person who has afforded a subject for so much bitter invective to one of our critics, existed in the Middle Ages. But this Man of Letters was not in the least like Chrysale's ["Monsieur Trissotin, forever talking poetry and Latin"] of the seventeenth century, that light of the drawing-room, nor the nineteenth-century man-of-fashion and ape of Baudelaire, that light of the boudoir. He was a man of no fixed abode, and above all no exponent of the art for art's sake doctrine of Voiture or Gautier. His concern was society, which on his poetical rounds he saw in its many-sidedness. While he kept a lord amused by skits of peasants drawn from life, he was carefully studying the lord and his household, and laughing at them behind his sleeve. One day or another he would read out a new satire in a village, and it would be the serfs who laughed at the lord. Thus, brisk and clear and lively as a running brook, carrying a drift of moral saws and witty sayings, its chattering waters a bond rather than a division between every region and every bank, satire flows in France from the thirteenth to the sixteenth century, enlarging little by little; and after its beginning as a trickle—this is the age of morality plays, bestiaries, and scolding apologues—it grows and swells until with d'Aubigné and Régnier it sweeps away all obstacles of decorum and timidity. Deep and chiding, it will seize on every vice, swallow up every social iniquity.

The seventeenth century will set itself to embank this headlong river and cleanse its waters, mighty in flow but laden with shingle and stained with yellow sand. Majestic but abated, satire will flow smoothly on its slow course between two stone walls. But this freeborn native child of France cannot be taught to chasten its frolics and laughter. Its nature is to respect nothing and laugh at everything. In the seventeenth century it revenges itself on restrictions and etiquette by backstairs giggles and organ-loft jokes. By the eighteenth century it has been embittered by enforced silence. It burns and ravages the narrow domain that is left open to it. Since Gilbert may only write about writers, instead of making game of them he thwacks and beats them. But presently satire sees too plainly all that society has lost since its ringing laughter, that alarum bell, has been silenced. It dares to expostulate. Then Chénier's *Iambes* are published. Henceforward, it will again attack society and government; it will no longer shut itself up for dead in books, it will come back to life, the authentic French satire; it will shake off the long torpor in which it has lain since Régnier. It begins to dart its "rankling" arrows all around. But now it is not content with rhyming on paper. From time to time during its two centuries of bondage it had turned its fancy towards the stage or the novel. Now it means to take possession of them. Beaumarchais did but inaugurate what the author of *Le Demi-Monde* calls *plays with a purpose*. Voltaire's novels are only the first of the satiric novels. Squibs and pamphlets give way to the daily column in various newspapers where the old satire is paid out in new coin. Finally, during the great period from 1800 to 1850, the lash of satire is for any hand that can wield it.

But nowadays, above all since Renan became fashionable in a society which an exceedingly scrupulous critic has called soft and crumbled, we are too detached to labour at destroying abuses or chastising vices. We can barely point out absurdities. The old French merriment survives as an appanage of the farcical stage, *La Vie parisienne*, and subversive newspapers. But this does not hinder the gentlemen of the Académie Française from periodically defining the French spirit as "a mordant spirit, shrewd and bantering," nor M. Sarcey from saying once a month that it is "light as the foam which tops a glass of champagne."

4

A *Sunday concert at the Conservatoire*[1]

At the Conservatoire concert yesterday, the pianist in the Mozart concerto was Saint-Saëns. Coming away, one met many people who had been disappointed and who, not knowing why this was so, gave different reasons for it; he had played too fast, he had played without expression, the music hadn't suited him. Well, here is the reason: it was because it had been truly beautiful. For true beauty is the only thing that cannot respond to what a romantic imagination anticipates. Everything else lives up to those preconceived ideas: dexterity is amazing, vulgarity, soothing, sensuousness, thrilling, claptrap, dazzling. But beauty which from the beginning of all things has been joined to truth in an eternal friendship has not got all these charms at its disposal. What disappointments it has given rise to since it came among men! A woman goes to look at a masterpiece feeling as thrilled as if she were reading the last instalment of a serial, or consulting a fortune-teller, or expecting her lover. Then she sees a man sitting near the window of a rather dusky room, deep in thought. She waits for a minute or two, as before a peepshow, to see if anything more is going to come out. And if hypocrisy seals her lips, in the depths of her heart she says: "What, is Rembrandt's *Philosopher* no more than that?"

In Saint-Saëns' playing there were no *pianissimos* where you feel you'll faint if they go on any longer, and which are cut off just in the nick of time by a *forte*, no broken chords sending instantaneous shivers

down your back, none of those *fortissimos* which
leave you bruised from head to foot, as if you had been
surf-bathing, none of those pianist's writhings and
tossed back locks of hair, which infect the purity of
music with the sensuality of the dance, which appeal
to the listener's senses, to her idle fancies, and supply
her with an element of pleasure, and a reason for enthusiasm, the framework of what she will remember
and the substance of what she will afterwards talk
about. There was none of this in Saint-Saëns' playing.
But his playing was regal. Now kings do not make
their appearance wearing golden crowns and being
carried in palanquins on slaves' shoulders. It is by
the way they bow, smile, hold out a hand, offer a chair,
ask a question, or reply, that great kings, like great
actors, can be recognised. It is the parvenu who is
stuck up, the charlatan who shows off. But the king's
grace and nobility are so natural to him that his nobility is no more astonishing to us than the nobility of
an oak-tree nor his grace than the grace of a rose-
wand. Every mannerism, over-emphatic or vulgar,
spontaneous or cultivated, [is eschewed]², and carriage and gestures are so stripped of all pomp and
formality that only simplicity remains. A great actor's
playing is barer than a clever actor's, and thus affords
less scope for the crowd's admiration, for the way he
speaks and moves is so scrupulously decanted from any
sediment, be it gold-dust or dross, that it seems clear
as water, like a window-pane which shows one nothing
but the natural objects beyond it. To this purity and
transparency Saint-Saëns' playing has attained. One
does not see Mozart's concerto through a stained glass
window or behind footlights, but as if through an air

interposed between us and our table, between us and our friend—so pure, that we do not even notice it.

That he should succeed in this is not of course surprising; for someone who has composed the finest symphony since Beethoven's, and so many operas, it was a small matter, a diversion, to play a Mozart concerto. But on those grounds, it seemed a great matter, too. For we do not think of human actions as being like violet blossoms which, once withered, are of no further use to the little plant, and do not make the other flowers open more beautifully, nor delay their fall. But rather we think of them in terms of branches yearly put out by trees, which even though subject to decay, hoist the future branches that much higher from the ground, so that the tree grows by the successive height of its branches; or again, in terms of the little white teeth of young horses which, as they come into place side by side in those large mouths, form a sure indication to the breeder of the animal's age and vigour. In such a way do we think of men's actions. And the slightest of them, like the newest, tenderest spike of chestnut-blossom, poised on the total stature of more ancient branches, is sensible of previous actions which, as if they were ancestors and respected old guarantors, now lend it the moral effect of their height and the support of their strength. Thus, when Saint-Saëns sat down, like a young student of the Conservatoire, to play a Mozart concerto, and played it so simply, there was not one single stroke of genius in the C Minor Symphony, not one of the sad strains in *Henri VIII*, not one of the lovely choruses in *Samson et Dalila*, not one of the richly inventive Bach transcriptions, which was not there, surrounding the mu-

sician with a choir as impressive as the choir of the
Muses, smiling on the genius which they maintained,
like a sacred fire, in his soul, and diffusing enchantment and enthusiasm and respect through ours.

5

Patriotism and the Christian Spirit[1]

To what intellectual guidance dare we commit ourselves? At the present day, the mind with the greatest aptitude for truth, the will with the strongest bent towards good, is probably Tolstoi's. In a world of lies and wickedness, he reacts as sharply as Socrates could have done. And now, in *Patriotism and the Christian Spirit*, the book he has written as a counterblast to the Franco-Russian celebrations, he sets himself to do away with the idea of love of country. Patriotism is absurd, he says, and self-contradictory, since to a German it means, "Germany is the finest country," to an Italian, "Italy is the finest country," etc. Then must we also dismiss the love of family, since it reposes on every son's preference for his father and mother? "Besides," adds Tolstoi, "patriotism, which governments artificially work up, leaves the masses unmoved, while socialism, which governments repress, daily appeals to them more strongly. A Russian peasant will choose to go and live in no matter what country, if wages are higher, etc." If this unhappily were true, it would only prove that concern for self tends to predominate over concern for others. How can Tolstoi find this a matter for rejoicing, how can he willingly attempt to dry up a fountain-head of disinterested feeling—and today, at least, patriotism is that—without being sure of causing another such to spring from the rock when he smites it? If socialism involves a predominance of altruistic over egoistic instincts in those of the moneyed classes who adhere to it of their own free will, among the poor on the other hand it marks a predominance of egoistic instincts over altruistic; but patriotism, in both the one and the other, subordinates egoistic instincts to altruistic.

In short, what angers Tolstoi most in warfare is that combatants to the death feel no hatred for each other. Is it not exactly because of this that war retains a certain moral character? It is not to glut a base appetite that a whole nation takes up arms, it is "for duty's sake." Besides, when war is over, there is often no hatred between officers on either side.

In the world of matter and material forces one can destroy in order to create, make use of evil, avail oneself of opposites, subordinate the means to the end. It is not so in the world of Justice and Love. Anarchists who fancy that after conquering the world by injustice they will establish the rule of Justice in it, who propose to enthrone Charity on violence, misunderstand what the words justice and charity mean, and the nature of those virtues. Force may bring about an equal distribution of private fortunes; never will Justice have been further from ruling the world. By practicing violence, slander, and ostracism, anti-semites may forcibly convert the whole world to Catholicism; on that day the whole world will be dechristianised, since Christianity means the indwelling God, a truth sought by the heart and assented to by the conscience. Let us never subordinate to a duty which is abstruse, remote, and uncertain, an explicit and immediate duty to deal justly and to love mercy.

6

On La Bonne Hélène[1]

I would like to pick a bone with M. Lemaître about the last scene of *La Bonne Hélène;* that done, I will praise the whole play.

In this otherwise flawless scene, Venus blames Paris for being jealous over his wife.

> *The eyes that she has charmed, do they steal light from*
> *   hers?*
> *Not so; a single flame will light a hundred fires*
> *And never be the less for it.*[2]

Then, playing like a goddess or like a critic with ideas and epochs, she defines another kind of love:

> *Which is like very hate.*
> *These would be singly loved, these would against life's*
> *   grain*
> *Be all the bliss, and if they fail in that, why, then*
> *Be all the woe of those they love.*[3]

(To appreciate the dexterity and reverence of this quotation from La Bruyère,[4] one has but to remember how clumsy the greatest poets have been in versifying interpolations from prose, believing, for instance, that they quote the Gospel in saying, one:

> *Suffer all those little ones to come before me;*

another,

> *Suffer the little babes to come before me;*

and a third,

> *Suffer these flaxen heads to come before me.*)[5]

But, adds Venus, it is not I who inspire that love:

Eros is grave and sad, he seeks I know not what
Out of this world. But I, I have a simple heart,
That knows naught of melancholy.[6]

Nothing could be more charming than this comparison of the yearning, dreaming, grieving love, Christian love, romantic love, love as it is today, with the love that is bounded by the senses; and nothing could be truer, were it not that jealousy is presented as a derivative, as deriving from the love which Venus disowns, as a pain the soul subjoins to bodily pleasure, as the sombre, blood-red flowering of the imaginative faculty.

Of course, our imaginations can work on jealousy, just as much as on any form of human suffering, and make the greatest but also the most straightforward of our afflictions as cunning and studied as a torture. But jealousy is not born of the imagination, or of melancholy, or of the mind. Jealousy is born of the body. Jealousy is pleasure's unacknowledged daughter, made in her image and to extort her dues, who resembles her in that intense thirst which nothing can appease. One is not jealous—to use the word in its strict and terrible sense—of the happiness, but of the pleasure of the women one loves, the pleasure she gives and the pleasure she takes. Jealousy was born long before intelligence; so they have never met, and intelligence can offer it no sort of consolation. The mind is weaponless in the face of jealousy as it is in the face of sickness or of death.

As is obvious, my objection is in no way a criticism, and has not the slightest bearing on the beauty of this scene—which my quotations have perhaps given some hint of—but is an idea which anyhow is very interesting and might—how mistaken I am, no doubt—be true. The whole play is handled with a control of fantasy, an absence of fuss in the lamination of several genres, a coalescence in the mixture of styles, which recalls the author of our only Racinean comedies. If the subject comes so home to us, it is because it is in the main, the power of Helen's beauty. In aligning Helen with our most harmless-hearted and most dangerous ladies of pleasure, M. Lemaître makes over to Helen's beauty—which is the further enhanced thereby —that mysterious power he denies to her abased character. And the more we are shown that she was not Helen the Good, the better we understand the extent to which she must have been Helen the Beautiful. Now if anything wields a sway over our souls comparable to the sight of beauty itself, it is to learn, by such an example as Helen, that they are at the mercy of beauty, of the dread power of its sweetness. When we read of the old men whose sons for the last ten years had gone to death for the sake of a woman whom they did not know:

And seeing Helen walk upon the walls of Troy,[7]

did not think themselves used unjustly:

If for even beauty 'tis we bear such hardship
One single glance of hers outweighs our total woe,[8]

we are as much moved as we would have been by seeing Helen herself. A beauty there is that we have never seen but whose sway we acknowledge from knowing the universal sovereignty of its charm. We know it, if to love it already is to know it. And never, be it the beauty of a work of art or of a woman, do we set eyes on it for the first time. Thus the power that the living Helen drew from her beauty survived her life and her beauty. Historians account for this by saying that the Greeks were an artistic race; I would rather say that the human race is beauty-loving. We experience no more than its sweetness. The Ancients could not have said as much. Three or four hundred years after Homer, the poet Stesichorus was struck blind for having spoken ill of Helen. But more quick-witted than Homer, he immediately guessed the reason for his misfortune and wrote a poem which begins: *No, thou didst not sail away with the many-decked ships. No, thou wast never in Troy. After all, the truth lies rather in the contrary of what I have said.* (Certain Monday articles in the *Journal des Débats* end no otherwise than this poem begins.) And we may suppose that Stesichorus, who also wrote his *Bonne Hélène* was, with a lesser brilliance, in other genres, and in a much smaller way, something like the Jules Lemaître of Antiquity.

Portrait of a writer[1]

In the case of some exceptional writers, the outer man, no less than the mind, has the mould of beauty, and we come to think of it as offering another and not the least self-expressive of their works to our speculations. These call out the painter's best as they do the critic's, and their portraits—be it a portrait of M. de Goncourt by Bracquemond, or of M. de Montesquiou by Whistler—unlike portraits of other literary men, do not exclusively conform to the expectations of the public, which yearly perambulates round the exhibitions, its nameless aspirations toward the wonderful equally appeased by the plumpness of a novelist or the bald head of a man who writes for the papers. Nothing remains to be said about M. Daudet the writer; it is M. Daudet the work of art I would like to talk about today.

If it is true that in every other case, force of feeling or power of expression has blurred the purity of the modelling, as the process of casting a medal effaces that of the effigy, then it is a work of art that is unique. In M. Daudet's face, intense suffering has not impaired a perfect beauty. That forehead, where the hair is parted as if in two strong buoyant wings, is not only glorious with martyrdom. It is the forehead of a god or a king. For kingly charm, sovereign ease of limb and posture, visible nobility, do not only exist in the fancy of snobs or in penny novelettes. Less physical than beauty, less spiritual than nobility of mind and character, one might call it the habit of that nobility, a nobility that has become second nature,

and been translated into the beautiful lines of face
and limb, the ample simple movements of the nobility which has taken flesh. (Only where the snobs go
wrong is that they look for it on the throne, where it
is seldom found.) In this sense, M. Daudet is a king, a
King of the Moors, with a thin alert face, like a Dam-
ascene blade. I know how to recognise in king or
pretender alike the true regal grace. King Charles I
has it in Van Dyke's portrait, and so has Prince Hamlet
in Mounet-Sully's acting.

But if I have momentarily allowed myself to think
of M. Daudet as a spectacle, it is so that I may be in a
position to say freely what a splendid, uplifting spectacle he is. When I was first introduced to M. Daudet,
I scarcely dared look him in the face. I knew that for
the last ten years he had suffered so appallingly that
he had to inject himself with morphia several times a
day. Almost as soon as he got into bed this anguish
became unbearable, and every evening he drained a
bottle of chloral in order to fall sleep. I could not understand how, nevertheless, he went on writing. Most
of all, I remembered to what extent bodily pain, so
slight compared to his that no doubt he would have
enjoyed it as a respite, had made me deaf and blind
to other people, to life, to everything except my
wretched body, towards which my mind was stub-
bornly directed, as a sick man lies in bed with his face
turned to the wall; and unable to comprehend how he
could have withstood these daily onslaughts of pain, I
felt that the sight of me must be a burden to him, my
good health, an affront, my mere existence, an impertinence. And then I saw something so sublime that it
ought to make us blush, cowards that we all are, or
rather—like the words of Him from whom we learned

that we were not sick men and bondsmen, but spirits and kings—ought to make us, arthritic or palsied, rise up, quiet us, a-fevered, dedicate us, egoists, to others, restore us, one and all enslaved to the pleasures or the pains of the flesh, to our right minds; I saw this beautiful sick man, whom sickness made yet more beautiful, this poet, in whose proximity suffering became poetry as iron melts and flows in the furnace, who, self-forgetful and out-going, his thoughts engaged on my future and the future of other friends, smiled on us who extolled happiness and the love of life, which he put to better use than how many of us did, continuing to think, and compose, and dictate, and write, as ardent for truth and beauty and bravery as a young man—saw him unflaggingly talking to us and, more heroically yet, listening to us. In the middle of a discussion he went out for a moment, and interjected some remarks, all fire and ardour, from beyond the doorway. Re-entering, he fanned the discussion with as much spirit as before. I knew that his pain had returned so violently that in order to show no sign of it he had gone to give himself a morphia injection. His forehead glittered with beads of sweat. He seemed to emerge from a struggle, but the serenity of victory breathed from him. On that beautiful forehead, in those eyes where, as in Hugo's beautiful line:

The persisting blaze of youth was light already,

I saw the combat of light and intellect and the Sungod with the treacherous spirits of darkness. Apollo had triumphed, slowly driving them back into their dusky kingdom.

During this last twelvemonth, M. Daudet has been getting better. After a journey, a final act of heroism which seemed bound to cost him his life, life came back to him. Physically, his condition was hopeless. Well, then—with the whole force of that energy which had faced the enemy in the Franco-Prussian War, and which must have increased a hundred-fold during that silent, terrifying combat, chair-bound or bedridden, against the foe, it is his soul which has won back life and hope.

M. Daudet is getting better. It is a sentence that no one can hear without a thrill, like every sentence which, awakening in us mysterious recollections of pre-existence, subjects the iron law of physical determinism to the shining law of the soul's omnipotence. That is why I often go—and I think every one would gain joy and spiritual profit from often going to the Rue de Bellechasse—as a pilgrim to that frail, glorious work of art which is M. Daudet, where Nature, in a language that is expressive and living after another fashion than ours, through eyes clearer than our style and deeper than our thoughts, through a complexion more finely coloured than our imagery, and with the stern vocabulary of muscles creased by suffering and controlled by energy of mind, exalts us with the whole meaning of pain, and beauty, and omnipotent will and spirit.

8

Poet and novelist[1]

The poet's life has its small events like the lives of other men. He goes to the country. He travels. But the name of the town where he spent a summer, written at the foot of the last page of a book, with the date, tells us that the life he shares with other men serves him for quite another purpose, and if, as sometimes happens, this name of a town, establishing at the *Finis* where and when the book was written, should be the very name of the town where the novel is set, the whole novel affects us like a sort of immense extension fitting into real life; and we understand that for the poet real life was something totally unlike the real life of others, something holding the precious vein he was in search of, and not yielding it up for the asking.

It comes rarely, that state of mind when under a sort of enchantment, he finds in everything as if for the asking, the precious vein it conceals. Hence, the debatings, the struggles to remount his winged steed, the recourse to reading, to wine, to love affairs, to travel, to revisiting old haunts. Hence, the projects that are broken off, taken up again, continually recommenced, sometimes, like Goethe's *Faust*, completed sixty years later, sometimes left unfinished and without inspiration having entered into them, so that a Mallarmé who for ten years had wrestled with a huge work, clear-sighted in the hour of death like Don Quixote, told his daughter to burn the manuscript. Hence, the sleepless nights, the misgivings, the aping of great writers, the bad books, the escape into all the things that do not require inspiration, finding excuses in the Dreyfus case, family concerns, a love affair that was unsettling without being inspiring, literary criticism, things noted down precisely as intellect perceives them but with an absence of that elation which is the only indication of things worth noticing, and the means by which we may distinguish them the moment they come our way. Hence the perpetual struggle which ends in the realm of the unconscious mind being invaded by the artist's anxiety, so that we still analyse the beauty of the landscapes seen in our sleep, so that we try to embellish the sentences we utter in our dreams, so that Goethe, at the point of death, and delirious, talks about the colouring of his hallucination.

We all come to the novelist as slaves stand before an emperor. He can free us with a word. Through him we abandon our former lot and know what it is to be a general, a weaver, a singer, a country gentleman, to live in a village, to gamble, to hunt, to hate, to love, to go soldiering. Through him we are Napoleon, Savonarola, a peasant—stranger yet, an existence we might never have experienced, we are ourselves. He lends a voice to the mob, to solitude, to the old churchman, to the sculptor, to the child, to the horse, to the soul within us. Through him, we become the true Proteus who puts on all forms of life in succession. Exchanging them thus, one for another, we feel that to our being, grown so agile and so strong, these forms of life are only a game, a mask that grieves or grins, but which is never quite real. Our good or bad fortune momentarily

looses its tyrannical hold on us, we play with it and
with that of others. This is why we feel such happiness when we reach the end of some beautiful novel
with a tragic theme.

9

The wane of inspiration[1]

All those who have experienced what is called inspiration know that sudden enthusiasm which is the only indication of the excelling quality of some idea that occurs to us, and whose coming sends us galloping in its train, and makes words malleable and clear and mutually illuminating forthwith. Those who have once known this know that not every idea, however apparently true, nor particular conception, however seemingly ingenious, is worth expressing, and they wait for the renewal of those raptures which are the only indication that what we are about to say is worth saying and may toss other hearts into a like rapture later on. So it is very sad, the era where these raptures are no longer renewed, where at the coming of each idea we look in vain for that enthusiasm, that re-minting of the brain when all the partition walls seem to give way, when nothing that restricts, nothing that resists, is left, when our whole substance seems a sort of lava ready to be poured into a mould and take what shape we may choose without either assistance or hin-drance on our part. Our grace still pleases those who have loved us in our works, for we can still keep it in what we write, as we keep the grace and sweetness of a cast of countenance, a look that still allows others to say, "that's So-and-so," as in talking to our friends we still—more frequently, perhaps—come out with those brilliant comparisons, those turns of thought, which belong to no one but ourselves. We can keep these in what we write—for the mysterious being whom we are, who possessed this gift of giving a certain form, pertaining only to himself, to all he took in hand, he is still with us, no doubt. But we know that such a page has been written without rapture, that the few ideas which pleased us did not engender others; and though all the discriminating readers on earth should say, "It's the best thing you've done," we should shake our heads with a sigh, since we would give all this for a minute of that former strange power which nothing can call back. No doubt in this latest concerto there is still the loveable, recognisable tone of voice, but an idea no longer engenders a thousand ideas and the material is both less precious and more exiguous. And the works which swept the composer off his feet when he had all his powers about him, let them go on sweeping others off theirs, this means nothing to him now. And he pines.

But during this period, while the winter makes no impression on him, for now one day is like another, and the mysterious power of the seasons no longer encounters any mysterious acclaiming power in him, behold, in that country town far away from where he lives, two officers who perhaps believe he is dead, for now one no longer really knows, have agreed to meet while their fellow-officers are out for a walk. And they have sat down at the piano. Then the [   ].

10

The artist in contemplation[1]

The spy stands rooted to the spot to pick up a plan, the libertine to lie in wait for a woman, sober respectable gentlemen pause to observe a new building going up or a notable old one being pulled down. But the poet is brought to a standstill in front of all manner of things not worth a sober respectable gentleman's notice, so that people wonder if he is a spy or a lover and what, during all this while he has appeared to be looking at a tree, he has really been looking at. He stands in front of this tree, trying to shut away the noises of the outer world and recapture what it was he felt just now when, as he was walking through the public gardens it caught his eye, alone on its grass-plot, so covered with white blossoms that it seemed as though countless little pellets of snow were still clinging, as after a thaw, to the tips of its branches. He stands in front of it, but what he is in search of is certainly something over and above the tree, since he no longer feels what he had felt—then, all of a sudden, he feels it afresh; but he cannot fathom it, and is at a loss. It seems natural for a traveller to stand in a cathedral wondering at the leaf-shapes of ruddy glass that the craftsman has spread in their thousands through the window's arboreal tracery, or at the countless little loopholes, by which he has breached the wall with an exquisitely proportioned pattern; but not so when a poet stands for hours in front of this tree looking to see how, with the coming of spring, the unconscious and infallible architectural mind called the double-cherry has disposed these in-

numerable little white blossoms,[2] lightly crisped and
ruffled, which will waft a delicate fragrance through
the tree's complexity of black tracery as long as they
remain in bloom.

The poet looks, and seems to be looking both into
the cherry tree and into his own mind, where what he
sees is from time to time blotted out by something
within him, so that he has to wait for a moment, just
as he has to wait for a moment when a passer-by blots
out the double-cherry. Or again, it might be the fragrance a lilac untiringly distills in each of its purple
turrets over which the poet is suspended; he draws
back for a moment, so that he may smell it better a
moment later; he smells it afresh, but the fragrance
the lilac affords him is still unchanged, and he learns
no more from it. And look as he may at Gustave
Moreau's *Death and the Young Man*, the young man
will tell him nothing further, nor will his expression
change. The poet stands in front of things like the
student who reads and re-reads the text of the problem set him, and which he cannot solve; he may
read and re-read, he will see no difference in it; it is
not from the text itself he can hope for a solution.
While he looks at a tree, the passer-by stops to look at
a carriage, or into a jeweller's window. But the poet
who welcomes the beauty of all manner of things as
soon as the mysterious laws he bears within him have
made him sensible of it, and who will soon make us
see it as charming by displaying it along with the
little bit of the mysterious laws, the little bit that con-
nects with them, reaching to their feet or issuing from
their brows,[3] and which in portraying them he will also
portray—the poet welcomes and makes known the
beauty of everything, of a glass of water as well as

diamonds, but of diamonds as well as a glass of water, of a field as well as a statue, but of a statue as well as a field. When one has looked at a Chardin, not only does one see the beauty of a homely meal—one believes that humble fare alone is poetical and averts one's eyes from gold and jewels. But when one has read *The Rajah's Diamond*, and when one has seen a Gustave Moreau, one pursues diamonds and precious stones as things which are beautiful too; and when one has seen a Gustave Moreau after having believed that things were only beautiful in their untrammelledness, flowers in fields and animals in their living state, while scorning all manner of *objets d'art* and leaving them to rich people with no imagination, when one has seen Gustave Moreau's pictures one acquires a taste for splendid attire, for things deflected from their natural virtue and taken for symbols, tortoises meant to be used in making lyres, coronals of flowers as symbols of death; and after having believed that a statue would spoil a field, so much did one want to drink deep of the real countryside, one feels and craves for the beauty of a classical landscape where statues stand conspicuous on the cliff's edge (as in Moreau's *Sappho*) and takes pleasure in viewing natural objects as mental images, through which the spirit of the artist, on whom they entirely depend for their disposal, makes its way, rising from one to another, from the flowers at the statue's base to the statue, from the statue to the goddess who is not far off, from the tortoises to the lyre, while the flowers on a bosom are almost of the nature of jewels and almost of the nature of silks and linens.

The poet's mind is full of manifestations of these mysterious laws, and when such manifestations become evident, gaining strength and standing out boldly against his mind's background, they are aiming to get out of him, since whatever is meant to be lasting tries to get out of whatever is frail and decaying and may perish in a night or no longer be able to give birth to it. Thus at all times the breed of man, whenever it feels vigorous enough and can find an outlet, attempts to escape in an inclusive seed which contains it entire, from the dated man who tonight, perhaps, will perish, who never again, perhaps, will hold it in such completeness, or in whom, perhaps (for inasmuch as it is a prisoner, he rules its fate), it will not be so vigorous again. In the same way, when the creature of the mysterious laws—or poetry—feels strong enough, it pants to escape from the decaying man who this night may perish, or in whom (for inasmuch as it is his prisoner, he rules its fate—and he may fall ill, or be led away, or grow worldly, or lose his vigour, or dissipate in pleasure the wealth he bears within him, and which under certain circumstances of his personal life will dwindle away, since its lot is still tied to his) it will no longer possess that mysterious energy by whose means alone it can completely unfold itself; it aims at escaping from the man in the shape of his works. When it is thus lipping the brim, mark the poet's gait; he is afraid of spilling it before he has the vessel of words to pour it into. If he meets a friend or abandons himself to some pleasure, its mysterious energy is lost. Doubtless, if it had come near enough to escaping to have clothed itself already in a few vague words, by saying them over to himself, one day when he feels its energy astir—keeping it till then beneath its words like a caught fish beneath grass —doubtless he may be able to give it life again. And

when, behind closed doors, he has begun to get to
work on it, with his invention every minute tossing
him a new set of words to breathe life into, a new bal-
loon to blow up, what a hallowed and dizzy labour it
is! For now he has exchanged his soul for the soul of
the universe. This splendid transference has been carried out, and if you should go in and compel him to be
himself again, what a blow! There he is, looking all
astray, ravaged by some unheard-of agitation. He looks
at you uncomprehendingly, then smiles, and hoping
you may go away again, won't risk as much as a
word, his idea lying as inert as a stranded jelly-fish
that will die if the tide does not flow back to it. For
your part, you try to make out why he has shut himself up, you can see nothing accessory to the crime you
interrupt—and yet that air of being all astray. What's
going on?—did the victim disappear the moment you
came in? But it is himself he is doing away with, as
soon as you find the one, the other's not there; as in
trying to make out what Jekyll had done to Hyde, if
you saw Jekyll there was no sign of Hyde, if you saw
Hyde there was no sign of Jekyll, you always find him
by himself.

Each time the poet is not switched through to the
line of the mysterious laws where he feels an identical life reaching him from all things, he is unhappy. Yet this often happens, since each time he
pursues something cold-heartedly, and with a purpose
involving a shift of his personality from an inner to an
outer world, he is no longer at home in that part of
himself where, as in a telephone or a telegraph box,
he can be in communication with the beauty of the
whole world. Even during those years when he has yet
to become aware of this property in his nature, what

every one calls pleasure does not please him, and he
feels very sad about life. But later on he gives up
looking for happiness except in the light of those
rarefied moments which seem to him authentic existence; so that after each such moment of bringing
forth a thing in which he has lodged his sense of the
mysterious laws, he can die without regret, like an insect that makes ready to die after it has laid all its
eggs. What makes a poet's flesh transparent for us and
allows us to look at his soul, is not his eyes, nor the
events of his life, but his books, into which the one
particular thing in his soul that with instinctive
passion wanted to perpetuate itself has made its way
in order to outlive his decrepitude. And so we see
poets scorning to write down their ideas about such
and such things, such and such books, however note-
worthy these may be, or to record the extraordinary
scenes they have witnessed and the historic remarks
they have heard from the lips of princes they have
known, things, for all that, which are interesting in
themselves and make even the reminiscences of cooks
and viceroys entertaining. But to them writing is,
rather, something to be kept in reserve for a sort of
procreation, to which they are invited by a special desire that intimates they must on no account hold out
against it—a procreation that other types of writing
can only impair, although these may be sighed for by
people who have heard them say things about this or
that aspect of art which they considered much more
brilliant than the very thing the poets had written
their books on purpose to say. But the books keep what
is their very essence, in all its singularity and unac-
countableness—whence, no doubt, that desire attaching
to the production of everything that is specifically

their own, while not to speculations that appear to be more remarkable but which an inward monitor tells them are less so, or, as one says, less personal, in that when thought about they do not exercise this charm, nor, when written about, this pleasure attaching to the preservation and reproduction of what is really one's own (which for the intellect corresponds to being in good health and making love); such as their liking for the coolness of shady squares in a town, or the flash of a diamond on a wise man's hand, or the drinks whose more or less high alcoholic content tempers personality and brings contentment, or a small town where for some time there has been living a man who is a stranger to the neighbourhood and of whom no one quite knows where he came from, but who is a person of standing there and does good; whose former crimes, living on in some sort of accomplice, and deemed forgotten,[4] come to the surface again and, being a potential threat to his good name, give an insistence to remorse which it would have lost in the totally new way of life and the sweetness of being universally respected: all things you would not see by going to visit the great man, or even wondering at the depth in his gaze, any more than by looking into a lover's eyes or even hearing him say, "How lovely she is!" you could imagine the particular charm, nor the dreams he is entwined in, which his love for such a woman has set dawning in his soul.

The creed of art[1]

Alas, Monsieur, we were not as yet so positive about our aesthetic faith, we were not as yet so sure it was truly catholic, applicable for all times and in all places —it was really too kind of you when, by giving the most inopportune bruit to a heresy which is perhaps the most disquieting that art's true believers have yet encountered, you broached a painful schism where we have to decide between the genius of Shakespeare and, if not the genius of Tolstoi—since one might try to place that beyond dispute—at least, and this is already saying a great deal, his ability to distinguish beauty, the First Cause of art. But in fact, has any one ever possessed this ability—at any rate, in cases of translation from one language to another (as well as from one art to another, witness all the times when the actual vehicle of a work of art baffles the critics, whether it be a foreign language or a technique he does not know about)? As it is beauty of statement alone that individualises the idea and marks at what depth of the creative mind the idea was worked out, if this vehicle of words obscures the work of art instead of throwing light on it, we are reduced to guesswork, and often guess wrong. Take Goethe's admiration for Béranger, the contemptuous abhorrence that Gothic architecture aroused in Stendhal, Ruskin's liking for Meissonier, Alphonse Karr, George Sand. But, Monsieur, down what paths are you hurrying us, and will this first concession be enough? Alas, Hugo admired Béranger no less than Goethe did, and in Stendhal's day even the most gifted artists despised Gothic as

much as he did. Renan, who saw George Sand at closer
range than Ruskin did, ranked her above Flaubert,
Sainte-Beuve preferred her to both Balzac and Stendhal. Where Sainte-Beuve is concerned, I grant that
he was too close, I don't say to the works of the
writers he pronounced on, but to the writers themselves. He had seen too often that Alfred de Vigny
had less social grace than Molé and was somewhat of
a simpleton compared to him, he had been too well
aware that in the circle of Mérimée and Jacquemont
and Ampère, Stendhal was by no means the foremost,
and far from being esteemed the man of genius we
have since decided—or as I think discovered—he was;
as if in the sight of even his most intelligent friends,
the superiority of the genius ought to clothe and trans-
figure the man it dwells in (and thus, in the delightful articles M. Jacques Blanche has written about
Whistler and Fantin-Latour, the brilliant painter-writer
has perhaps slightly scaled down his models because he has "seen so much of them"). But if too much
information is a dangerous thing, too little does not
help matters either. The fact that in the nineteenth century, men of genius could have been mistaken about
Ossian ought to put us on our guard. A good grapholo-
gist who has to appraise the value of a letter ought to
know all that is to be known about its writer. We do
not even know whether Shakespeare existed, and we
carol over the fact that everything was grist to his
mill [   ].

PORTRAITS OF PAINTERS

1

Watteau[1]

I often think with a mixture of fellow-feeling and pity about the life of the painter Watteau, whose work lives on as the portrayal, the allegory, the apotheosis of love and pleasure, and who was, by the report of all his biographers, physically such a weakling that he could never, or rarely, taste the sweets of love. So in his art, love, and even pleasure, is overcast with melancholy It has been said that he was the first to have painted modern love, implying by this, no doubt, a love in which conversation, the pleasures of the table, strolling in parks, the sadness of masquerading, of water flowing and time fleeting, are more to the fore than actual pleasure—a sort of garlanded impotence. It is told of him that having many friends he made many enemies; for his disposition was even more fickle than it was affectionate, so that when he had spent half a year under a friend's roof he could live there no longer, chafed at not being elsewhere, fell in love with some other place and sickened until he got to it. And the deserted friend thought what an ungrateful fellow he had had to do with. Today too, I daresay, there is not an artist who would not recognise himself in this aspect of Watteau, and against whom quantities of people would not feel a like grievance. "To think that at one time he dined here every evening!" In this, more innocently and with less to show for it, artists resemble careerists. A devil impels them towards new places and fresh souls, but does not allow them to settle. It can be urged that in Watteau's case this changeableness was a physical condition. It

increased with the tuberculosis which was to carry
him off. During the last months of his life it was not so
much his sufferings that fretted him away as not being able to go to Flanders. He thought he would recover in his native air, but he could not be moved.

Though I think his disease had some bearing on
the way he perpetually fell out with things and people, I do not mean to say that it was the cause of it.
Our bodily ailments are not the cause of what is ailing
in our characters, but body and character are so
closely linked that they share in the same adversities.
I myself do not believe for a moment that Watteau's
fickleness was due to ambition or to self-interest. On
the contrary, one is struck at every turn by his sincerity and goodness of heart. Feeling himself mortally ill,
he begged that his pupil, Pater, whom he fancied he
had offended, should be fetched to Nogent, to his bedside; and every day during the space of two months,
and up to the day of his death, he taught him everything he knew about painting and drawing. Pater said
afterwards that he owed all his acquirements to that
apprenticeship.

In M. de Caylus's life of Watteau, which M. de
Goncourt—the great writer who has stolen the rarest
secrets of the painter's brush in order to portray him
—discovered in a bookseller's shop, there is a touch
which shows Watteau's guilelessness. He had been im-
mensely taken by a rather worthless wig. The wig-
maker cunningly refused to accept money for it, saying that if Watteau would do a sketch for him, that
would be payment enough. Watteau felt obliged to
paint a full-sized canvas, and even so was afraid that
it was too trifling a return, and far below the value of
the wig. M. de Caylus adds on a note of disdainful pity

that the wig was hideous, and Watteau's delight in it absurd. I shall not take it on myself to say that of the two, Watteau was in the right, although to feel such a degree of longing for the wig he must have had infinitely more interesting reasons for wanting it than those for which M. de Caylus scorned it. But the predilections of an artist are not always grounded on reason. If he has an overbearing, calculating character, the oddity of his tastes will rouse the public to gaping admiration; but if, like Watteau, he is easygoing and puts up with being laughed at, the people he lives among feel sure that the precision with which they measure his departures from the normal gives them a great advantage over their friend, and triumphantly make this plain to him. Inattentive to all the things that others give their minds to, sensitive to other things which he alone has eyes for, an artist is easily worsted in debates of this sort. Watteau, a sick man, must have suffered more than most from these walk-over victories by domineering ironical familiars. The victim of his bad health, he was also the victim of all the bores and cadgers who came to visit him, and whose request for a picture he never knew how to refuse.

This good man who was so ill-starred found consolation in being a good painter. It is pleasant to learn that he was fond of the Luxembourg Garden, and spent long hours there painting "because this garden was not kept so tidy as the other royal domains." But I find even more significance in the fact that he got together, by purchase or gift, a regular collection of all the *Commedia dell' Arte* costumes. It was his chief delight, when friends came to see him, to make them dress up in these costumes. Then he would ask

them to pose for him, consoling himself, by the spectacle of living, smiling, chattering people in such lovely
unreal attire, for having to drag a soul enamoured of
light and happiness through a lifetime of fog in
which it was always a-cold. When his friends had left
him, he pulled together the sketch he had begun,
and brought it into a full-scale composition later on.[2]

2

C*hardin*

Let us imagine a young man of limited means and artistic tastes sitting in a dining-room at that dreary daily moment when the midday meal has been eaten but is still not completely cleared away. His imagination is full of the splendours of art collections and cathedrals, seas and mountains, and he eyes with discomfort and boredom, with a sensation approaching nausea, feelings akin to black despair, the pushed-back tablecloth dangling on the floor and a knife still lying beside the remains of an oozing unappetising cutlet. On the sideboard a ray of sunlight, glinting on a tumbler of water that a quenched thirst has left almost full, accentuates as cruelly as a sarcastic laugh the dreary familiarity of this inartistic spectacle. At the further end of the room he sees his mother who with the tranquillity of everyday habit has already settled down to her work and is slowly winding off a skein of red wool. And behind her, perched on a cupboard beside a piece of biscuit-china that is only used on "special occasions," a stout squat cat seems the puny evil genius of this middleclass home.

The young man shifts his gaze, and it falls on the bright array of domestic silver-plate, polished and spotless, and from there descends to the glowing fire-dogs. More exasperated by the tidiness of the room than by the untidiness of the table, he thinks enviously of artistically-minded plutocrats who never stir foot except among objects of beauty, in rooms where everything from the tongs to the doorknob is a work of art. Execrating the ugliness of his surroundings, and ashamed of having spent a quarter of an hour in finding them, not disgraceful, but disgusting and somehow enthralling, he gets up; and if he cannot catch a train for the Hague or Italy, he goes to the Louvre to feed his eyes on palaces by Veronese, princes by Van Dyke, harbour scenes by Claude—visions which that same evening will be sullied and intensified anew by the recurrence of everyday scenes in their familiar setting.

If I knew that young man, I would not deter him from visiting the Louvre, I would be more inclined to go with him. But leading him into the Lacaze Room and the Room of the eighteenth-century French School, or the Rubens Room, or some other room of the French School, I would halt him before the Chardins. And when he stood amazed by this sumptuous painting of what he had called commonplace, this appetising painting of a way of life he had considered vapid, this greatness achieved in a kind of art he had supposed paltry, I would say to him, You're happy, aren't you? But really you have seen nothing more than a well-to-do tradesman's wife pointing out to her daughter where she had made mistakes in her wool-work (*La Mère laborieuse*), a woman with an armful of loaves (*La Pourvoyeuse*), a kitchen where a live cat walks across a heap of oysters while a dead skate hangs against the wall, a half-cleared sideboard with knives still lying about on the cloth (*Fruits et Animaux*), and even worse, table and kitchen ware, not just Dresden chocolate-pots and pretty things of that sort (*Ustensiles variés*), but such as you consider ugliest, a shiny saucepan lid, crocks of all sorts and sizes (a salt-jar, a skimmer), sights you shudder at, like raw fish lying about on a table, and sights that turn your stomach, like half-drained tumblers and a plethora of tumblers filled to the brim (*Fruits et Animaux*).

If all this now strikes you as beautiful to the eye, it is because Chardin found it beautiful to paint; and he found it beautiful to paint because he thought it beautiful to the eye. The pleasure you get from his painting of a room where a woman sits sewing, a pantry, a kitchen, a sideboard, is the pleasure—seized on the wing, redeemed from the transient, ascertained, pondered, perpetuated—that he got from the sight of a sideboard, a kitchen, a pantry, a room where a woman sat sewing. Your pleasure and his are so inseparable one from the other that if he had not been able to credit yours, you would not credit his, and if he had chosen to become absorbed in feeling and conveying his, you would inevitably recant from yours. You have already experienced it subconsciously, this pleasure one gets from the sight of everyday scenes and inanimate objects, otherwise it would not have risen in your heart when Chardin summoned it in his ringing commanding accents. Your consciousness was too sluggish to reach down to it. It had to wait for Chardin to come and lay hold on it and hoist it to the level of your conscious mind. Then you knew it, and for the first time in your life knew it as enjoyment. If you can say to yourself when you look at a Chardin, This is home-like, this is comfortable, this is living, like a kitchen, you will say to yourself, walking round a kitchen, This is singular, this is grand, this is beautiful, like a Chardin. Chardin will have been but a man who took pleasure in his dining-room among its fruits and glassware; but a man of intenser sensibilities whose uncontainable pleasure brimmed over in caressing brushwork and deathless colours. You will be a Chardin, less great, to be sure, but great to the extent to which you will love him, to which you will re-constitute yourself to be, like him, one for whom metal and pottery will come to life and fruits have language.

When they see that he has confided to you the secrets he learned from them, they will make no more ado about confiding in you themselves. Still life will become eminently alive. Like life itself, it will always have something new to tell you, some witchery to dazzle you with, some mystery to disclose; daily life will be full of charm for you if for a matter of days you have gone to school with his art, and when you have understood the life of his painting you will have possessed yourself of the beauty of life.

Into these rooms[1] where you see nothing but a representation of other people's limited minds and the reflection of your own boredom, Chardin enters as does the light, giving its colour to everything, conjuring up from the timeless obscurity where they lay entombed all nature's creatures, animate or inanimate, together with the meaning of her design, so brilliant to the eye, so dark to the understanding. As in *The Sleeping Beauty*, they are all brought back to life, resume their colour, begin to talk to you, put on life and duration. On the sideboard everything, from the stiff creases of the turned-back cloth to the knife lying askew and jutting out by the length of its blade, records the hurry of servants, witnesses to the gluttony of guests. The dish of fruit, still as glorious and already as ravaged as an autumnal orchard, is crowned with swelling peaches, rosy as cherubs, smiling and inaccessible as the gods on Olympus. A dog with outstretched neck cannot reach up to them, and makes them the more desirable for being desired in vain. He eats them by sight, divining their fragrant flesh from the downy skin that it moistens. Wine-glasses, clear as daylight, enticing as spring-water, are grouped together, those in which a few sips of sweet wine display themselves as though lingering in a gullet standing beside others already almost drained, like emblems of a lively thirst beside emblems of a thirst allayed. One glass has half tipped over, tilted like the bell of a withered flower; the luck of its position discloses the pontil mark at its base, the delicacy of its stem, the purity of its crystal, the elegance of its contours. Freed henceforward by the crack running through it from the claims of a household it will serve no longer, its useless grace has the aristocracy of a Venice glass. Oyster shells, light as cups of mother-of-pearl, cool as the sea-water they offer us, lie about on the cloth like charming fragile symbols on the altar of gluttony. Cold water in a bucket, swirled all to one side by the kick of a hasty passing foot, spills over on to the floor and a knife, token of an appetite that could not wait to begin, quickly tucked away by someone and heaving up the golden rounds of lemon that seem to have been put there by appetite's own hand, these complete the mouth-watering array.

Now come into the kitchen, where the entrance is strictly guarded by a feudality of crocks of all sizes, faithful, hardworking servants, a handsome industrious race. Knives, brisk plain-dealers, lie on the table in a menacing idleness that intends no harm. But a strange monster hangs above your head, a skate, still fresh as the sea it rippled in; and the sight of it mixes the foreign charm of the sea, the calms, the tempests it matched and outrode, with the cravings of gluttony, as though a recollection of the Museum of Natural History traversed the delicious smell of food in a restaurant. It has been gutted, and you can admire the beauty of its delicate immense structural design, painted with red blood, azure nerves, and white sinews like the nave of a polychrome cathedral. Near by are other fish, prostrate as their death agony left them, contorted in a stiff despairing curve, their eyes bulging out. Then there are oysters again, and a cat, counterpointing this fishy creation with the covert vitality of its subtler contours and with its glittering eyes fixed on the skate, picks its velvet-footed way in unhurried haste among the opened shells, and discloses at once the prudence of its character, the lust of its palate, and the daring of its enterprise. An eye practised in trafficking with the other senses, and in reconstituting by means of a few strokes of colour not merely a whole past, but a whole future, can already feel the freshness of the oysters that will dabble the cat's paws, and hear their tiny splintering exclamations and the thunder of their fall, as the precarious heap of frail splintered shells gives way under the cat's weight.

Like ordinary objects, everyday faces have a charm of their own. It is pleasant to see a mother examining her daughter's woolwork, the experienced eyes of the one—knowledgeable, assessing, foreseeing—and the artless eyes of the other. The wrist and the hand are no less revealing and to the sight of a discriminating onlooker even a little finger has a great deal of interpretive ability, and performs its character part with delightful truth. He is a poor-spirited artist—artist at any rate by the jargon and the painter's smock—who looks for nothing in nature except persons in whom he can recognise the ideal symmetry of allegorical figures. For the real artist, as for the naturalist, every type is interesting, and the least little muscle has meaning. You disliked the sight of old people whose features are lacking in any kind of elegance or stateliness—old people whom the years, like a rust, have abraded and reddened. Go to the Pastel Room, and look at the self-portraits Chardin painted in his seventieth year. Above an enormous pair of eye-glasses, that has slipped down to the tip of his nose and compresses it between two brand-new lenses, his hard-worn pupils are screwed high up in his dulled eyes with a look of having seen a great deal, found much to laugh at, much to love, and of saying, with a sort of wistful brag, "Yes, I'm an old man sure enough." Beneath the dimmed gentleness that age has strewn on them, they sparkle still; but the eyelids, grown slack as a clasp that has been too long in use, are red-rimmed. His skin, too, like the old coat he is wrapped in, has stiffened and faded. Like the material, it has kept and almost brightened its shades of pink, and in places a sort of golden opalescence glazes it. And at every turn the wear and tear of the one recalls the worn tints of the other, being, like the tints of all things nearing their end, whether dying embers, rotting leaves, sinking suns, garments wearing out or men growing old, extremely delicate, rich, and soft. It is astonishing to see how exactly the fold of the lips is determined by the raised eyelids, which the wrinkles on the nose also comply with. Character, life, mood of the moment, the three component factors, are faithfully, fastidiously translated by the slightest pucker of the skin, the least emergence of a vein. I hope that from now on, whether in the street or in your own home, you will stoop with respectful interest over these worn inscriptions which, if you know how to decipher them, will tell you infinitely more things, and more arresting, and more vital, than the venerablest manuscripts could.

In the portrait we have been talking about, Chardin's casual undress and the nightcap he has already put on make him look like an old woman. In the other pastel self-portrait we have of him, it is a match for the ludicrous eccentricity of some elderly English tourist. From the eye-shade shoved down over his forehead to the Madras neckerchief knotted under the chin, everything about it makes one want to smile, to smile without a thought of concealment, in the face of this old oddity who is patently so intelligent, so crazy, so amiably prepared to be taken as a joke—above all, so much of an artist. For every detail of this startlingly casual get-up, all equipped for going to bed, is as much an index of discrimination as it is a flout to convention. If that pink Madras neckerchief is so old, it is because a faded pink is softer. Looking at those pink and yellow crumples which seem to have left their reflection on the sallowed and rosied skin, seeing the dull glitter of the steel spectacles confirmed by the blue lining of the eye-shade, the first astonishment provoked by the old man's extraordinary attire melts into serene delight—and into the aristocratic pleasure, too, of finding the stately hierarchy of precious colours, the ordered laws of beauty, in the seeming disorder of an old commoner dressed at his ease.

But looking more closely at Chardin's face in this pastel you will think again, and feel perplexed, not daring to smile, nor justify yourself, nor shed tears before the ambiguity of his expression. It is what often happens to a young man confronted with an old man, and never if he is with a man of his own age—to be baffled, I mean, by that language we call the play of physiognomy, which is representational as a picture, but swift, direct, and disconcerting as a retort. Does Chardin here look at us with the bravado of an old man who makes light of himself, exaggerating the vaunt of his unabated good health, of his unquenched love of mischief, in order to entertain us or to show he is not really taken in by them: "Aha! So you believe you young ones know everything?" Or has our youth wounded him in his impotence, does he hit back with a passionate defiance, useless, and grievous to see? One could almost believe it, there is so much stern intent in the alertness of the eyes and the quiver of the lips. How many among us have been thus at a loss over the meaning and purpose of something an old man has said, above all over some glance of his, some twitch of the nose, some compression of the lips. We sometimes smile at the aged as if they were charming old madmen. But sometimes too we tremble at them as though they were madmen. During their long lives their hinged jaws have so often swung open for a smile, rage or tenderness have so often kindled fire in their eyes or breathed in the trumpet of their voice, the vivacity of their quick blood must so often have rushed in a flood to the transparent wall of their cheeks, that the mouth whose mechanism is worn out, fails to open under the stress of a smile, or closes imperfectly when the serious mood returns. The fire of the eye blazes up no longer, the smoke smothers it; cheeks redden no longer or else redden too much, stagnant as wine-coloured lakes. So the face, no longer translating every thought, every emotion of the soul, by its exact and proper expression, but leaving out, here, the emotion without which an assurance becomes a jest, there, the affectionate irony without which a bluster becomes a threat, turns from the representational but precise transcription of our feelings it was before into a sort of riddling depressing rigmarole, which from time to time may suddenly leave room between contradictory and inconsecutive expressions for our uneasiness, our glosses, our musing melancholy.

You have seen objects and fruits having a life, like people, and the skin on people's faces having a bloom, a significance of colour, like fruit. Chardin goes yet further by combining things and people in those rooms which are more than a thing and perhaps even more than a person, rooms which are the scene of their joint lives, the law of their affinities or contrarieties, the pervasive secreted scent of their charm, the confidant, mute yet a blabber, of their soul, the shrine of their past. As befits people and things who have lived quietly together for a long time, either needing the other, and finding as well an obscure pleasure in each other's company, everything in such a room breathes friendship. The arrogance of the old fire-dogs, like family servants who take a pride in their master's good name, is mollified when a gentle cordial glance from the fire rests on them, and the dignified bearing of the motionless armchairs holds out a welcome to the room where their days are passed, and where every morning when they are moved to the window to have the dust switched out of them, their punctual elderly stroll, or their slow twirl, takes place at exactly the same hour.

How many special friendships we come to learn about in some apparently uneventful room, as in a current of air, stirring or sleeping beside us, we can distinguish if the sun shines through it an infinity of eddying atoms. Look at *La Mère laborieuse* or *Le Bénédicité*. Friendship reigns between the tuffet and the old dog who comes every day to lean his indolent comfort-loving back against its soft well-wadded material —always in the same place, always in the same attitude. Friendship guides that woman's pretty feet so naturally towards the old spinning-wheel where they will be so comfortable, while she, her thoughts elsewhere, her body obedient to habits and affinities she ignores and complies with, scarcely knows what she is doing. Friendship exists, wedlock even, between the colours of the hearthrug and those of the tuffet and the skein of wool, between the stooping body, the happy hands, of the woman who is laying the table and the old tablecloth and the still unchipped plates, whose gentle tenacity she has felt for so many years always holding its own in her careful grasp, between the tablecloth and the sunlight which as a keepsake of their daily encounters has given it the smoothness of cream or of a linen lawn, between the sunlight and the whole of this room that it fondles, where it falls asleep, where now it loiters, now frisks into when least expected—exists with all with the tenderness of years between warmth and materials, between beings and things, between past and present, between light and shade.

Here we reach the end of this journey of initiation into the unnoticed life of inanimate objects that any one of us can accomplish who takes Chardin for his guide, as Dante let himself be guided by Virgil. To go further, we would now have to entrust ourselves to another master. On the threshold of Rembrandt, let us pause. Chardin has taught us that a pear is as living as a woman, a kitchen crock as beautiful as an emerald. He has proclaimed the divine quality of all things under the light which beautifies them and to the mind which reflects on them. By opening the world to us, he has made us leave behind a false idealism in order to explore an ample reality where, on all sides, we have rediscovered beauty, no longer the dwindled prisoner of convention or false good taste, but free, strong, universal; and it is into the open sea of beauty that he launches us. For with Rembrandt, even reality will be left behind. We shall learn that beauty does not lie in objects, since then it would certainly not be so unsearchable and so mysterious. We shall see that objects in themselves are nothing, empty eye-sockets in which light is the play of expression, the borrowed beam of beauty, the aspect of the eternal. In *The Two Philosophers*, for instance, we see the irruption of light redden a window to a furnace or colour it to stained glass, or let loose in a plain everyday room the majestic many-coloured splendours of a cathedral, the awesomeness of a crypt, the horror of darkness, of night, of the unknown, of crime. In the same way, in *The Good Samaritan*, where in two matching windows a figure already benighted steals away from the smile of a figure still day-lit, we shall see a similar shaft of light that makes earth at one with heaven set a mysterious beauty vibrating like a fiddle-string, alike in the distant hillside, and in the back of a horse, and in a bucket dangling[2] from a window, and transmitting to all these familiar usual things the reflection and as it were the tremor of that being which we feel to be everywhere and can nowhere seize on—that light which all day long is the beauty of objects and at dusk all their mystery, which by withdrawing from them alters their being to such a degree that we realise it is light they live by, so that in those beautiful unnerving moments they seem to undergo all the rigours of death. At that moment, each of us is like Rembrandt's *Philosopher*. We tremble at seeing the words of power written on the wall in letters of fire. Above the river or the dazzling or darkened sea, above the glittering enamelled burning windows, the transfigured housetops, we behold the sky whose reflection we have recognised everywhere on earth, that light we shall never know and know so well, which is the beauty of all we have seen, and its mystery and unknowability too. We all copy the Philosopher in looking at the sky, but unlike him we do not try to apprehend our joy or our anguish, what they are, what they mean. We have no reason to suppose that even the painter of the *Philosopher* thought philosophically. Still, like the Philosopher, he must have studied the sky, since he painted it—and that is all I shall assert by way of justifying myself to the painters, since they are constantly inveighing against writers for talking nonsense about painting, and finding things in pictures which they, the painters, never meant, never wanted, to put there. But put it there they did, and that is enough for me.

As for Chardin, I have shown what the work of a great artist could mean to us by showing all that it meant to him. Since it was in no way a parading of out-of-way qualities, but the expression of what had lain nearest to him in his life and of what lies deepest in things, it is our life that it appeals to, it is our life that it makes contact with, and gradually disposes towards things, and acclimatises to the heart of things. To the painters who are constantly reproaching writers for not being able to talk sense about pictures, and for the bland way they attribute to painters intentions they never had, I would add that if painters really do what I described, or, to be categorical, if Chardin had done all that I described, he never intended it, and it is even highly probable that he was never aware of it. Perhaps he would have been greatly astonished to learn that he had put so much fervour into conveying the animation of what we believe to be still life, had supped delight from iridescent oyster-shell cups and from cool sea-water, sympathised in a tablecloth's affection for a table, in shadow's affection for light. In the same way a gynæcologist might astonish a woman who has just given birth by explaining to her what had taken place in her body, by describing the physiological sequence of the act she has had the mysterious energy to carry out but of whose nature she knows nothing; acts of creation, in fact, proceed not from a knowledge of their laws but from an incomprehensible and obscure capacity which is not made any the stronger by enlightenment. A woman does not need to know about doctoring in order to give birth, a man does not need to know the psychology of love in order to love, a man does not need to understand the mechanics of anger in order to [   ].

3

Rembrandt

Picture galleries are dwellings that house only thoughts. Those who are least capable of sharing these thoughts know that what they look at in these pictures hanging in a row is the thought, that the pictures are precious and that the canvas, the paint that has grown dry on it, even the gilded wood of the frame, is not. When one looks at a picture by Rembrandt, one sees an old woman cutting a young woman's nails, a string of pearls glimmering on a piece of fur, table-covers of red carpet-work or some reddish Indian material, a kindling fire which lights up the depth of a dusky room while the evening light coming in through the window lights up the doorway, a young woman's long silky hair that an old woman is combing out, a burst of sunlight falling on the weir of a river and the men riding along the river bank while windmills twirl their sails in the distance; and one thinks that all these things make part of nature and that Rembrandt painted them as he would have painted any others. But if you see a succession of Rembrandt pictures you will come on another old woman about to cut a young woman's toe-nails, and the same dull gleam of pearls on a different piece of fur. Now it is no longer Rembrandt's wife, it is *The Woman Taken in Adultery*, or *Esther;* but she too has a submissive sad face, she too wears gold brocades or a red cashmere shawl beneath her pearls. It is no longer the house of a philosopher, it is a carpenter's workshop, or the bedroom where a young man sits reading; but at the back of the room, now only dimly or partially lit by daylight still persisting out of doors, the fire blazes up and casts a brighter light. Here is a bullock's carcase in a butcher's shop; it is not the picture where a kneeling woman on the left is washing the floor, but on the right a woman looks back as she is going out; so that the old women, cutting nails or combing out fine tresses, the sad modest woman with her furs and her pearls, the house where a fire blazes up in the shadow of a dusky room, these are not just the things that Rembrandt painted, they are things that appealed to him—those ideas in which every great man finds himself, the self for whom a thing has significance and is rewarding, if it is something in whose recesses he may suddenly come on those ideas anew, and begin to rejoice in them, and to fasten on them with a stronger hold.

To a thinking man how devoid of any real interest a stroll through a picture gallery will be except when it suddenly brings him face to face with one of those ideas, whose richness and readiness to parent other wonderful ideas is immediately apparent to him. At first, an artist's works may bear more resemblance to nature than to himself. But later on, that essential self of his, which has been further aroused by every fruitful encounter with nature, impregnates them more completely; and towards the end it is obvious that now this alone is real to him, and that he strives increasingly to convey it in its entirety. The portraits that Rembrandt painted as a young man have very little in common with each other, and can look like portraits by other great masters; but after a certain point, all these sitters appear in a sort of golden medium, as if they had all been painted in a similar light, which is seemingly the light of sunset, when the levelled rays

of the sun gild every thing they touch. So that in all
Rembrandt's pictures, this feature of resemblance has
much more force than the resemblances obtaining
among those old nail-trimmers and combers of fine
tresses, or even among his effects of sundown and his
fires blazing up. These are Rembrandt's predilections;
but the light that bathes his portraits and his pictures
is in some way the very light of his thought, the kind
of personal light in which we view things when we are
thinking for ourselves. One cannot doubt that he had
realised that this was his own proper light, and that
when he saw by it, what he saw became full of riches
for him, and fitted to parent other profound pieces of
observation in him, and that then he felt the joy
which portends that we are nearing some high event,
that we are about to create. So he scorns all other
lights as less fertilising to him and less hallowed, and
henceforward paints by none but this. And we confess
to his right of genius to do so by the joy the sight of
his golden medium arouses in us, a joy to which we
give way without reservation, conscious that it admits
us to a profoundly intimate view of what Rembrandt
saw; his sister's sad face, or the bucket which in the
hush of evening, in the last scattered gleams of a sun
long set, is lowered in front of the house where the
Good Samaritan ended his happy days.

And in what we call the Third Manner of Rembrandt it is obvious that this golden light, in which it
was essential—and in consequence of that, so fruitful,
and in testimony of that, so moving—for him to see
things, has become the whole of reality for him, and
that he will go on exerting himself, more and more,
and with the utmost obsessedness, to convey it as a
whole, without further care for beauty or any other

outward verity, but sacrificing everything to this, halt-
ing himself, going over it again so that nothing of it
should escape, feeling that this is the one thing that
mattered. Now, from the depth of each of his canvasses, it seems as if his gaze, while still bent on the
reality he had tried to encompass, were already relax-
ing in the release of accomplishment, and somehow asking us, "Is this it?" or saying, "Look!"—that
gentle understanding gaze his Christ turns on the
woman taken in adultery, that gaze in the *Homer* of
the poet saying over his lines to himself with the full
sense of all they mean, that gaze which beholds every
sorrow, and contains every tenderness, and seems
hardly able to hold back its tears, of the *Christ on the
Journey to Emmaus;* and all of whom, the Christ beside the adulterous woman, the Homer, the Christ of
Emmaus, have the pinched neck, the slackened gesture
—piously subservient to the thought it fears to break
in on, to falsify, by a positive movement—of those who
are engaged in thought and whose whole body waits
upon their thinking; and the eyes, not bold or staring,
but fixed, and full of a thought which our own thought
gathers and recognises, in orbits that respect what
they contain and unwinkingly safeguard it; and the
bowed, acquiescent back and the humble look—as
though every great thought, be it Homer's, be it
Christ's, were greater than themselves, as though
thinking nobly and deeply were summed up in thinking so attentively that one allows no part of the
thought to escape. But having finished his picture, a
Rembrandt less encumbered with thought looks out
of the canvas at us, untormented—say what one will
of the artist's craving for recognition—by any great
anxiety; since the end for which artists are made is

not fame, but the complete statement of this or that conception, and (as regards the work in hand) he is at rest as soon as he has finished it, insofar as he feels it is faithful to what he meant. Besides, Rembrandt has left portraits of himself where from the young man's vehement longing that later on will become a sort of qualm of solicitude, we can make out the inward reality—his genius ablaze in him, and recognised by him, and the difficulty of getting it all down on canvas.

Thus all these pictures are extremely serious matters, fit to preoccupy the greatest minds among us during a whole lifetime—beyond it, no, because of a material impossibility in which they can have no say—but compellingly so to the last, like something whose meaning the flight of years does not lessen and which in the last years or the last weeks that remain to one, will still appear full of import and reality. At a Rembrandt exhibition[1] in Amsterdam I saw an old man come in, together with an old housekeeper. His hair was long and curly, his demeanour, in spite of a fine countenance, was doddering, he had blear eyes, a doting expression—such extraordinary beings are the aged or the sick, who already look like the dead or look like idiots, and in whom we suddenly discover, violently manifested by a shaky arthritic hand, an amazing willpower that disconcerts a whole family, or changes the destiny of a state, or reprieves a man from the scaffold by the signature that no threat, no persuasion had been able to arrest, while he sat drowsing in his warm room, benumbed by sad dreams, and which an illegible scribble traced by his octogenarian fingers, will testify by the explosion of the deed to the intact survival of his intellect—that amazing and smiling in-

tellect!—in the form of a book, of a poem sparkling
with the irony of a wrinkled soul, through the same
lapse of time when intellect was tracing those endur-
ing grieved wrinkles in a palsied face, which when we
meet it makes us suppose we have met an idiot out
for an airing. But the old man who came in had, on
the contrary, a fine countenance beneath his long curling white hair, though he was doddering and blear-
eyed. It seemed to me I knew his face. Just then someone near by spoke his name, which being already
immortal seemed to be spoken of the dead: Ruskin.
He was nearing his end, and yet he had come from
England to see these Rembrandts, which in his twenti-
eth year already seemed essentially great to him, and
had no less reality for him now, in his last days. He
went up to the pictures, looking at them without
seeming to see them, all his movements, because of
the exhaustion of old age, being directed to some one
of the innumerable material necessities—the need to
keep hold of his cane, the effort of coughing, of turning
his head—which swaddle the old man, the infant, and
the invalid like a mummy. But through the foggy
stretch of years thickening over his sombre face and
over his eyes, in whose depths, now so far away one
could no longer catch sight of the soul, the life, of
Ruskin, one sensed that still the same, although in-
discernably so, he had come from the depth of years,
on his doddering legs which were nevertheless the
legs of Ruskin, to pay his incomparable respects to
Rembrandt. It was he, Ruskin; two such incompatible
things, this unknown groping old man and the idea of
Ruskin one had made for oneself, that it was very
difficult to contain them in one thought; and that
so much soul and genius was enwrapped in those

vile lendings of his senility had something almost
supernatural about it, the moment in which a spirit
takes a body, in which the insignificant body is acknowledged a spiritual person, a mind independent
of any body, dead or not, and immortal. What, Ruskin, that discarnate thing, is in the flesh, and the man
he was is still alive, and here? He is the same Ruskin
who as a young man went to look at Rembrandt and
wrote so many impassioned pages about him. Black-
ened like a Rembrandt by the shadow of nightfall, by
the patina of time, by the obliterating years, he was still
led on by the same endeavour to understand beauty.
It suddenly seemed that the Rembrandt canvasses
had grown worthier to be visited since Ruskin, from
so far away, had come into the room; it seemed too
that for Rembrandt this was like a reward which he
might have found sweet, and that if his gaze which
seemed to be studying us out of the depth of his con-
summated pictures had been able to see Ruskin, the
master would have been at his service, like a king who
recognises a king among the crowd. Yes, Rembrandt's
pictures seemed worthier of admiration since Ruskin
had come in—or painting itself, rather, in that it bears
potentialities of more excellent gifts, seemed something more essential, since we had witnessed such an
exalted spirit, so near death, still studying it, and at a
juncture when even the most exquisite of enjoyments
does not mean so very much to us still holding fast
to it as though to one of those realities which are
stronger than death, if death, nevertheless, prevents
our further recourse to them.

But perhaps—so much are our pleasures rooted in
habit and the way our senses come to feel at home
with certain objects—we must also consider whether

for him too this was not one of these enjoyments which, since they are determined by temperament and the course of time, no one can prescribe off-hand for us; so much so that the doctor who hopes that a little of what we fancy may do us some unspecified good, must learn from someone of the household what that fancy feeds on. In Ruskin's case, the sight of a Rembrandt might set going that sweet familiar play of old ideas, familiar likings, habitual pleasures, as would in a grandfather the sight of his little granddaughter, in an inveterate bezique player a game of bezique, in a madman some old private incomprehensible trick. Perhaps his housekeeper took him to see the Rembrandts as she would have taken some other old man to watch a game of cards, or brought him a bunch of grapes. For those who live with us can always name what it is we love. And we often smile at hearing majestic names spoken without understanding by familiar lips, smile from pleasure, too, seeing our predilections given a greater reality, as it were, by being thus matter-of-factly dealt with by people more subject to reality than we.

4

Gustave Moreau

It is not always easy to understand why certain birds
flying across a landscape, a swan rising skywards from
a river, a courtesan taking the air on a lofty terrace
among birds and flowers, should unceasingly preoccupy the thoughts of a man of genius, and these,
recurring in all his pictures as essential characteristics,
be the admiration of posterity and the especial delight of that collector who buys no canvasses but his
and discovers with delight that the swan in the *Descent from the Cross* is the swan in *Love and the
Muses* too, while with an inversion of the same delight
he rejoices at possessing the artist's only blue bird.
We can ask ourselves what the great man intended by
it, but to no purpose; there is little likelihood that
any one can answer us since even he has not been able
to find an answer in himself except by painting the
courtesan on her terrace in the cool of the evening,
and the flight of that swan which the Muses point to
—the exactest images he could achieve of what he had
caught a glimpse of, and no doubt infinitely more exact than any explanation, since a statement of what
we meant to do amounts to nothing, we can produce
that at any time, whereas to reconstruct the idea that
has visited us, we must wait for inspiration, try to see
it as it was, steal up on it, and paint it from life.
But these landscapes of Moreau's are so patently the
landscape where some god walks or some vision appears, and in them a reddened sky is such an infallible portent, and the intrusion of a deer such a good
omen, and the mountain so hallowed a spot, that by

comparison a straightforward landscape seems quite vulgar, and as if deprived of its intellectual faculties; as if mountains and sky and animals and flowers had been suddenly drained of their ichor of history, as if the sky and the flowers and the mountain no longer bore the imprint of a tragic hour, as if the light were not the light in which the god walks, or the courtesan came forth, as if nature deprived of its intellectual content forthwith became vulgar and more extensive, Moreau's landscapes being as a rule contracted in a ravine or closed by a lake wherever and whenever an aspect of the divine manifests itself at some indefinite moment that the canvas perpetuates like a heroic myth. And like this landscape which is natural and yet seems full of awareness, like these mountains whose stately summits where people go to pray are almost temples and have temples crowning them, like these birds who perhaps conceal the soul of a god, who look at us almost humanly through their feathered disguise and whose flight seems directed by a god as an admonition, the face of the hero himself seems to participate as indeterminately in the mystery which the whole canvas expresses. For the courtesan has the air of being a courtesan just as the bird flies—by a destiny which is in no way the result of her choice or her disposition—but her face is sad and beautiful and she gazes while she plaits her hair among the flowers; and the Muse seems to move onward willy-nilly, shaping a tune on her lyre; and Saint George as he slays the dragon seems to be tranquilly submitting to his own valour, and to be the legendary, vaguely musing site of that mythological deed, like the mountains around him, like the rearing horse, fiery and gentle, caparisoned with gems and darting vexed glances—classic pictures that one sees at a glance are not by an Old Master but by this man who, a law to himself, in painting his dreams gathered together these red draperies, these green garments studded with flowers and precious stones, these grave heads that are the heads of courtesans, these mild heads that are the heads of heroes, this country of mountain defiles in which everything he paints takes place; because life has not withdrawn from things and wholly percolated into beings, because the mountain is legendary and the person is no more than a legend, because the mystery of what is taking place is expressed by all that the face of the person withholds, the hero with the mild air of a virgin, the courtesan with the grave air of a saint, the Muse with the inconsequent air of a traveller, casting no sort of light on the action which they do not seem to carry out, and by all the secreted complicity of the landscape —because the caves conceal monsters, the birds utter auguries, the clouds drop blood, and the hour of day is mysterious, and seems to grieve in the heavens over what is mysteriously accomplished on earth.

A picture is a kind of revelation of some little part of a mysterious world of which we know various other aspects, which are canvasses by the same artist. We are in a drawing-room, we are conversing, all at once we look up and catch sight of a picture we have never seen before and yet have already recognised, as though we remembered it from some previous existence. Those horses that look untamed and full of sensibility, trapped with gems and roses, that poet with a woman's face, a dark blue cloak, and a lyre in his hand, and all those beardless men with feminine faces, garlanded with hydrangeas and swaying branches of

tuberoses, that bird, also dark blue, who follows the
poet, the poet's breast, swelling with a solemn melody
which strains the rose-branches that encircle it, and
the colouring of all this, the colouring of a world
where each several colour is, not the colour it is in
this world of ours, but the colour it is in that canvas;
and beyond this, the aura of that world where the sun
often sets and wild mountain-sides are crowned with
temples, and where, if a bird follows that poet and a
flower grows in that valley it is by virtue of other laws
than those of our world, laws which appoint the bird
to single out the poet, to follow him and remain with
him, so that in the wings that flutter about him there
is something sacred and instructed, by which that
flower grows in the valley near that woman because
the woman must die, and the flower is the flower of
death, so that there is a kind of foreboding in the fact
that it should have sprung up there, and in its springing growth a kind of swelling menace, so that she
seems to look at it and feel her last hour upon her.
. . . In a flash, because of various glimpses into that
strange country we have had already, we recognise
that what we are looking at, and have never seen till
now, is a Gustave Moreau.

The country which works of art thus show us fragments of, is the poet's soul, his true soul, of all his
souls that which lies deepest, and his true native clime,
but where he can only live for a few precious snatches
of time. That is why the light that bathes them is an
intellectual light, and the colours that glow in them
and the people who figure in them are intellectual
colours and intellectual beings. Inspiration is the moment when the poet is able to break through into that
innermost soul. Being at work is the struggle to re-

main entirely there, so that while he is writing or painting there may be no contamination from the outer world. Hence that revision of wording, retouching of colours, before a model which is as actual and imperious for the poet as for the painter, as personal and cerebral for the painter as for the poet. And so we love to see these canvasses, brought back by the poet from the mysterious country where he has a right of entry and which retain a sort of mysterious colouring from it, dazzled[1] by their return to broad daylight amidst the realities of the world, not the true world but the most commonly accepted, the one that corresponds to the outermost of our souls—which in the poet is almost comparable to that of other men. Such a moment of inspiration hangs before my eyes, held fast for ever behind the impenetrable frail prism of its soft colour, one that not long since floated so swiftly on the high tide of Gustave Moreau's thought, a delicate jelly-fish on the shore now, but still keeping the pale freshness of its hyaline tints. It is called *The Persian Singer*. And he sings indeed, this rider in kingly trappings, with a woman-like, priest-like countenance, whom the mysterious bird follows, before whom women and priests bow down and bow their flowering branches, and whose horse looks at him with an eye animated by the soul that circles on through all creation, looks at him tenderly as though it loved him, while it raises an untamed muzzle towards him as though it hated and would devour him. He sings, his mouth is open, his breast distends the rose-garland that entwines it. It is the moment when one gets out of one's depth, when solid earth melts under one's feet, when the ship puts to sea and is afloat and already miraculously moving forward, when words, lifted on the tide of rhythm, become song. And that visible pulsation throbs on for ever in the rigid canvas.

Thus it is that poets do not altogether die, and the true soul, that innermost soul where alone they felt authentically themselves, is to some extent preserved to us. We may believe the poet is dead, we may make our pilgrimage to the Luxembourg as though we were simply going to visit a grave, we go, as simply as the woman carrying the head of the dead Orpheus, to look at the *Woman Carrying the Head of Orpheus*, and in that head of Orpheus we see something that looks at us through those lovely sightless eyes that are the colour of pansies.

The painter looks at us—we dare not say that he sees us; and of course he does not really see us, but we, however dear we may have been to him, we meant so very little to him. What he saw is still to be seen, it is before our eyes, that is all that matters.

Now that Gustave Moreau is dead, his house is to become a museum. That is as it should be. A poet's house is never quite a house, even while he still lives in it. We are aware, for one thing, that what has been achieved in it has already passed from his ownership to the ownership of mankind; and that often—whenever he has ceased to exist save in his innermost soul, that is—it does not house a man. It is like a geographical concept, like the Equator or the poles, a meeting-place of mysterious currents. But it is in a man that this soul from time to time becomes active. The man, no doubt, is always to some extent consecrated. He is a kind of priest, whose life is vowed to the service of this god, who feeds the sacred animals the god delights in, and wafts the incense-fumes that encourage the god to appear. His house is half a church, half a presbytery. Now the man is dead, nothing is left except what was divine in him and had been able to break away. By an abrupt transformation the house turns into a museum even before it is made over as such; the bed and the kitchen stove have no more business there. The man who from time to time was God and lived for all men lives on as God alone, he no longer exists for himself, only for others. There is nothing about his house that could call home a self which exists no more. The palisade of personal individuality within which he was a man like other men is down. Take away the furniture. Nothing is needed beyond the pictures that relate to the inner soul he often had access to and address themselves to all of us. Besides, he had increasingly striven to break down that palisade of personal individuality, striving to stimulate inspiration (that is, to redouble those moments when he could have access to his inner soul) by industry, that same industry by whose means he strove to record them in their integrity, and without any contamination from the everyday soul. Little by little, pictures encumbered all the rooms, till only a room or two was left for the purposes of the man who required to eat, sleep, entertain his friends. Little by little the hours in which he was not taken over by his inner soul, in which he was still the man whom he was as well, became rarer. His house was already almost a museum, his flesh and blood little more than the place where a work of art was being accomplished.

It is bound to be so with all those who possess an inner soul into which they can sometimes penetrate. A private joy admonishes them that the hours they spend there are their only authentic hours. The re-

mainder of their life is a kind of exile, often volun-
tary, not sorrowful, but morose. For they go into an
intellectual exile; no sooner are they exiles than they
lose all memory of their native land, and only know
that they have one and that it is sweet to dwell in it,
but not how to find their way back. And also that as
soon as they desire some other country they are no
longer in their own, for their country is a frame of
mind, and the desire for something other is exile from
it. But insofar as they are themselves—when they are
not exiles, I mean, when they inhabit their inner souls
—they act by virtue of a sort of instinct which, like an
insect's, is reinforced by a privy knowledge of the mag-
nitude of their task and the shortness of their days,
and so they put by every other obligation in order to
create the dwelling where their posterity will live, and
to lay that posterity in it; and that being done, are
ready to die. Look at the fervour of the artist as he
paints his picture, and tell me if the spider spins her
web more fervently than he.

And all these inner souls of poets are knit in friendship and call to one another. I was no different from all
the other men in that drawing-room; I glanced up and
I saw that *Indian Singer*, who had neither voice nor
motion, but whose breast heaved the roses that lay on
it and before whom women bowed down their flowers.
And instantly, in me too the singer awoke. And inasmuch as he had been awakened nothing could have
turned him aside from what he had to say. And a privy
instinct instructed me, word by word, in the words I
ought to say. And did more striking thoughts occur to
me, or chains of thought that would have made me
seem more intelligent, I listened to them without being able to turn away from the task before me—invis-

ible but assigned. For the singer who inhabits me also has a woman's gentleness, but he has a priest's gravity, too. And it is because this mysterious country, which then extends before us, exists in very sooth when we scour over it in such intoxication of mind, that all the pictures of it we bring back, if indeed we have been there to fetch them, that is, if we have really been inspired, all resemble it,[2] and if we have been at pains to let nothing from the everyday soul mingle in them—if we have been conscientious, that is, if we have laboured—all resemble each other. And that was why when I looked up in that drawing-room and saw, on his horse with its fierce muzzle and gentle eyes and trappings of roses and precious stones, that grave mild singer heaving the roses that bound his breast with the vehemence of his inaudible song, followed by the bird *that knew him,* and backed by a *customarily* setting sun, I could say, It's a Gustave Moreau. Perhaps it is even more beautiful than the others, as though it were song, where they are beautiful speech. Enthusiasm dilates it, like the young singer's rose-wreathed breast. But like all the others, it comes from the land where colours have that colouring, where poets have women's faces and the insignia of kings, are loved by birds, acknowledged by their horses, decked with gems and roses—in short, where it is allegory that gives the law to life.

Recalling how I felt about this picture of Gustave Moreau's, I, who feel like this once in a twelvemonth, I envy those people whose lives are so well ordered that every day they can devote some part of their time to the joys of art. At moments, too, above all when I notice how much less interesting they are in other re-

spects than I myself, I wonder if they claim to experience these feelings so often only because they have
never known them. Those who have once been in love
know how far the easy-going attachments to which the
name of love is applied, fall below the true love. Perhaps if it were within everyone's capacity to be smitten
with love for a work of art, as it is within everyone's
capacity (or at least, appears to be) to be smitten with
love for some person of another sex (I speak of true
love), we might similarly know how rare a thing it is
to be in love with a work of art, and how far the countless artistic enjoyments which gifted people with harmoniously ordered lives talk about, are removed from
that love.

Nothing has reality for a writer except what may
mirror his individual mind, that is, his writings. That
he may be an ambassador, or the bearer of some distinguished princely name, counts for nothing. If his van-
ity as a man pursues such ambitions, it may be disas-
trous to the writer, though perhaps he might otherwise
let himself be stultified by indolence or stupefied by
debauchery, or preyed on by sickness; but at least, he
ought to know that it has no validity in literature.
This is what embarrasses me in Chateaubriand, who
seems gratified at having been a person of eminence. A
person of eminence in the world of letters even, what
has that to do with it? It is a materialistic outlook on
literary grandeur and consequently false, since literary
greatness is entirely spiritual.

For all that, he cuts a fine figure, and there is a quality of grandeur in his charm. But this is because he had
a noble imagination, not because he was nobly born.
Do circumstances count for nothing? There are times

when it would appear so. Rodenbach, however, said that Baudelaire was Baudelaire because he had been to Africa.[3] I myself think circumstances count for something. But any circumstance is one-tenth chance and nine-tenths being disposed to fall in with it. That Gustave Moreau seen on a day when I was feeling out of my element, and disposed to hearken to inner voices, enriched me more than all that tour of Holland, hurried through, my heart dutiful, but untouched.

5

Monet

A lover of pictures, of Claude Monet's landscapes, let us say, or Sisley's, will inevitably come to know and feel a liking for rivers where a sailing boat streaks its wake between grassy banks, for the blue sea at Antibes, for various times of day, for certain aspects of Rouen where the cathedral shows among the houses, with its spire and ribbed Gothic walls standing out among flattened roofs and smooth house-fronts—just as a man who loves a singer inevitably loves the character of Juliet or of Ophelia, in which, as in the bread of the altar, the being he adores is made manifest to him. Picture lovers who will make a journey to look at a Monet painting of a poppy-field will not, perhaps, take a walk to look at a field of poppies; but meanwhile, like astrologers who had a speculum that showed them everything in the world, but which had to be consulted in some place of solitude, since astrologers did not mingle in the world's affairs, they have hanging on their walls mirrors of a no less magic kind called pictures, in which, if one knows how to look at them steadily, slightly withdrawing oneself the while, important constituents of reality are unveiled. There we stand, bent on the magic mirror, standing a little back from it, trying to drive out every other thought, seeking to understand the purport of each stroke of colour, each of them calling to mind past impressions which gather into a construction as atmospheric and multicoloured as the strokes of colour on the canvas, and build up a landscape in the imagination; mirrors consulted by old men with long beards who do not know that the wind parches and the sun scorches, but who are entranced to discover all these truths, which besides, are based on the real wind and the real sun. Just as the singer's lovers know the author whom she admires and whose characters they see her playing, a picture by Monet [1] makes us love the landscape which pleases us in it. He often painted the banks of the Seine at Vernon. No doubt we can be of the opinion that he would have seen things as lovely elsewhere, and that perhaps it was his personal circumstances that took him there. Never mind. To draw out the truth and beauty of a place we must know that they are there to be drawn out, that gods are everywhere latent in its soil. Apart from those places where, on some high and holy day, we ourselves have been granted a revelation, we can only pray on consecrated ground. Certainly it is not a vain idolatry for Monet or Corot that will do our loving for us. We shall love ourselves. But on the threshold of love we are bashful. There has to be someone who will say to us, Here is what you may love; love it. And then we love. Monet's pictures show us the magic vein in Argenteuil, in Vétheuil, in Epte, in Giverny. So we set off for these holy lands. They show us too the heavenly pasturage our imaginations can find in things less localised, islet-dotted rivers during those motionless hours of afternoon when the river is blue and white with sky and clouds, and green with trees and lawns, and pink with sunbeams already sloping on tree-trunks, and splashed with scarlet in the shadow of the garden hedges where the tall dahlias push through. The pictures make us adore a field, a sky, a beach, a river, as though these were shrines which we long to visit, shrines we lose faith in when we see, strolling through the field, walking briskly along the shore, a lady drawing her shawl closer, a man and woman holding hands. We rank the divinities of our worship so high that whatever brings them down to the level of the already known breaks the spell for us. It is the ideal we give our hearts to. Believing that the painter is going to tell us about the place itself, a mysterious personage with a vast countenance of cliff, a sunset glance reddening through the rain into the very depths of the sea, we see a couple thrust themselves between it and us. And we who believed this personality of places to be such a mystery that we believed the painter entirely given over to calling it up amid the silence and the furrowing boom of waves on that beach, we are astounded to see that he was in the upshot no more concerned with it than with this couple, who strike us as in no way mysterious and whom he has put into his picture too. We thirsted for parts of the world that are themselves and nothing but themselves, beaches that never see more than a particular corner of the cliff and hear the sea's lament all day and all night, towns built on the slope of a hill that see only a river and in summer, lilac groves; the sight of mankind imbedded in these things irks us, since it was them only, them unbelittled, that we wanted to see. Such is the unreasonableness of our ideals. When we are children, and we try to find the moon and the stars in books we are enraptured by the moon in *Picciola* because it is a glistening luminary, and are disappointed by it in *Colomba* because it is compared to a cheese and a cheese seems vulgar to us and the moon appears divine. And in Musset's *Histoire d'un Merle blanc*, so long as it is a matter of white wings and a rosy beak and little drops of water, we are charmed, but after the white blackbird has addressed the dove as *Madame la Marquise*, these men and women who then represent the real world to us, which we think to be ugly, to be unpoetical, irk us and take away all our pleasure. It is the period of our life when the only things we enjoy in a picture gallery are works by Gleyre or Ingres, when we require faultless symmetry, moons like silver crescents in a star-strewn heaven, and when all the colouring of the *Marriage at Cana* seems as far removed from the world of poetry, and as vulgar, as the coat-tails over the chair or the winestains on the tablecloth.

PROUST THE READER
(*Journées de Lecture*)

1

G oethe[1]

The topics we habitually recur to in our books show
what has fired our inspiration, and it is easy to see what
has made a strong impression on our minds. In Goethe,
sites are extremely important. We often come on a
place where there is a wide and varied prospect. Valleys extend before us, with villages and a fine river on
which the light of morning dazzles, and we look down
on all this from a little mountain. Various private collections, too, are dwelt on with pleasure, collections of
pictures, natural history collections. One feels that
these things were not merely put in to please, but that
they had an extremely serious bearing on his intellectual life; that the concern of his intellect and its essential aim was to analyse the pleasure he drew from
them (for it is by an essentially higher kind of pleasure that things important to the intellect first impose
themselves on it and declare their importance) and to
ascertain their effect on the mind. Although his characters may often debate the importance of various
things, and though among those characters who are
most congenial to him one may be a young man who
likes talking about the Eternal Verities, doesn't mind
laying down the law, and speedily grows eloquent,
which enables him to be very cogent in his statements
as to how the various things are related to reality, this
is still an insufficient vehicle for all that Goethe has in
mind. Nor is a "Therefore" followed by a maxim
enough for him, either. The narrative is often interrupted by an extract from a diary, or a book of Reflections kept by one of the characters. According to Goe-

the, these Reflections will show what preoccupations habitually engaged that character's mind. But the character himself, embodying as he does such a type of mind, and seeing the world in such a light, stands in relation to Goethe as the extracts from the diary stand in relation to him. The character shows us the habitual preoccupations of Goethe's mind. Such and such reflections in the diary are certainly rather awkward to fit into the character's life. We wonder what could have given rise to them, and part of the story remains unknown. In the same way, Goethe's novels cannot give us a complete statement of Goethe, but they show his preference of mind as plainly as an intimate diary could do. For it is not in our diaries but in our books that we record ourselves, our true selves.

Goethe's novels are much taken up with the arts, and the means whereby we can master them. The actor's art, the architect's, the musician's, the art of teaching, are much to the fore, and with all this goes the question of the true nature of art. The problem of getting every one in the cast up to scratch obviously struck him as being part of the very essence of the artistic effort; hence, the part played by private theatricals and charades, and by that first performance in which Wilhelm Meister wants to act but does not know what to say, or that masonic ceremony where every one wishes to throw something into the foundations but being taken unawares does not know what to throw in. In *Elective Affinities*, a great deal is said about the art of laying out gardens, and planning buildings. And it is pointed out to what an extent lives are vainly devoted to these arts, a mistaken point of view having been adopted towards them, since for some minds—for example, Goethe's—a particular reali-

sation of the function of perspective, or of the grouping of tombs in a churchyard, can become one of those
things whose inner reality we are so sensible of that
trying to lay it bare we constantly hark back to it, and
are very ready to symbolise what it means to us by
stories and by characters. Apparently Goethe must
also have attached great importance to the need to
symbolise what is unseen and essential in our lives by
ceremonies; allegorical ceremonies which strike us as
extremely cold and trifling (a point on which it would
be absurd to raise theoretical quibbles, as each one of
us is enslaved to some aspect of things through which
the spirit of truth and inspiration is communicated to
him—for such a one, a scent which recalls the past and
breathes poetry into it, for others, something else).
Thus in *Elective Affinities* and *Wilhelm Meister*
there are Utopias where the virtues are celebrated in
such ceremonies, where very odd temples exhibit images, not of the old gods but of what ought to be vene-
rated, and pageants such as may strengthen man's will
to good.

Natural history seems to have been a negative pole
for his mind, as for some men debauchery is, for
others, the critical frame of mind, for others, luxury
and pleasure; in a word, whatever banishes inspiration, whatever is inimical to our true growth. Several of his Reflections relate to the folly of attrib-
uting so much importance to the study of human
phenomena or the perplexing and curious aspects of
the animal creation. The people in these novels are
dealt with pretty much like those of a puppet theatre,
so strongly is one made aware that Goethe is holding
the string that leads them on to a mysterious end—
moreover, this is what constitutes the charm of his

characters. In the rooms there are toy theatres. In the private museums, pictures or implements. In the narrative is inserted another narrative, told by one of the characters, which the real narrative cuts short. Characters are purposely left in bare outline, being merely "two lovers of the drama" (*Wilhelm Meister*), or "two people for whom there is no such thing as morality" (the Count and the Baroness in *Elective Affinities*). Characters are brought in at the beginning of the narrative only to reappear at the end, or here and there in the action. Again, encounters often take place with people who are encountered for some end known only to themselves, so that something very mysterious is imparted to their greetings. And finally, various incidents are foreshadowings of what will happen later on. Some of the characters are symbolical of a side of nature that Goethe seems to have been concerned at: the futile display of false activity by women (Philine, Luciana in *Elective Affinities*). And the author delegates and shares out his role of judge and mentor among various characters who are in some way moral specialists (like Mittler in *Elective Affinities* and the Genii of the Tower in *Wilhelm Meister*).

2

Chateaubriand

Shadowy figures, what are we beside these famous men? We vanish past recall. You, wild sweet-william, lying on my table beside this sheet of paper, whose belated little flower I gathered on the heath, you will grow up again; but we, we shall have no second spring with the fragrant recluse who beguiled me from myself. (Memoires d'Outre-Tombe, *Vol. II, p. 463.*)*

I love reading Chateaubriand because when on every second or third page I hear him sounding (as on a summer night after an interval of silence one hears the two notes, always the same two notes, that make up a barn-owl's cry) what is his own personal cry, just as monotonous, just as inimitable, I feel sure this is a poet. He tells us that there is nothing lasting on earth, that soon he will die and oblivion bear him away; we feel he speaks truly, since he is a man like other men; but all of a sudden, by the secret power within him, he has discovered among these events and ideas that poetry which he peculiarly seeks for, and behold! the thought which by rights should sadden us, enchants us, and proves, not that he will die, but that he is alive, that he is something of a higher order than things and events and the years; and we sigh for pleasure, remembering that this something is identical with what we have loved in him before. This very persistency ravishes us, for we feel that there is something higher than

---

* All page 485 in Vol. II, and numerous metaphors at the close, Christ of the Middle Ages as an image of the poet's wounds, the pierced veins as an image of the relief of writing.

events, nothingness, death, universal futility; and because that something which overcomes all else in him
is always one and the same and true to itself, we know
a new delight, as if we had seen that this marvellous
and transcendent power not only exists but has be-
gotten marvellous and transcendent persons whom we
recognise by their common identity. And when Chateaubriand while bemoaning Chateaubriand slips the
jesses of that marvellous and transcendent person who
is himself, we sigh for pleasure, since at the moment
when he declares himself annihilated, he makes his escape and enters upon a life where there is no such
thing as dying.

To be sure, he has not always been that person. Often, and above all when he sets out to be witty,
sprightly, Voltairean, though we may admire we do
not recognise him. But gradually, by force of sincerity, he has become it; and then, when it is that person
speaking, even when it is to convince us by every possible argument that he is but dust, he inspires an exactly contrary opinion because we feel he is alive; and
we sigh for pleasure, because we had previously known
him come alive, so that we can reassemble in him the
living person for whom there is no such thing as dying
and who lives with an intermittent but immortal existence in his works. We are sure that this person is a
poet, a *rara avis*, since what he says is always identical,
and does not borrow any grandeur, any authenticity,
from any of the things he relates, which do not alter it,
whereas quite suddenly, whether it is a matter of the
great Condé or of a little flower gathered at Chantilly, one feels that beneath his sentence there lies another reality, which shows through from beneath it

and whose physiognomy is made apparent, beneath the several clauses of the sentence, by their lineaments which correspond to it.

It is not possible to say why this reality is of a higher order than the reality of quite another kind which makes for the historical importance of events—higher than the intellectual validity of ideas, even, or the realities of death and annihilation. And yet there is something in it which surpasses events, since when he has just spoken of the fall of empires and of the mote he is in that whirlwind, the way he speaks of a little flower gathered at Chantilly—a way which ravishes us and is identical with that by which he ravishes us on other occasions—gives us the feeling of being something which, if not outlasting empires, in this sense of still retaining a personality, is at any rate so superior to time that even if one had known that the page was to be burned as soon as one had written it, one would have gone on writing in the same ecstasy, and relinquishing all else for it, so strong would be one's feeling of having given life to something real and of a reality inherently incapable of death; from which it follows that, as I said thirdly, it is of a higher order than the realities of death. And as I said, it is also higher than the intellectual validity of ideas; since in saying things patently more lofty, more searching, more universal, than what he says of that little blue flower, he might not have given us any comparable sensation nor (to turn from the reader to the maker) have found any trace of what was to inspire him and make us say in the same breath, This is Chateaubriand, and, This is beautiful. For perhaps the sole proof of the subservience of the noblest ideas to that mysterious thing, one's self, is that only when we meet with it is that high excitement at hand which makes our own words an enchantment to us, and makes others say, That is beautiful.

3

Joubert

One can see that Joubert's letters were intended to please. The fine passage about old men in the letter to Fontanes was certainly put in because he thought well of it, he "leads up to it." The wish to make a good impression on one's friends is compensatory, so to speak, to ambition; and those who, like Joubert, have renounced the thought of fame because deficient health, deficient talent too, may be, and lack of determination and driving force prevented them from working for it, are on the other hand stimulated into minor exploits, impromptus or little more, in order to make the most of themselves in the sight of younger members of their circle whom they would like to be admired by. And so we find in Joubert an abstemious distinction whose accents tell of solitude (inspiration, the moment when the mind makes contact with itself, when the inner voice leaves off being conversational and repudiates the talking and debating part of man), and yet, for all that, something perpetually sociable, all letter-writing and talking and allusions to his own Joubertian self, and assumptions that man is a social animal (which is Stendhal's weakness, too—but in other respects, how different). Nevertheless, what he says is coloured from within by his latent genius, and one understands how, feeling so superior and yet being unrecognised and having produced nothing, he set himself to prove his worth in the letters to Fontanes, and Molé, and Mme. de Beaumont, if nowhere else. Only it is a little egoistic (done with himself in mind). And he enhances his effects by adding: "Goodbye, I'm cold, I must go and get warm. That's all I remember. I feel tired." All truths, moreover, and all tricks to show that what seems so wonderful to them is only a little something struck off at random, when in fact it is only a little something struck off at random.

I would like to draw a parallel between this need for appreciation felt by those who are not "recognised" and the love of advertisement felt by those whose work seems unable to reach the public because it is too far above people's heads. When they write, their own approval is all they aim at, they don't give a thought to the public, and the public returns the compliment. And then they try to influence it by purely mechanical means, so that their work, in lieu of being widely read, should be violently talked about (Montesquiou). This is partly to give a little hoist to their reputation among their friends, too, I don't doubt.

Culture is, as it were, the intellectual equivalent of knowing how to behave. Among cultivated minds there reigns the freemasonry of fashionable society. One makes an inexplicit allusion to a writer, and every one knows who is meant by it, people don't require to be told what's what and who's who. One belongs to the same world. All this has its drawbacks too, involves too much of the personal element, imputes too much validity to the outer self and an absolute, or at any rate a vestigial importance to the sort of learning which is valueless except as having been instrumental in reaching the truth.

4

Notes on Stendhal[1]

Eighteenth-century style of irony (Voltaire, although Beyle didn't like him).

". . . so that one could have instanced old millionaire shopkeepers, old lawyers, old money-lenders, who during that period forgot to look morose and make money." (*Chartreuse*, p. 10.)

". . . had a hundred and fifty patriots arrested; these were the best men that Italy then had to show . . . damp . . . lack of food did speedy justice on all those rascals." (*Chartreuse*, p. 12.)

"There was a great deal of talk about this species of duel, and those who had found themselves involved in it thought it best to go travelling in Switzerland." (*Chartreuse*, p. 22.)

Ironical treatment of the characters, and Voltairean elegance. "Oh, a thousand times rather, let us be duped! That evening was appalling." (*Le Rouge et le Noir*, Vol. II, p. 87), and all the chapters following "*Moments Cruels . . .*"

"The misfortunes of jealousy could not go further." (*Le Rouge*, Vol. II, p. 100.)

"Twenty-four hours after the vase of old Japanese porcelain was broken, Julien was decidedly one of the unhappiest of men."

Voltairean elegance: the conversation between Prince Korasoff and Julien in the Strasbourg chapter that ends with: "I am demented, I am foundering, I must do as a friend advises and not as I think myself."

Weakening of a great mind and a good heart linked

to bodily weakening. The virtuous man grown old;
pessimistic morality; the Abbé Chélan visits Julien in
prison. Fabrice's last visit to the centenarian Abbé
Blanès's tower.

Rejection of all but spiritual emotions, renewed vitality of the past, indifference to ambitions, and tedium
of scheming, either when near to death (Julien in
prison; no longer ambitious. Love for Mme. de Rênal,
for nature, for reveries) or consequent on indifference
caused by being in love (Fabrice in prison, though here
the prison represents, not death, but love for Clélia).
This loftiness of soul linked to actual height (Julien's
cell very high up, fine view from it, Fabrice's cell very
high up, fine view from it).

Which leads to the third cause for indifference (in
this case, temporary); emotion at the sight of nature
and almost always on heights: the cave from which
Julien had such a wide view (it is true that he felt ambition there, but he says, "It was a passion, then"—
closing pages of *Le Rouge et le Noir*) and he says it
would have suited a philosopher. The tower where
Fabrice spends "one of the happiest years of his life."
The rock where one night he looks out over Lake
Como, and resolves to be so much more than the
nephew of ordinary private life to the Duchesse Piet-
ranera (difference between what one wills in moments
of exalted feelings and when those feelings have sub-
sided). Besides, this love of nature is the eighteenth-
century love for the beauties of nature, for beautiful
situations, always high up, whether the Vergy woods or
the terrace at Verrières, the Farnese tower or Grianta.
The feelings are very straightforward, in keeping with
picturesquely situated places: the stream at Verrières

or the beautiful expanse of Lake Como, mountain colouring, daybreak showing through trees (twice over in *Le Rouge et le Noir*, I think, from Mme. de Rênal's room and from Mathilde's. No doubt in *La Chartreuse* too).

Remorse, sheer weakening, a sad form of love, not more virtuous.

A maxim of Stendhal's: Never repent.

"This creature, weakened by too unremitting a sorrow. . . . That sorrow was Julien's absence, she called it remorse."

So remorse, with the aversion to pleasure it sets up, is always followed by an outburst of intense passion and sensual surrender. Scenes where Mme. de Rênal repulses Julien, then, after breaking off with him, kisses him (two instances, I think). Ditto for Fabrice and Clélia (in this second example, the refinement about *seeing* is in order to mark an Italian mentality, and, a double stroke, to show the inanity of religious enjoinments, their formal character).

In a manner of speaking these great books[2] reinforce the events of the narrative by giving a corresponding layer of the spirit behind the deed. Every action in *Le Rouge et le Noir* is followed by a clause showing an unconscious psychological process; it is the novel of motives. "Mme. de Rênal, sitting at the further end of the table, was startled into thought by this"; hatred and envy can be understood.

5

George Eliot

In *Adam Bede* the thing that strikes me is the careful, detailed, respectful, poetic and sympathetic portrayal of the humblest and most hardworking walk of life. To keep one's kitchen spotlessly clean is a prime duty, almost a religious duty, and a duty that is a pleasure too. Another striking thing is the sense of gravity attached to an evil intention or to a failure of resolution, which because of the interdependence of mankind spreads its fatal repercussions in every direction; and another, the sense of the mysterious greatness of human life and the life of nature, the solemn mysteries in which we play a part while knowing no more about them than does the growing flower (cf. *Silas Marner*). Then there is the sense that above the sequence of our vices and misfortunes a mighty providence somehow sustains a higher order that turns our evil into the incomprehensible instrument of our good (cf. *Silas Marner*). Adam loses Hetty, and this had to be, so that his heart might be opened to love the child (cf. Emerson, *Compensation*, and "man hurries about and God leads him"). Extremely sensitive feeling for nature, entering into it rather than describing it; above all, for nature in tranquillity; sweetness of autumn days, beauty of meadows and woodland, evenings of fast-travelling clouds. An exact, colourful, shrewd, eloquent way of fitting dialogue to humorous characters without lapsing into farce, with a dry wit as in Anatole France. Sense of the changes taking place in us and in things during the course of our lives. Silas's return to [Lantern] Yard, etc. Here and there, proofs of being familiar with philosophy (terms . . . imagery, etc.).

Freshness of imagery, springing from a sensitive, unjaded way of looking at things, that discovers unobserved feelings in them and so can describe them as symbols of feelings that are analogous (hearts thawing like little brooks); rather ponderous jokes about the nobility and gentry.

Sense of the good wrought by suffering, of moral growth, of counterpoising moral reactions through the social scale: here, about a flight of birds, here, about a church-going, elsewhere, about a gambler's losses.

A conservative spirit; not too much book-learning, not too many railways, not too much religious reform.

A genuine feeling for the bent of mind in a carpenter, a weaver, etc.

A lively sense of the development of sympathy and liking between people. Dinah, Silas Marner and his neighbours. . . .

Progressive capitulation of will power; we leave the baby's mother in *Silas* resolved against taking any more opium, and we find her with the bottle emptied. M . . . resolved not to see Hetty again, a moment later in her arms.

Sense that suffering is greater in a person who has no spiritual life, no moral solidarity with the others.

One of the conclusions to be drawn from these books (and which is not pointed out) is that the evil we do *is* evil (we work evil to ourselves and to others). And that on the other hand the evil which befalls us is often the necessary condition of a greater good that God intended for us.

6

Tolstoi[1]

Nowadays people set Balzac above Tolstoi. This is lunacy. Balzac's books are repulsive, posturing, full of absurdities; in them, humanity is judged by a literary man anxious to write a great book; in Tolstoi, by a serene god. Balzac succeeds in giving the impression of greatness; in Tolstoi everything is great by nature —the droppings of an elephant beside those of a goat. Those great harvest scenes in *Anna Karenina*, the hunting scenes, the skating scenes, etc., are like vast unbroken surfaces that space out the rest, and make everything seem on an ampler scale. It seems as though there were the whole meadow of standing hay, the whole summer, between two conversations of Levine's.[2] One loves different things by turns in this great world, and scenes that are like nothing else—the emotion of the man riding a race (O my beauty, my beauty!), of the man who has laid a wager, sitting on the window-sill, the gaiety of life under canvas, of the life of the little hunting squire, of old Prince Stsherbatski at the German Spa when he talks about the good old days of feudal Russia (getting up late, in the chapter about taking the waters, etc.), of the aristocratic spendthrift (Natasha's brother) in *War and Peace*, of old Prince Bolkonski. This is not the work of an observing eye but of a thinking mind. Every so-called stroke of observation is simply the clothing, the proof, the instance, of a law, a law of reason or of unreason, which the novelist has laid bare. And our impression of breadth and life is due precisely to the fact that none of this is the fruit of observation, but that every deed, every action, being no other than an expression of a law, one feels oneself moving amid a throng of laws—only, since the truth of these laws is established for Tolstoi by the inward authority they have exercised over his thinking, there are some which we are still baffled by. It is not easy to understand what he means when he speaks of Kitty's sly look when she talked about religion, nor when he speaks of Anna's delight at humbling Vronsky's pride.

We are pleased to see how the man of splendid intellect really draws on much the same kind of wit we often draw on ourselves (Ruskin's witticisms about his dog Vizir and his servant Anne, Tolstoi's witticisms setting the tone of the opening of *Anna Karenina*). And for all that, in this apparently inexhaustible fund of creation it seems as though Tolstoi were repeating himself, as though he had no more than a few themes at his disposal, disguised and reshaped, but the same in both novels. The stars, and the sky that Levine rivets his gaze on are pretty much the same as the comet that Peter saw, as Prince Andrew's wide blue sky. What is more, Levine, first discarded by Kitty in favour of Vronsky, then loved by her, reminds one of Natasha leaving Prince Andrew for Peter's brother-in-law, then going back to him. And might not the same memory have "sat" for Kitty passing by in the carriage and Natasha in the carriage following the army?

7

Dostoievski[1]

Dostoievski mentions among the worst miseries of his convict-life never, during the space of four years, being able to be by himself. But it would seem that even when continually exposed to the presence of others one should be able to isolate or abstract oneself. That is in everyone's power, and should have been more so, one would suppose, for Dostoievski than for any, he who ought to have known so well how to abolish what was around him by the hallucinating power of imagination. Anyhow, there are more incommoding presences to put aside than human ones, which at least are exterior to you and who, though able to incommode the process of thought, cannot prevent it. These presences are inmates. A man who has a disease lodged in him, who during these same four years (and often for much longer) has experienced frightful suffering and is never free from the stupefying discomfort that attends an incessant fever, so that it is an effort for him to turn over in bed, that man, always at the mercy of his disease, is much less alone than Dostoievski among the convicts, to whom, besides, he paid no attention and who paid no attention to him. But pain and fever compel you to attend to them.

For Dostoievski, forced labour was probably the stroke of good fortune which set free his inner life. It is strange how from that time on his letters resemble Balzac's: request for money, promises, based on hopes of fame, to repay at a hundred per cent. "*The Idiot* will be a fine book" (like *Le Lys dans la Vallée*) because he feels a new man awakening in him. Whatever Gide may say, there are dissertations interpolated in the narrative, those long reflections on capital punishment in *The Idiot,* for instance.

Crime and Punishment could be the title of all Dostoievski's novels (as all Flaubert's, *Madame Bovary* above all, could be called *L'Education sentimentale*). But probably he makes two persons by dividing what really appertained to one. There was certainly a crime in his life, and a punishment (which perhaps had no connection with the crime), but he has preferred to allot them severally, to attribute in case of need the impressions of punishment to himself (*The House of the Dead*), and the crime to others. His genius—contrary to what Rivière says—was for construction.

8

J*ules Renard*[1]

I admire him because he does not look for means of escape—contrary to almost all those who, unable to fathom what they feel, instead of persisting in the attempt to discover what there is in it, give up, glide on to something else, fail to get any deeper into that and scrabbling here, scrabbling there, end by covering a vast amount of ground, and believe that this will result in pleasing more readers than at some one point having persevered and dug right down. Renard does fathom a sensation, and seizes on its hidden truth. The whole truth?—No. He too, but not, after all, until he has already got down to a certain depth, has his little means of escape—or rather, he has two different kinds of base metal with which he completes the body of his little poem, which without this addition could not be coined into truth. And these two other things which qualify the absolute truth of the poem, and on which, when he feels truth running short, he pounces so that he may make the poem all the same and preserve the truth which without this alloy would be infinitesimal, are Drollery and the Conceit. (The Peahen: "Because of her hump, she dreams only of sores; and on the ground, she wallows like a humpback." The Hen: "She never lays golden eggs." The Butterfly: "This love-letter folded in half is looking for a flower's address.")

Note that the drollery is nearly always a Conceit—that is, a drawn-out image (like the Peahen quoted above). And that the conceit is sometimes the truth. For instance, the butterfly "looking for a flower's address" is not merely a conceit: that is, when one has run out of truth, going on with the image which turns into a play on words and supplies an ending which has only a verbal connection with the truth. But the butterfly "looking for a flower's address" is true because of the way the butterfly flits tentatively from flower to flower, and enquires, and must have been mistaken since it goes on to another flower. The *Chasseur d'images* is poor stuff.

9

Robert de Montesquiou[1]

M. Robert de Montesquiou, like Wagner, is much admired by persons of fashion. People who at heart only enjoy musical comedies and *La Favorita*, and when it comes to books find M. Leconte de Lisle incomprehensible and M. Mallarmé crazy, swoon over *The Valkyrie* and swooned over *Le Chef des Odeurs suaves*, comforting themselves for being so idiotic by imagining they are among the prophets. So the popularity enjoyed by M. Robert de Montesquiou cannot be urged in his favour, but neither should it be held against him, as it is by some. It has not the slightest bearing on his talent, which is vigorous enough to withstand anything, even fashion. But more emancipated spirits—still subject, however, to some rather wilted paradoxes which already look more like prejudices—understand him, in my humble opinion, no better when they cherish him as a sort of Prince of Decadence, ruling as a whimsical despot over every corruption of the mind and every refinement of the imagination. This is an attractive property but not extensive, and increasingly seems open to any offer. There is nothing profound about elegance and vice. One soon comes to the end of satanism, and of dandyism too. True sovereignties must be founded on a higher lineage or on a more transcendant conquest. Even supposing that no one happened to dethrone him, if M. de Montesquiou were no more than this, he would only be a sumptuous archetype of the ordinary young man of today. But comparing them, one will see the difference, or rather, the antithesis, and perhaps one will reach a clearer understanding of the true quality of the poet who wrote *Chauves-Souris*.

The generation of authentic Decadence took its charter from those lines in Théophile Gautier's preface to *Les Fleurs du Mal*, which not only made the young men of the day become aware of their worst intellectual failings but persuaded them that these were eminent qualities, well worth preserving and making more of. He proclaims that the style of decadent epochs, "the language already streaked with the tartness of decay and, as it were, well-hung," is by rights "the requisite and destined idiom of nations where civilisation and the artificial way of life have supplanted nature and taught man to feel new needs." This artificial way of life and even the depravity that results from it surpass the intellectual and moral values of the classic epochs, "as a maturer woman using all the resources of an accomplished charmer at a dressing-table spread with bottles of scent, face-washes, ivory-backed brushes and steel tweezers" surpasses "a simple young girl whose only cosmetics are soap and water." "As for depravity, it is a token of greatness. For depravity—in other words, the departure from the normal—is impossible for the beast, fated to obey an inflexible instinct." These theories, which seemed novel and already look curiously old-fashioned—provoking one to apply Dostoievski's profound remark that "a paradox is an axiom inside-out, one is no truer than the other"—had, among others that need not be gone into here, two serious consequences. The first, that the admiration which every superior mind should vow to Baudelaire, as the greatest poet of the nineteenth century and as the only intellectual and outspoken champion of classical poetry against romanticism, was

replaced by feelings which a mere satanist and decadent could inspire—feelings inevitably bound to fluc-
tuate between infatuation and exasperation, and to
obscure the reality of Baudelaire's genius by a legend
which even today has not been done away with (M.
de Montesquiou is in process of being victimised by
just such another legend); the second, that there
has ensued a generation of young men who with
scarcely an exception persist in resembling each other,
and whom we would like to distinguish most emphat-
ically from M. de Montesquiou, instead of making him
out to be their leader, as he is their god. If we know
one of these young men, we know them all. They are
all alike. To begin with, they all suffer from "impaired volition." They have no will to anything, so
they do not know how to act and do not wish to think.
The greater number plume themselves on this, others
make a show of deploring it as though it were some
indescribably distinguished ailment. One or two realise how deep their sickness goes, and how it eats into
thinking and doing, but cannot change their ways,
since to do so they would have to will so. If this
were not the most pitiable wretchedness, it would be
all too nauseatingly familiar.

Now the first thing that strikes me about M. de
Montesquiou is a deft, tenacious, commanding, all-
powerful will. His conversation reflects it, his fame
canonises it. From the moment he begins to talk one
is subjugated by a tremendous lilt which at first is
startling, accustomed as one is to the tame level voices
of today. His richly melodious tones recall those wonderful lines in the *Fleurs du Mal* about:

> . . . *The rich metallic strains*
> *Of regimental bands that sometimes flood our parks,*

And in the golden dusks when one draws breath again
Shed a brief heroism into the town-bred heart.[2]

He bears more resemblance to those conquistadors immortalised by M. de Heredia than to the neurotics of today. Does he not himself say in one of his flights of eccentricity which always have so much truth in them, that he would like to cancel that fatuous law which ordains that bad writers should make fortunes and good ones die in garrets, and that the reward of talent should be, not *that at least,* but *that as well?*

The decadent is usually ignorant, at any rate of all that is not the literature of decadence. He has never thought deeply, and his work, if he has not already attained literary sterility, reflects along with the morbid play of his feelings the nullity of his thought. M. de Montesquiou has drunk deep of classical literature, as his mottoes, chosen with exquisite skill, serve to prove. But above all else—and it is this which on setting out we reproached his most fervent admirers for being blind to, so that in their most eloquent praises they fall short of the truth—M. de Montesquiou does not stop at having the most exquisite sensibility, he is also one of the few nineteenth-century poets who can think. First and foremost, he is an intellectual. And so, as happened with Baudelaire, his poetry is rich in pithy lines, lines which recall Corneille as often as Baudelaire's recall Racine. Try this experiment. Ask who wrote these lines on *The Dying Peacock:*

His eyes are quenched, but not those of his plumes,
Living, he shone, and in his death he shines,
He tutors us in how to die serenely.[3]

Or this:

Who to proud modesty vowed eyelashes unwet.[4]

Or again this:

And the soul's inward sight strengthens as daylight fails.[5]

From Corneille? No, from Montesquiou.
  These (except perhaps the third):

And there is still, O Lord, no surer title-deed
That we can show in proof of human dignity
Than this impassioned sob that swells from age to age
And dies upon the brink of your eternity.[6]

And these:

O Lord my God, give me the strength and fortitude
To look upon my heart and flesh without disgust,[7]

should have been Racine's but are Baudelaire's.

As I write, I have before my eyes a photograph of
M. de Montesquiou which has caught the impeccable
beauty, the pensive nobility, of his face. One would
like to see "the Olympic laurel-wreath of exiled spirits"
on that head where the lightly-crisped locks are like
those of Greek statues, which have this same airy brilliant charm. Beneath, the poet has written the first line
of one of the *Chauves-Souris* poems:

I am the prince of transitory things.[8]

That is (whatever the clumsiness involved in recapit-
ulating what is so perfect) the sovereign of the shimmer of opals and the shadows of ghosts. Should not the
conclusion of these brief considerations be that his
kingdom is not only of this world, and that he has
been as often concerned with things eternal as with
things transitory? Since *Le Coucher de la Morte* has
been so often retailed this year, let us listen for once

to *Laus Noctis*. We have kept the best argument for the last.

II

I went to Versailles a few days ago.[9] Not far from the Allée des Marmousets

With its full flock of two and twenty bantlings[10]

I saw the oleanders—

Oleanders like bouquets of blooming lips[11]

in full flower,

Showering down their exculpating kisses
Us to absolve for having greatly loved.[12]

I went for a minute or two into the royal apartments, where I saw the wax mask of the Grand Monarch in which he is no more than "an old doll,"

Strange termination for so great a splendour.[13]

But soon I abandoned them for

Those green apartments that Le Nôtre designed,[14]

and walked about in the groves where formerly Bossuet took his solitary walks among figures out of Benserade's Fables,

A peopled solitude that pleasured the great churchman,[15]

and where today the great churchman would find them no longer. The sun was mottling the ornamental waters with gold and purple once more:

So many suns have died in these famed marble basins.[16]

Persuaded that in the crimsoned western sky I saw the distant gules of kingly France, I could say with the poet:

> *There is a pageant in the sky tonight*
> *And nature wears the borrowed light of history,*[17]

while the last rays of the sun, striking on the palace windows

> *Poured into them the jewelled panes of Chartres.*[18]

Then "this lovely bloodstained sky" turned into pink muslin and I went slowly back by the palace

> *Where grass grows up between the courtyard*
> *flagstones,*[19]

having given a parting glance at those deities

> *Of whom [   ] required a ducal mien,*[20]

and who already saw themselves less distinctly in the tanks whose waters were now tinged with blue under the rising moon,

> *Feeding their eyes upon themselves a-dying.*[21]

On my way home I thought about the poet whose noble figure, "youthful and of ancient race," had invisibly led me on this walk, where those lines that I adore, splendid lines that one knows by heart, start up before each statue like its shadow, before each shrub like its scent, before each figure of the past like its soul—so unshakably founded are they, so deeply and mysteriously rooted in this hallowed soil, in its landscape and in its history. This constraining power that enforces them on the mind in face of the reality and makes them inseparable companions of our strongest impressions, honoured guests in our memory, is no slight proof of their beauty. Today this poet is known to all of us and revered by the best of us: he is Robert de Montesquiou.

It is an added charm when the writers who in their varying degrees are great figures in literary history have been engaging, entertaining or poetical figures to boot. We enjoy seeing them, they for their part enjoyed displaying themselves in their books, Chateaubriand with his wind-blown locks, Lamartine followed by his greyhounds, or skating, like Goethe, or mounted on one of those horses "he had loved so much." It would take too long to explain, but it can be felt easily enough by any one of sensibility that M. de Montesquiou is of the same breed, that everything to do with him is poetical and that not only are his ideas those of a poet but that the circumstances of his life are artistically, and even symbolically, arranged. For *Les Perles Rouges*, the new book from which come the lovely lines we quoted (thinking, talking, writing, how often they come to mind!) and which will be both a compelling and an exquisite source of wonder to every lover of letters, M. Besnard has drawn the poet in the setting of Versailles—of all settings the stateliest, the richest in proud, fine, melancholy associations—and assuredly, the poet is not unworthy of the setting, nor do I know of anything statelier, finer, prouder, than that melancholy length of limb. Disdaining light literature and plebeian little stories, living in the austere fraternal company of the illustrious dead, whose memory I have evoked because he evokes it, this thinker and poet who is at once so majestically towering in his flights and so artistically scrupulous in his craftsmanship, adds yearly and sometimes even oftener, a fresh stone to an already hallowed monument—a massive slab, beyond the scope of weak minds to weigh or measure, and engraved with delightful hieroglyphics of deep mysterious meaning whose variety matches the thousandfold variety of the natural world. This time the poet has become an historian, but the historian has remained a poet. It is a strangely powerful poetry, nourished on facts, thirsty for life, not flinching from what is ludicrous, what is horrible, what is erudite; a singular kind of poetry, and singularly beautiful, of which M. de Montesquiou, inheriting from the romantic movement, and beyond that, from the neglected seventeenth century, is today perhaps the only exponent. Every outstanding mind of our time, from Leconte de Lisle to Verlaine, has singled it out and loved it. And this tireless and amazing artist is one of the most eminent thinkers, one of the most astonishing "eccentrics" (in the best sense of the word) now alive. At each fresh volume we should duly bow, and salute. . . .

10

Henri de Régnier

While I find myself over again in Régnier (myself—
and I think more than one writer of today and other
periods) not only in regard to what is the real core
of writing and what we all try to express, but in regard
to what is not, perhaps, my strongest suit, the way of
expressing it, the way that someone who is not a novelist tries to spill his feelings into a novel (for instance, I
am sure that what gave Régnier Antoine going to the
war is the transference into a different person's case of
what was true and universal in his feelings at the
time of his duel; the dinner with the Marshals must
also have a substratum of actual experience—however, one can be sure of nothing; when Régnier wrote
La Double Maîtresse he had never been to Rome! At
bottom, this actuality, whether or no someone has
killed, lain with, etc.—that is something which can
only be drawn from emanations of the deed itself, its
"waves" and material repercussions; reason knows as
much, knows more, but not exactly that); well then,
while I find myself over again in Régnier, I am also
conscious of things that make him different, his predilection for such and such a "type" or "feature," which
in conversation makes him say with a donnish air of
respect and comical admiration, outwardly extremely
formal, inwardly a mingling of affectation and cre-
dulity: "He only shakes hands with dukes, and just
waggles himself for a commoner. Quite admirable."
Then, a laugh. One can't qualify this as snobbery, even
as a traditional, retrospective snobbery. It comes
down from Flaubert and Leconte de Lisle, from the

taste for Simple Simons, from admiring what appears odd and picturesque. It must have been this that makes him take delight in the seventeenth century and resort to it for the amalgam between the language he took to studying there and his natural complexity of mind—the amalgam which is his language in *La Double Maîtresse*, and in which, although it may be the language of a great writer, one finds those seventeenth-century mannerisms of Faguet, Hervieu, Brunetière, etc., all the same. But of course in addition there is picturesqueness.

11

Léon Daudet[1]

Now a fresh volume of *Mémoires* by the Saint-Simon we call Daudet has come out, before the reading public can have had time to exhaust the merits of those wonderful books, *L'Hérédo*, and *Le Monde des Images*. I have said before that these were epoch-making, like the *Discours de la Méthode*. No less vitalising, they will little by little give rise to a new school of medicine, a new kind of literary criticism, a new morality and a new sociology. Apart from these proliferations, whose half-emerging shoots prick up from every page, they are masterpieces in themselves. That often-quoted hoarfrost passage in *Le Monde des Images* is typical of one of the most searching and sensitive clairvoyants into the life and spirit of man that I know.

It is a totally different aspect of this prolific mind which we are shown in these extraordinary *Souvenirs*. I shall venture to say that they and the author's polemical writings (in spite of their frequent similarity as regards subject matter, or rather, contrariwise, because of it) are poles apart. This is one of the differences between Saint-Simon and Léon Daudet—who is not only a Saint-Simon, but a Saint-Simon in between being other people, just as he is a Balzac, a political doctrinaire, and at the same time a very Balzacian Ferragus, Destroyer-in-Chief. There are many resemblances between Daudet and Saint-Simon. The profoundest, I take it, is the alternation with equally successful handling between portraits which are triumphs of ruthlessness and portraits which are all sweetness and light and veneration. In the former, the style is colloquial, the words, charged with a gunpowder energy, go off in irresistibly pictorial fireworks, that have an inspired, ingenious comicality out of all reason, but whose testimony prevails and always will prevail on something which, though not rational, is part of every literate mind. So, after the delightful La Fontaine fable which "epitomises" M. Noblemaire's speech, we have M. Loucheur launching himself with giant strides on the speaker and "biting him on the wrist," we have Casimir-Périer, sad and sober "as a spectacle case," we have Faguet, Judet, d'Avenel, and the rest of them. But side by side with all these figures, etched as bitingly as Saint-Simon's Président de Harlay, Duc de Noailles, Villars, Vendôme, are the portraits of Doctor Potain and Général de Castelnau. Did Philippe de Champaigne ever paint anything purer, more austere, more serenely composed than these? It is as though it were Saint-Simon writing about Beauvilliers or the Duc de Bourgogne or Rancé.

There are many differences. That which strikes me most is this double personality of Léon Daudet's thought, shown in his polemics and in his *Souvenirs*. I have only lately come to know the polemic Daudet. One paper being as much as I can read, instead of those I used to read I now read *L'Action française*. I may claim to have this counted unto me for righteousness. Since the thought of what a man could suffer had earlier made me a Dreyfusard, it can be imagined how a "daily" infinitely more merciless than *Le Figaro* or the *Débats* that I had previously been content with often gives me much the same sensation as the oncoming of a heart-attack. But what other daily paper has its front page decorated with frescoes by the very hand of Saint-Simon—by which I mean the hand of Léon Daudet? Further on, Bainville's luminous column, upright and incomparable in its crystalline irrefutability, guides me unerringly through the desert of foreign politics. Maurras, who today appears to hold the record for altitude, has but to give a bird's eye view of Lamartine, and it does me more good than a flight in an aeroplane—an altitude treatment for the mind. And at the opposite point of the horizon flashes the constellation of Orion.

But Léon Daudet's *Souvenirs* show his polemicism strangely and wonderfully translated. This man who is so unpretentious, so warm-hearted towards the "small fry," the common people, who is in very truth the least snobbish of mankind, and who has attacked wealth and worldliness in pages that are absolutely capital and ring absolutely true, this man who seems to have imposed on himself, from patriotic motives, a "heroic" obligation to loathe—in the meaning of the word he employs where he speaks of the "sham heroics" of Colonel Henry (that I do not consider heroic at all, however disillusioned I may be with all the Dreyfusards who try to establish a footing in the Faubourg Saint-Germain), this man, writing on the same subjects and about the same people—true, at a different period—allows himself the solace of being kind, of leaving

The harsh-voiced string where hatred had vibrated [2]

unplucked in his lyre.

Doubtless he knows that these are the very people whom he will now daily accuse of being Bolsheviks; and he is too much of a philosopher not to connect effects with causes. But in these books, it is the poet, as Schumann says, and only the poet who speaks. And so he will tell in the gentlest way about these same people as they were in private life, twenty years ago. They, for their part, when they read the book must surely believe that the articles are some appalling nightmare, or, when they read the articles, that the book is a blissful dream that one can put no belief in. I who myself in the articles and in the books of Léon Daudet have met with nothing but his delightful friendship, I can speak impartially of this double vision, which views the same beings in the light of action and in the light of recollection, and can say that, in these volumes of the *Souvenirs*, it gives me, quite apart from the incomparable liveliness of narrative and description, a mysterious impression of a kind of golden age. What must this be like for his victims? Judet himself, I imagine, whose portrait one cannot read without being rocked by Homeric laughter, must fancy on reading our Saint-Simon's story of how the militarist de Neuilly's mass of war material fell on Henry Houssaye's foot, that it is only in a dream that he has been accused of communicating with the enemy. There is so much poetry in this double vision that to convey some idea of it I should need (did not the savage limitations of journalism oblige me to break off just when I was getting into my stride) the words that Léon Daudet had at his command when, a propos of *Soir des Rois*, he talked of Shakespeare's fairy-tale period.

Notes

*I should make it plain that the G. (for Gallimard edition)
in these notes is merely a textual reference. I have no doubt
that most, if not all, of the few instances where I have
found myself in disagreement with the text are exactly
transcribed from Proust's manuscript. But as it would only
be possible to make a just apportionment of these disputed
readings by collating the printed text with the original, I
have no choice but to cite the printed text as source.*

*Method. In points of dispute, or needing elucidation, the
translation is given first and the Gallimard text after it.
Thus:*
*until his cronies Arthez, Rastignac and Marsay are dragged
through the mire:* l'heure où ses fidèles d'Arthez recevront
le baptême de la boue, de Rastignac et de Marsay.
the true Daughter of Fire: Sylvie *makes part of a series to
which de Nerval gave the general title* Les Filles du Feu.

The text of the quotations from Les Fleurs du Mal *is taken
from the Basil Blackwell edition, edited Enid Starkie, 1924.
The quotations from Proust's letters are taken from* Letters
of Marcel Proust, *translated by Minna Curtis, Chatto &
Windus, 1950.*

Prologue

[1] This and other titles, except where noted, are supplied by G. Proust made an N.B. for this opening. "Begin by mistrust for intellect." G.

In Slumbers

[1] Take yourself off, my boy: *Ote-toi de là, mon petit, que je m'y mette*. A catchword, dating from the French Revolution.
[2] Square brackets indicate gaps in Proust's manuscript. Any text between such square brackets is supplied by conjecture.

The Article in Le Figaro

[1] Proust's notebook contains this outline: "In the morning Mamma tells me to go back to sleep, gives me my article, more light through the window curtains, rain at dawn and mild weather, the butcher's step in street enough to make me see the day that's beginning and to follow it while at the same time I keep my body asleep. Smell of cars in the country. Maeterlinck and Barrès, both wrong." G. The latter part of this note was used in *The Days*.

The Sunbeam on the Balcony

[1] The title is Proust's.
[2] Félicie, afterwards Françoise. This piece is of earlier date. G.
[3] *Il faut que mon maître ait pris le soir pour le matin.*
(Molière, Amphitrion.)

Talking to Mamma

[1] *Son départ ne pouvait plus à propos se faire.*
(Molière, Le Misanthrope.)
[2] It would be a fine set-out:
(Labiche, La Grammaire.)
[3] *Si vous n'êtes Romain, soyez digne de l'être.*
(Corneille, Horace.)
[4] *Point d'ordre, point de bruit sur la ville.*
(Amphitrion.)
[5] *Eh là là! Madame la Nuit*
Un peu doucement, je vous prie,
Que vos chevaux, aux petits pas réduits,
De cette nuit délicieuse

Fassent la plus longue des nuits.
Proust's memory has furnished him with two passages from
the first scene of *Amphitrion*, which he has put together.
* *Cette nuit en longueur me semble sans pareille.*

(ibid.)

* *Peut-il donc ignorer quelle sévère loi*
Aux timides mortels cache ici notre roi,
Que la mort est le prix de tout audacieux
Qui sans être appelé se présente à ses yeux?

(Racine, *Esther*.)

Here the quotation is slightly manipulated by the speaker.
* *O douce paix,*
Beauté toujours nouvelle,
Heureux le cœur épris de tes attraits!
O douce paix,
O lumière eternelle,
Heureux le cœur qui ne te perd jamais!

(ibid.)

* *C'est vous Esther qui sans être attendue. . . .*
Sans mon ordre on porte ici ses pas.
Quel mortel insolent vient chercher le trépas.

(Racine, *Esther*.)

Thus in G. Proust's memory has recalled the last line first. In
Esther:
Sans mon ordre on porte ici ses pas!
Quel mortel insolent vient chercher le trépas?
Gardes! . . . C'est vous, Esther? quoi! sans être attendue?
* *Que craignez-vous? Suis-je pas votre frère?*
Est-ce pour vous qu'est fait un ordre si sévère?

qu'on fit. G.

* *Défendez, chère Alcmène, aux flambeaux d'approcher.*

(*Amphitrion*.)

The Method of Sainte-Beuve

[1] Projected opening for the first version of the essay, in orthodox essay form. G. Proust's outline: "That mistake consists of. Mistake over Stendhal. People who have known us
poets. Really, poetry is something secret. Sainte-Beuve has
not understood this. From the beginning, salons. Later, *Lundis* better, more society, women, but still the surface: method
for salons, Louis XIV, politics, no posterity, fine season for
poetry this year, those who come after us. Became of this,
bad writer. Go further: intellect." G.

[2] Proust's italics.

[3] This passage from *On Heroes, Hero-Worship and the Heroic in History* would seem to be what Proust had in mind.

[4] The "illusion to be described" is Flaubert's phrase.

[5] He drew no dividing line between the state of being engaged in a piece of writing and the state when in solitude: *Il ne faisait pas de démarcation entre l'occupation littéraire, où, dans la solitude. . . .* G.

[6] . . . something more superficial and empty in a writer's authorship, something deeper and more contemplative in his private life: *quelque chose de plus extérieur et de plus vague, quelque chose de plus approfondi et recueilli à l'intimité.* G.

[7] G. supplies the passage in question. "It is not that the poet's talent has in any way grown less. It is the use and misdirection of that talent which invites a sort of repression."

[8] Pontmartin: M. de Pontmartin, who probably suffered at the hands of Sainte-Beuve, put a rather spiteful sketch of him into one of his books. "It is affirmed that he spends his time hunting up weapons of offense and defence, with which to overwhelm those whom today he loves and tomorrow may hate, or today detests and will wreak vengeance on later." Sainte-Beuve replied in an indignant article. "Understand this, Monsieur, that if you were not a trifler who does not weigh his words, you would be a slanderer." G.

[9] . . . replied to the . . . : Proust may have had in mind Sainte-Beuve's reply to the Goncourts, who asked him what had become of his promised article on *Madame Gervaisais.* "On thinking it over, it seemed to me that I should be embarking on a difficult, almost impossible operation: to amplify, amid much praise of details, an adverse criticism on the method and general effect, and to do so not only without wounding the authors, but also without provoking more or less well-intentioned comments—and certainly very animated comments—in their immediate circle.

"I was led to this conclusion by my own judgment, and also, I will admit, by one or two of those rumours which, though not serious in themselves, are danger-signals.

"As my purpose in writing these articles, and the spirit in which I reckoned on writing them, was quite definite, and as these would have remained the same in six months' time, I shall brook it ill if any of this is attributed to a change of environmental temperature—as our friend Taine has it." G.

[10] *Cet être, comme il est gauche et laid.* Proust, quoting by memory from Baudelaire's *L'Albatros*, makes a conflate of:

Ce voyageur ailé, comme il est gauche et veule!
Lui, naguère si beau, qu'il est comique et laid!

Sainte-Beuve and Baudelaire

[1] In G. this is preceded by the essay on Gérard de Nerval. But as Proust in *Sainte-Beuve and Baudelaire* refers to de Nerval's poetry "which we ought to turn to next" (p. 139), I have accordingly reversed the order. The title is Proust's. Note is Proust's, as are all other footnotes appearing with the text.

[2] . . . drafting in anonymity a plan for the defence: which he headed, *Petits Moyens de Défense.*

[3] *trop gaie: trop sage.* G.

[4] . . . our spiritual man, in the outward man imposed on it by our body . . . : . . . *notre personne, dont l'apparence que lui donne notre corps. . . .* G.

[5] *Même quand l'oiseau marche, on sent qu'il a des ailes.*

[6] *Ces yeux sont des puits faits d'un million de larmes. . . .*
(*Les Petites Vieilles*) *un millier:* G.
Toutes auraient pu faire un fleuve avec leurs pleurs,
(ibid.)

[7] *Flagellés par les bises iniques,*
Frémissant au fracas roulant des omnibus . . . ,
Se traînent, comme font les animaux blessés,

[8] . . . any cruel detail: Proust notes here, "His poem, *Les Aveugles,* begins: *Contemple-les, mon âme; ils sont vraiment affreux!*"

[9] *Ou dansent, sans vouloir danser, pauvres sonnettes. . . .*
Celle-là, droite encore, fière et sentant la règle. . . .

Avez-vous observé que maints cercueils de vieilles
Sont presque aussi petits que celui d'un enfant?
La Mort savante met dans ces bières pareilles
Un symbole d'un goût bizarre et captivant. . . .

A moins que méditant sur la géométrie
Je ne cherche, à l'aspect de ces membres discords,
Combien de fois il faut que l'ouvrier varie
La forme de la boîte où l'on met tous ces corps. . . .

[10] *Mais moi, moi qui de loin tendrement vous surveille,*
L'œil inquiet, fixé sur vos pas incertains,
Tout comme si j'étais votre père, ô merveille!
Je goûte à votre insu des plaisirs clandestins.

[11] *Débris d'humanité pour l'éternité mûrs,*

[12] *Le violon frémit comme un cœur qu'on afflige,*
(*Harmonie du Soir.*)

[13] . . . perhaps this subordination of sensibility: *omnibus*. Peut-être, and new paragraph. G.

[14] *Pour que tu puisses faire à Jésus, quand il passe,*
Un tapis triomphal avec ta charité.
(*La Rebelle.*)

[15] *Un ange furieux fond du ciel comme un aigle,*
Du mécréant saisit à plein poing les cheveux,
Et dit, le secouant: "Tu connaîtras la règle!
(Car je suis ton bon Ange, entends-tu?) Je le veux!
Sache qu'il faut aimer, sans faire la grimace,
Le pauvre, le méchant, le tortu, l'hébété,
Pour que tu puisses faire à Jésus, quand il passe,
Un tapis triomphal avec ta charité."
(ibid.)

[16] *Toutes m'enivrent! Mais parmi ces êtres frêles*
Il en est qui, faisant de la douleur un miel,
Ont dit au Dévouement qui leur prêtait ses ailes:
"Hippogriffe puissant, mène-moi jusqu'au ciel!"
(*Les Petites Vieilles.*)

[17] *L'une, par sa patrie au malheur exercée,*
L'autre, que son époux surchargea de douleurs,
L'autre, par son enfant Madone transpercée,
Toutes auraient pu faire un fleuve avec leurs pleurs!

[18] . . . idea of *patria: la patrie des anciens.* G.

[19] *Les uns joyeux de fuir une patrie infâme.* . . .
(*Le Voyage.*)

C'est la bourse du pauvre et sa patrie antique.
(*La Mort des Pauvres.*)

[20] . . . like the splendid idioms . . . : *Comme les belles formes* and new paragraph. G.

[21] *Dans le pain et le vin destinés à sa bouche*
Ils mêlent de la cendre avec d'impurs crachats;
Avec hypocrisie ils jettent ce qu'il touche,
Ils s'accusent d'avoir mis leurs pieds dans ses pas.

Sa femme va criant sur les places publiques. . . .
Je ferai le métier des idoles antiques, . . .

Ah! que n'ai-je mis bas tout un nœud de vipères,
Plutôt que de nourrir cette dérision!
(*Bénédiction.*)

[22] *Tous ceux qu'il veut aimer l'observent avec crainte.*

(ibid.)

[23] *Elle-même prépare au fond de la Géhenne*
Les bûchers consacrés aux crimes maternels.

[24] *Des trônes, des vertus, des Dominations.*

[25] *Je sais que la douleur est la noblesse unique*
Où ne mordront jamais la terre et les enfers,
Et qu'il faut pour tresser ma couronne mystique
Imposer tous les temps et tous les univers.

[26] But soon: I read what follows as one long sentence which comes to its end with *Gustave Moreau's country.* G. breaks it twice; first, with a full stop and new paragraph after *O prince's daughter;* and again with a full stop after *serpent.*

[27] *Je traîne des serpents qui mordent mes souliers*

(La Voix.)

[28] How beautiful are thy feet: cf. Canticles 7.1.

[29] . . . *et ces serpents sous les pieds comme sous les pieds de Jésus,* Not traced.

[30] *Où des vaisseaux glissant dans l'or et dans la moire*
Ouvrent leurs vastes bras pour embrasser la gloire
D'un ciel pur où frémit l'éternelle chaleur

(La Chevelure.)

G. has *nageant* for *glissant*, and prints the quotation as part of Proust's own sentence, except for the last four words which are between quotation marks.

[31] *Que les soleils marins teignaient de mille feux.*
baignaient for *teignaient*—G.

[32] *Les cocotiers absents de la superbe Afrique*
Derrière la muraille immense du brouillard. . . .

(Le Cygne.)

[33] *Des cocotiers absents les fantômes épars.*

(A une Malabaraise.)

[34] . . . *ses beaux reflects de cierge*
Sur la nappe frugale et les rideaux de serge

(Je n'ai pas oublié: Tableaux Parisiens.)

[35] . . . *ces concerts, riches de cuivre,*
Dont les soldats parfois inondent nos jardins,
Et qui, dans les soirs d'or où l'on se sent revivre,
Versent quelque héroïsme au cœur des citadins.

(Les Petites Vieilles.)

[36] *Le son de la trompette est si délicieux*
Dans ces soirs solonnels de célestes vendanges

(L'Imprévu.)

G. omits *solonnels.*

[37] *. . . nous monte et nous enivre,*
Et nous donne le cœur de marcher jusqu'au soir.

(*La Mort des Pauvres.*)

[38] *Brick ou frégate dont les formes au loin*
Frissonnent dans l'azur

a summarized quotation of

. . . brick, tartane ou frégate
Dont les formes au loin frissonnent dans l'azur

(*Lesbos.*)

[39] *Le Plaisir vaporeux fuira vers l'horizon*

(*L'Horloge.*)

G. has *printemps* for *plaisir;* an extremely odd mistake for
Proust to have made, but possibly his mind was still claimed
by the elaboration of the passage about the precious stone—
which we call cat's-eye.

[40] *Le printemps adorable a perdu son odeur*

(*Le Goût du Néant.*)

[41] *Bâton des exilés, lampe des inventeurs. . . .*
Toi qui fais au proscrit ce regard calme et haut
Qui damne tout un peuple autour d'un échafaud.

(*Les Litanies de Satan.*)

[42] *C'est l'auberge fameuse, inscrite sur le livre*
Où l'on pourra manger, et dormir, et s'asseoir;

Et qui refait le lit des gens pauvres et nus;
C'est la gloire des Dieux, c'est le grenier mystique,
C'est le portique ouvert sur les Cieux inconnus.

(*La Mort des Pauvres.*)

[43] *Je fume comme la chaumine. . . .*

(*La Pipe.*)

[44] *. . . c'est ici qu'on vendange*
Les fruits miraculeux dont votre cœur a faim.

(*Le Voyage.*)

[45] *Vous êtes un beau ciel d'automne, clair et rose!*

(*Causerie.*)

[46] *Et les soirs au balcon, voilés de vapeurs roses*

(*Le Balcon.*)

[47] *Beaux écrins sans joyaux, médaillons sans reliques*

(*L'Amour du Mensonge.*)

relique—G.

[48] *Et les grands ciels qui font rêver d'éternité*

(*Paysages.*)

[49] *Et tes yeux attirants comme ceux d'un portrait*
                    (*L'Amour du Mensonge.*)
[50] *O toi que j'eusse aimé, ô toi qui le savais*
                         (*A une Passante.*)
[51] *Tous ceux qu'il veut aimer l'observent avec crainte*
                         (*Bénédiction.*)
[52] *O charme d'un néant follement attifé*
                         (*Danse Macabre.*)
du néant—G.
[53] *Et dont l'aspect aurait fait pleuvoir les aumônes*
Sans la méchanceté qui luisait dans ses yeux
                         (*Les Sept Vieillards.*)
les yeux auraient; qui brillait—G.
[54]   . . . *ce petit fleuve,*
Pauvre et triste miroir où jadis resplendait
L'immense majesté de vos douleurs de veuve. . . .
                         (*Le Cygne.*)
triste et pauvre—G.
[55] *Nul trait ne distinguait, du même enfer venu,*
Ce jumeau centenaire, et ces spectres baroques
                         (*Les Sept Vieillards.*)
nul œil—G. Second line supplied.
[56] *Aux captifs, aux vaincus!—à bien d'autres encor!*
                         (*Le Cygne.*)
[57] *Au fond de l'Inconnu pour trouver du nouveau!*
                         (*Le Voyage.*)
[58] *Et mon âme dansait, dansait, vieille gabare*
Sans mâts, sur une mer monstrueuse et sans bords.
                         (*Les Sept Vieillards.*)
sans (bords)—G.? Brackets suggest that the sentence fol-
lowing should be read as a footnote.
[59]   . . . *sa raison s'en alla.*
L'éclat de ce soleil d'un crêpe se voila;
Tout le chaos roula dans cette intelligence,
Temple autrefois vivant, plein d'ordre et d'opulence,
Sous les plafonds duquel tant de pompe avait lui.
Le silence et la nuit s'installèrent en lui,
Comme dans un caveau dont la clef est perdue.
Dès lors il fut semblable aux bêtes de la rue,
Et quand il s'en alla sans rien voir, à travers
Les champs, sans distinguer les étés des hivers,
Sale, inutile, et laid comme une chose usée,
Il faisait des enfants la joie et la risée.
                         (*Châtiment de l'Orgueil.*)

⁶⁰   *. . . les vastes éclairs de son esprit lucide
Lui dérobent l'aspect des peuples furieux.*

(*Bénédiction.*)

Dérobaient—G.

⁶¹ But like Gérard: Here Proust incorporates in his text, chang-
ing the tense:
*Il joue avec le vent, cause avec le nuage,
Et s'enivre en chantant chemin de la croix.*

(*Bénédiction.*)

⁶² no fool: Here Proust notes: Check.

Gérard de Nerval

¹ *Je suis le ténébreux.*

(*El Desdichado.*)

² a sicklied resolution in which the predetermining instinct is
lacking: *maladie de la volonté ou manque d'instinct déter-
miné.* G.

³ *Le ciel pur où frémit l'éternelle chaleur.*

⁴ *Un ciel pur où se perd l'éternelle chaleur.*

⁵ *Et la treille où le pampre à la rose s'allie.*

(*El Desdichado.*)

⁶ *. . . où le pampre s'enlace aux rosiers.*

⁷ *Il est un air pour qui je donnerais. . . .*

(*Fantasie.*)

⁸ *Une femme que dans une autre existence peut-être
J'ai vue et dont je me souviens. . . .*

(*ibid.*)

Sic. in G. Proust's compression of
*Puis une dame. . . .
Que dans une autre existence, peut-être
J'ai déjà vue—et dont je me souviens.*

⁹ *. . .* goblets he might have put there: the reference is to the
story of Joseph and his brethren. Gen. 44.

¹⁰ no steelier point: *Car il n'est pas de pointe plus acérée que
celle de l'Infini.* Baudelaire. *Petits Poèmes en Prose.*

¹¹ the true Daughter of Fire: *Sylvie* makes part of a series to
which de Nerval gave the general title *Les Filles du Feu.*

Sainte-Beuve and Balzac

¹ Madame de Beauséant shows no surprise: Proust's note,
"Compare, as regards delicacy of feeling, the amazement of
the heroine in Mme. de Noailles, *La Nouvelle Espérance,*

when the man who seemed to be wooing her said, 'Do ar-
range a good marriage for me.' "
² semblance of fiction: *des mines de romans.* G.
³ historical disquisitions: *de courts historiques.* G.
⁴ The greatest grief of my life? "One of the greatest griefs in
my life is the death of Lucien de Rubempré." Said by Vivian
in Wilde's *The Decay of Lying.*
⁵ . . . until his cronies Arthez, Rastignac and Marsay are
dragged through the mire: *l'heure où ses fidèles d'Arthez recevront le baptême de la boue, de Rastignac et de Marsay.* G.

Monsieur de Guermantes' Balzac

¹ The title is Proust's.

A Race Accursed

¹ I bowed and began to talk to her: *je le saluai d'abord.* G.
² sight of Christ: in French law-courts a crucifix hangs on the
wall behind the judge.

Names

¹ belfry: *cloches.* G.
² Jacques Cartier: navigator and explorer, 1491-1557. When
Proust was writing "old Chinese pottery" was fashionable,
and some of it was, as he here implies, of very dubious antiquity.
³ a Duchess in Debrett: Proust uses the English form of the
word, *de cette duchess,* and italicises it.
⁴ beneath two bridges: *sous deux toits.* G.

The Return

¹ Crippled Men of Jumièges: *les énervés de Jumièges* were sons
of Clovis II. Revolting against him while he was on pilgrimage to the Holy Land, they were punished by being ham-
strung. Set adrift in a boat on the Seine—"God will know
where to take them"—they were cast ashore at the Abbey of
Jumièges.
² *Quelle importune main en formant tous ces nœuds,*
A pris soin sur mon front d'assembler mes cheveux?
³ . . . that the view of Chartres had upset me: *que la vue de
Combray m'avait remué.* G. The view, on p. 262, is certainly
of Chartres. What Marcel at the opening of this paragraph

speaks of having seen (p. 261) is in the singular: *C'est comme cela que je l'avais vu,* and a footnote in G. says *Le clocher de Chartres;* but as Chartres has two, this is not wholly satisfactory. In fact, we have to deal with two different "states" of Proust's creation, and the discrepancies cannot be resolved.

The Return to the Present

[1] This is headed *Conclusion* in G. It seems, rather, a new departure, since it has no bearing on what has gone before, and except for one mention of Sainte-Beuve, makes no reference to it. But in deference to M. de Fallois, I have chosen a title which links it with the rest of *Contre Sainte-Beuve.*

[2] hurrying the words: *les notes.* G.

[3] an equally beautiful shepherd. Proust's marginal note: "So the variant readings and emendations in the critical editions are not all that important. Various versions of Verlaine's *Titus and Bérénice* sonnet."

[4] questions of wider import. Here Proust interpolates between brackets: "Take out this horrible writing."

[5] *Ne dites pas: la vie est un joyeux festin;*
Ou c'est d'un esprit sot ou c'est d'une âme basse.
Surtout ne dites pas: elle est malheur sans fin;
C'est d'un mauvais courage et qui trop tôt se lasse.

Riez comme au printemps s'agitent les rameaux.
Pleurez comme la bise ou le flot sur la grève.
Goûtez tous les plaisirs et souffrez tous les maux.
Et dites: c'est beaucoup, car c'est l'ombre d'un rêve.
G. supplies these verses of Moréas's from Proust's indication: "Quote the verse that has *d'un esprit trop sot et d'une âme trop basse,* and ends with that old tag which has been said hundreds of times after Leconte de Lisle, *l'ombre d'un rêve.*"

Against the Young Writers of the Day

[1] M. de Fallois dates this as not later than 1896. There is a certain resemblance in tone to parts of the essay on Robert de Montesquiou on which Proust was working in 1894 (p. 384 *et sup.*) and perhaps de Montesquiou's influence may be traced in both.

On Taste

[1] Similarly dated by M. de Fallois.

A History of French Satire

[1] Of earlier date.
[2] *Gringoire:* a comedy by Théodore de Banville (1886).
[3] Mathurin Régnier, a satiric poet (1573-1613); Nicolas Gilbert, satirist (1751-1780).
[4] Monsieur Trissotin, *qui parle toujours de Vers et de Latin.* (*Les Femmes Savantes*, Act II, Scene X.)

A Sunday Concert at the Conservatoire

[1] Appeared in *Le Gaulois*, 14 January 1895.
[2] every mannerism . . . [is eschewed]: *Toutes les mauvaises manières, emphatiques ou vulgaires, spontanées ou apprises, et les mouvements du corps sont dénudés. . . . G.*

Patriotism and the Christian Spirit

[1] Dated by M. de Fallois from the French translation of Tolstoi's work, which came out in 1900.

On La Bonne Hélène

[1] Dated by M. de Fallois as contemporary with the article on Saint-Saëns.
[2] *Les yeux qu'elle a charmés font-ils les siens moins beaux?*
Non, une seule torche allume cent flambeaux
Et garde intacte sa lumière.
[3]   *. . . qui ressemble à la haine elle-même.*
On veut être aimé seul, on veut, que d'embarras,
Faire tout le bonheur, ou si l'on ne peut pas,
Tout le malheur de ce qu'on aime.
[4] The passage in La Bruyère runs: *L'on veut faire tout le bonheur, ou, si cela ne se peut ainsi, tout le malheur de ce qu'on aime.* (*Caractères; du Cœur.*)
[5] They quote the Gospel:
Laissez venir à moi tous ces petits enfants. . . .
Laissez venir à moi les tout petits enfants. . . .
Laissez venir à moi les petits enfants blonds.
The first of these lines may be an authentic quotation, but more probably the whole thing is invented.
[6] *Éros est grave et triste, il rêve on ne sait quoi*
Par-delà le réel, je suis très simple, moi,
Et n'ai pas de mélancolie.

Dessus les murs troyens voyant passer Hélène,
Si pour telle beauté nous souffrons telle peine
Notre mal ne vaut pas un seul de ses regards.

Portrait of a Writer

[1] Alphonse Daudet, who died in 1897.

Poet and Novelist

[1] This contains two evidences of its date. Mallarmé died in 1898. The repercussions of the Dreyfus affair continued even after the re-trial had taken place in 1899. Proust was a Dreyfusard, and it seems unlikely that he would have written about "finding excuses in the Dreyfus Affair" during the thick of the agitation.

The Wane of Inspiration

[1] M. de Fallois suggests no date. The metaphor of the partition is used in the preface to *Contre Sainte-Beuve*.

The Artist in Contemplation

[1] M. de Fallois suggests no date. In style, matter, and argument, this essay is related to the critical section of *Contre Sainte-Beuve*, and reads almost as if it were a statement of just what it was in Proust's own reaction to art that made him find Sainte-Beuve's so inadequate.
[2] innumerable little white blossoms: *innombrables petites blanches gaufrées.* G.
[3] The passage about "the mysterious laws" is perhaps easier to accept than to explain. What is meant, I think, is that some aspects of the beautiful are demonstrations of those laws, and others, annunciations of them ("issuing from their brows").
[4] whose former crimes . . . and deemed forgotten: *les anciens crimes survivant dans tel complice qu'on croyait oublié.* G.

The Creed of Art

[1] Dated by M. de Fallois as written in 1905 or 1906.

Watteau

[1] These five studies of painters are dated by M. de Fallois as having been written between 1894 and 1904. Moreau, the subject of the fourth essay, died in 1898.

[2] . . . and brought it into a full-scale composition later on.
The full-scale composition may be read as *Jean Santeuil* (for the fellow-feeling for Watteau is much more the subject of this study than Watteau's painting) or even *La Recherche*. That Proust found even more significance in the *Commedia dell' Arte* collection may cover a reference to his *Fragments de Comédie Italienne* in *Les Plaisirs et les Jours*.

Chardin

[1] Into these rooms: *Dans ses chambres.* G.

[2] a bucket dangling: *un sceau qui descend.* G. (I would not think this slip of spelling worth mention if it did not support the presumption on which I have read *dans* for *dont:* see note to p. 128.)

Rembrandt

[1] At a Rembrandt exhibition: "I met Whistler one evening," Proust wrote in a letter to Marie Nordlinger, "and he told me that Ruskin was absolutely no judge of pictures. It is possible; but in any case, even while he was rambling on about other people's pictures, out of his misjudgments he painted and drew marvellous pictures which must be loved for what they are." Similarly, this account of Ruskin coming in his old age to look at an exhibition of Rembrandt must be loved for what it is; but it is fiction.

Moreau

[1] . . . which retain a sort of mysterious colouring from it, dazzled by their return: *qui en gardent une sorte de couleur mystérieuse, éblouie, d'être revenues. . . .* G.

[2] all resemble it: *se ressemblent toutes.* G.

[3] had been to Africa: *a été en Amérique.* G.

Monet

[1] . . . based on the real wind and the real sun. Just as the singer's lovers know the author . . . whose characters they see her playing, a picture by Monet . . . :

*. . . ont comme matière le soleil, le vent, comme les amants
d'une chanteuse connaissent l'auteur . . . dont ils lui voient
jouer les rôles. Un tableau de Monet. . . . G.*

Goethe

[1] M. de Fallois dates the essays on Goethe, Chateaubriand, Joubert, and George Eliot as contemporary with the period of *Jean Santeuil:* 1896-1904.

Notes on Stendhal

[1] Before 1908. G.
[2] these great books: *les beaux livres.* G.

Tolstoi

[1] Contemporary with *Contre Sainte-Beuve.* G.
[2] conversations of Levine's: *de Vronsky.* G.

Dostoievski

[1] After 1918. G.

Jules Renard

[1] Jules Renard died in 1910. The present tense need not mean that this was written during his life-time. Reading post-obit judgments on Renard may have impelled Proust to note down his own opinion.

Robert de Montesquiou

[1] In a letter of April 1893, Proust, thanking Robert de Montesquiou for a copy of *Les Chauves-Souris,* says: "I discovered long ago that you stood far above the type of exquisite decadent"; and in a subsequent letter he returns to this, and says that he intends to write a study "to show how much you differ from the banal decadents of our time." This study, never published, was to be called *De la Simplicité du comte de Montesquiou.*
[2]   *. . . ces concerts, riches de cuivre,*
Dont les soldats parfois inondent nos jardins,

Et qui, dans les soirs d'or où l'on se sent revivre
Versent quelque héroïsme au cœur des citadins.
(Baudelaire.)

³ *Ses yeux se sont éteints, mais non ceux de sa traîne.*
Il rayonnait vivant, il rayonne défunt,
Il enseigne à mourir d'une façon sereine.
(Robert de Montesquiou.)

⁴ *Ceux que la pudeur fière a voués au cil sec.*
(Montesquiou.)

⁵ *L'âme y voit mieux en elle au déclin des clartés.*
(Montesquiou.)

⁶ *Car c'est vraiment, Seigneur, le meilleur témoignage*
Que nous puissions donner de notre dignité
Que cet ardent sanglot qui roule d'âge en âge
Et vient mourir au bord de votre éternité.
(Baudelaire, Les Phares.)

Et c'est encore, Seigneur. G.
⁷ *Ah! Seigneur! donnez—moi la force et le courage*
De contempler mon cœur et mon corps sans dégoût!
(Baudelaire, Voyage à Cythère.)

⁸ *Je suis le souverain des choses transitoires.*
(Montesquiou.)

⁹ This second project of an article about Montesquiou can be dated by the publication of *Les Perles Rouges*, its subject. In G. it precedes the other. All the quotations are from *Les Perles Rouges.*

¹⁰ *Où vingt-deux bambins font un troupeau complet*
¹¹ *Lauriers-roses pareils à des bouquets de bouches.*
¹² *Laissant pleuvoir sur nous leurs baisers que disculpe*
Une absolution d'avoir beaucoup aimé.
¹³ *Étrange aboutissant d'une splendeur si grande,*
aboutissement. G.
¹⁴ *Ces verts appartements dessinés par Le Nôtre.*
¹⁵ *Solitude peuplée, agréable au grand prêtre*
¹⁶ *Tant de soleils sont morts dans ces bassins augustes,*
¹⁷ *L'horizon est vraiment historique ce soir,*
La nature à l'histoire emprunte ses effets.
¹⁸ *Y versaient les joyaux des verrières de Chartres.*
¹⁹ *Où l'herbe croît au dallage des cours*
²⁰ *A qui [   ] voulait des airs de ducs*
²¹ *Heureux de se mirer à l'heure de mourir.*

Léon Daudet

[1] Dated by M. de Fallois from the publication in 1918, 1919, of the books by Léon Daudet referred to. In a letter dated November 26, 1921, Proust sounds Jacques Boulenger, editor of *L'Opinion*, as to whether he would accept "an article— very dithyrambic—which I might do on Léon Daudet—not about his politics, naturally. . . . I know that Daudet is detested and that by praising him I shall put up the backs of the few people who are loyal to me. But admiration and gratitude are both very strong feelings that demand expression . . . when the whole press (except Binet-Valmer) deserted me about *Sodome et Gomorrhe*, Léon Daudet, in *L'Action française*, a ridiculously straight-laced paper, never failed for a single day to support me. . . . I never do articles; it is like opening a wound from which the rest of my blood will flow. But it so irritates me that he is never mentioned, that people pretend to ignore, or to take for a simple Rochefort, such a remarkable journalist."

Admiration and gratitude and loyalty to a friend were all very strong feelings in Proust. So, too, was the resentment aroused in him by that time-serving caution which by 1921 had prompted people to ignore Léon Daudet, or, at the time of Baudelaire's prosecution, prompted Sainte-Beuve to the niggardly anonymity of his *Petits Moyens de Défense*—a resentment which may, indeed, have been the genesis of *Contre Sainte-Beuve*. M. de Fallois does not say whether the article on Léon Daudet was published; presumably, it was not; but in the last year of Proust's life, when he was fighting against time to finish *La Recherche*, it was written.

[a] *La corde injurieuse où la haine a vibré.* (Not traced.)